I Am Giorgia

I Am Giorgia

My Roots, My Principles

GIORGIA MELONI

Translated by Sylvia Adrian Notini
Foreword by Donald Trump Jr.

Skyhorse Publishing

© 2021 Mondadori Libri S.p.A., originally published by Rizzoli, Milano, Italy
English translation copyright © 2025 Skyhorse Publishing
Foreword copyright © 2025 by Donald Trump Jr.

All rights reserved. No part of this book may be reproduced in any manner without the express written consent of the publisher, except in the case of brief excerpts in critical reviews or articles. All inquiries should be addressed to Skyhorse Publishing, 307 West 36th Street, 11th Floor, New York, NY 10018.

Skyhorse Publishing books may be purchased in bulk at special discounts for sales promotion, corporate gifts, fund-raising, or educational purposes. Special editions can also be created to specifications. For details, contact the Special Sales Department, Skyhorse Publishing, 307 West 36th Street, 11th Floor, New York, NY 10018 or info@skyhorsepublishing.com.

Skyhorse® and Skyhorse Publishing® are registered trademarks of Skyhorse Publishing, Inc.®, a Delaware corporation.

Visit our website at www.skyhorsepublishing.com.

Please follow our publisher Tony Lyons on Instagram @tonylyonsisuncertain.

10 9 8 7 6 5 4 3 2 1

Library of Congress Cataloging-in-Publication Data is available on file.

Cover design by David Ter-Avanesyan

Print ISBN: 978-1-5107-8356-0
Ebook ISBN: 978-1-5107-8357-7

Printed in the United States of America

Contents

Foreword ... vii
Introduction ... ix

I Am Giorgia
Little Women ... 1
Baptism by Fire ... 17

I Am a Woman
The Stronger Sex ... 39
The Open Sea ... 63

I Am a Mother
When a Mother Is Born ... 85
The Things That Count ... 104

I Am on the Right
It All Began When Everything Was About to End ... 127
Saving the Future ... 153

I Am a Christian
I Believe in Us ... 173
The Racism of Progress ... 191

I Am an Italian
It Didn't All Go Well ... 217
Attacking the Decline ... 241
For Ginevra ... 269

Foreword

Very few people in today's political world can honestly say that their election marked the tip of the spear for radical change in their nation, but just like my father here in America, Giorgia Meloni has effected lasting change in Italian politics. Meloni has taken on the globalist elite, stood up for her country, and brought to her office a courage and clarity that most so-called "leaders" could only dream of. But what makes her story even more powerful is that long before she led Italy, she was simply a young working-class woman with a deep love and vision for her nation.

I Am Giorgia is the unfiltered story of the patriotic tidal wave that Meloni would ride to becoming one of the most significant political figures in the world. This isn't just another political memoir. It's the real deal. In her own words, Meloni walks us through the trials, fights, successes, failures, and principles that made her who she is. This book lays it all out, beginning from her roots in a working-class Roman neighborhood, through her days as a young political activist, to leading Fratelli d'Italia and eventually becoming the leader of a significant European power.

When her memoir was first released, Giorgia hadn't become Prime Minister yet—but her talent, drive, and keen understanding of the populist issues animating the Italian people were crystal clear. While establishment politicians ignored the issues that their voters cared about, Meloni spoke up for them on everything from faith and family to patriotism and national identity.

If you want to truly understand the worldwide conservative revolution, then read this book.

—Donald Trump Jr.

Introduction

October 19, 2019. Assembled before me in Piazza San Giovanni were thousands of Italians who had traveled to Rome to join our Center-Right protest. They had come to express their "Italian pride" against the formation of the second Conte administration—yet another government that had come to power without heeding the will of the people. The square was a sea of flags waved by the Brothers of Italy, the Lega Nord, and Forza Italia, all blending together in a spirited dance. The crowd was united by its shared purpose: the fight for the right to be heard and to achieve self-determination against those who sought to exploit institutions for their personal gain.

On the massive stage that had been set up for the occasion, I faced 200,000 people, flanked by my allies Silvio Berlusconi and Matteo Salvini. When it was my turn to speak, I addressed the crowd for twenty minutes, speaking from the heart. I had no script, relying instead on my instinct and passion. My tone was that of a political rally, but—as always—I also tried to convey my vision. On that day, I reiterated a theme I had often emphasized at other events: the value of identity. I spoke of the ongoing clash between those who defend identity—like us—and those who seek to wipe it out—our adversaries. I pointed out how all the key pillars of our identity—family, nation, faith, and even gender—were viewed as the enemy. Our identity is under attack, not by coincidence but by deliberate design.

I concluded my speech with these words: "I am Giorgia. I am a woman, a mother, an Italian, a Christian. You will *never* take that away from me." There was a roar of applause from the people in the square, and the event was a resounding success. But I could never have anticipated the lasting impact those words would have in the months to come.

In the days that followed, my phone was flooded with a curious remix of my speech from different sources. The broadcaster and writer Tommaso Zorzi (who would later win Italy's version of the reality show *Big Brother*) had posted a critical commentary on Instagram. Meanwhile, MEM & J, two young DJs from Milan, had remixed my words over a disco bassline. They intended to satirize and mock my message, to turn my words against me. But something unexpected happened. The remix was too catchy, too danceable and, in its own way, too revolutionary to serve its intended purpose. Instead, it became wildly popular. Within weeks, it was playing in clubs across the country, with people dancing to it. It even earned a gold record, which (ironically) fulfilled my most secret childhood dream: to be a singer.

As I reflected on this unlikely turn of events, I thought of my Nonno Gianni and how proud he would have been of me. My grandfather was a Sicilian through and through, but he had his moments of tenderness and sharp wit. He had often made my sister, Arianna, and me compete in a family version of *X Factor*. His favorite request was always the same: *Parlami d'amore Mariù*, a song from the 1930s made famous by Vittorio De Sica. Unfortunately, Nonno Gianni was also the most demanding judge in the history of talent shows, so neither of us ever won the 5,000-lire prize that was up for grabs.

Nevertheless, that strange blend of political rally and dance music, complete with a viral dance routine, had made me popular—especially with Gen Z. What was meant to undermine my message had become a megaphone amplifying it. Suddenly, I was no longer just another dull politician; I was an unexpected pop phenomenon.

That song was what convinced me to write this book. I realized that too many people were talking about me and my ideas without truly knowing me. So, I decided to open up and write about what I believe in and how I got to where I am today, directly from me to you.

I can imagine the reviews: "Barely forty and Giorgia Meloni is already writing an autobiography? Power must have gone to her head." Or, "Giorgia Meloni thinks she's qualified to draft a manifesto for the Italian Right, but she still has a long way to go." Comments like these might have some merit. But let me be clear: this book is not a theoretical manifesto for the Italian Right. At most, it is the story of a life spent contributing to the growth of the movement, without hiding from its challenges. There are others more suitable to write our political manifesto. If I were ever to do so, I would need to take a page from the books of those who have spent their entire lives working on these matters. These pages, meanwhile, aren't really even an autobiography—not in the traditional sense. Autobiographies belong to those nearing the end of their journey, and I'm not planning on leaving this world any time soon.

This book is different: it is my effort to share who I am and what I believe in, here and now. It is for anyone with the patience to read it, and also for myself.

In a political landscape where the majority lie about who they are, I see support for the Brothers of Italy continue to grow, and I want to be truthful and earnest with people about who I really am. I want those who choose to vote for me, support me, or believe in me to do so fully informed, knowing me for me: as a human being, with merits and limits, strengths and myriad weaknesses. A person who believes in what she does and tries to do it as best she can. In Italy, we always talk about politicians as though they are a separate species, as if they had suddenly landed on Earth from another planet. But politicians are also simply Italians, just like everyone else. There are good ones and bad ones. The challenge lies in distinguishing between the two. And we can't recognize them or choose the right ones if they don't tell the truth. So, here is my truth, whether you like it or not.

Perhaps I started writing this book mostly for myself. I'm at a crossroads in my life—far enough along to make a difference, but still vulnerable to losing my way. I've always believed that the greatest challenge for anyone in politics is to leave their mark while remaining loyal to the sincerest part of their life—what first inspired them to go to the front line. In the end, we all face the same inescapable question: *Did I change the system, or did the system change me?* I want to document who I am today so I can look back in ten, twenty, maybe thirty years' time and hold myself accountable. But I also want this book to be a tool for those who believe in me and in the things I do and say. Let this be a weapon should I betray my ideas and promises. No deception, no tricks.

In a world where everyone is trying to be someone, my goal is to remain true to myself, whatever it takes. To do so, I need to be honest—with you and with myself—about who I really am.

I am Giorgia, and this is my story so far.

I AM GIORGIA

Little Women

I owe everything to my mother. A strong-willed, cultured woman, she concealed a fragile soul beneath the armor she wore to face her life.

I owe her my love of books, my curiosity, my pride, my resilience, my dedication to work, my sense of freedom, and my unwavering need to speak the truth. She taught me everything with her no-frills approach that alone could fill a book. Today, once and for all, in front of everyone, I wish to thank her. Because most importantly, I owe her my life. Of course, every child could say that about their mother—but with mine, these words are even more profound. In fact, my exact words should be: "I owe everything to my mother and to her alone." The truth is, I wasn't even supposed to be born. When she became pregnant, Anna was twenty-three, already had an eighteen-month-old daughter, and was in a struggling relationship with my father—and he already had his suitcase packed, one foot out the door. Theirs was a wounded family.

My mother was a stubborn and free spirit, yet she had almost let herself be convinced that it didn't make sense to bring another child into the world under these circumstances.

I remember when she told me this and how long it took for me to fully process it. At times, I've thought that silence might have been better, sparing me from that morbid need adults have to bare their soul. But eventually, I came to understand the immense struggle of a single mother who held the power of a High Court in her hands: she could choose to let life begin, or send it back into the void.

The story she told me is always the same. The morning she was scheduled to undergo the routine pre-abortion tests, still fasting from the night before, she began walking toward the clinic. As she reached the door, she stopped, hesitated, and asked herself: *Is this truly my choice—to give up on the chance to become a mother for a second time?* Her answer came instinctively: *No, I don't want to give up. I don't want an abortion. My daughter will have a sister.*

It was a spring morning, the air gentle and pure. She felt a deep sense of having made the right choice. All that remained was to solidify her decision somehow, in whatever way she could.... She noticed a café across the street and went inside. "Morning. A cappuccino and a croissant, please." With that, her fast was over, the lab tests abandoned, and the scheduled abortion averted.

I owe everything to that breakfast, to my mother, to her resolute decision against all the odds.... In the words of Oriana Fallaci, "Some months later, I was lolling victoriously in the sun."

There are so many things I never knew about my mother's early life. I never even asked her how her relationship with my father began, how it evolved, or why it fell apart. I never asked about her thoughts, dreams, or illusions during those complicated times. It was the infamous 1970s, a period fueled by youthful fervor soon overshadowed by the cynical, ruthless power and logic of opposite extremist ideals. There were clashes in the piazzas, people using wrenches to attack each other, and a grim succession of bodies on the streets. Yet, those are not the only things to define that decade. It was also a time of relentless drive to change everything, share everything, and debate everything—an ethos that feels enviable in today's age of disposable values. My mother lived through that era, having just emerged from adolescence. She had been a sympathizer—perhaps even a militant one at times—with the right-wing youth movement back then. But she shared little of this with me. I know that, at some point, she had become infatuated with an older man who had already charted his path in life. It's never easy to decipher someone else's loves. Over time, though, I began to suspect that my mother wasn't so much pursuing love as she was seeking an escape from a strict family environment that felt suffocating to her rebellious spirit.

Her parents embodied the meeting of two very different worlds. My grandfather was Sicilian to the core, his face etched with an unwavering sense of duty. My grandmother, on the other hand, was thoroughly Roman, controlling my mother's fiery temper with the discipline of a Prussian general. She had an authoritative frown that we grandchildren never experienced. That's often how it goes: human beings, unlike trees, tend to grow softer, not harder, as time passes, becoming as tender as sapling wood.

My grandparents, however, were not so tender with their daughter. To them, whatever she did was wrong. Admittedly, my mother was always a unique personality, but I'm not sure whether her rebellious nature provoked this strictness, or whether their lack of leniency is what made her a rebel. Toward the end of her life, I often debated this with my grandmother, pushing for the latter possibility. I never managed to change her mind.

My mother's yearning to leave her parents' home was so strong that, as soon as she reached adulthood, she began building her own family—one piece at a time, like assembling a structure with Lego bricks. One of those pieces (perhaps the most important one) was my father, an accountant from northern Rome—however, he was deeply flawed.

For instance, when my mother was discharged from the hospital after giving birth to me, he didn't even come to pick us up. Suffice it to say, he wasn't exactly the ideal partner.

When I was still very young, he decided to take off for the Canary Islands on a boat named *Cavallo Pazzo* (Crazy Horse). He set sail and vanished from our lives.

I don't remember the day he left. Frankly, I can't remember ever living with him.

I must have come to realize this bit by bit.

The awareness of a father who is no longer there, who vanishes into thin air, is something that's hard to explain. It may leave a deeper wound than a father's death. At least then you can imagine him looking down at you from heaven. But when he chooses to leave, you're left grappling with the ghost of a person who isn't there.

I think he lived with us for a few months in the upscale Roman neighborhood Camilluccia—the district of well-heeled Romans, reputed for their affluence and reserve. We stayed in that house for a while, even after he had left.

Two events from our time in that house left an indelible mark on my life. One felt straight out of a scene from the detective movies that were so popular at the time. The other was more like something from a Stephen King novel. Although I've always loved his stories, living through one is an entirely different matter.

We had two German shepherds, Ettore and Eva. Eva, as is often the case with bitches around newborn babies, became like a mother to us. She would sleep beneath the cradle and bark at anyone who approached—even my father, which gives you an idea of how perceptive she was.

As I mentioned, our neighborhood was rather upscale, and our neighbor was a political bigwig in those days.

One evening, perhaps due to some noise they'd heard, agents from the neighbor's security detail decided to conduct a routine check, sneaking into the garden outside our building. Alarmed, my mother ran outside shouting, "I'm armed!" She froze, terrified in the semidarkness, just as Ettore and Eva rushed out, barking furiously. Quite a commotion ensued, but the evening ended peacefully.

A few nights later, though, the same security detail returned to sweep the area. This time, Ettore and Eva leaped over the fence and went on the attack. Seeing the two huge German shepherds charging at them, the agents drew their weapons and shot, hitting Ettore in the leg.

Hurt and frightened, Ettore began digging under the fence to get away. Besides being injured in the leg when he was shot, in the struggle to get away he also lost his sight in one eye.

Ettore was a marvelous animal. Despite his handicap, he remained the same. He allowed us to do anything to him—he even loved it when we put skates on his paws. But at the slightest hint of an external threat, his wolflike instincts kicked in. I was twelve when he died, having spent every one of those years with him. Losing him was devastating, and he remains the animal I have loved most in my life.

That brings me to the second memory that left a lasting impression on me: the image of a large stuffed panda devoured by flames, its glass eyes staring hauntingly at me.

My sister, Arianna, and I loved to experiment. We once dismantled Barbie's house to convert it into an unlikely rocket ship. We'd set paper and small objects on fire just to observe how they crumpled or melted. We rearranged furniture to create elaborate sets for stories that we invented. We were a dynamic duo. Until my daughter, Ginevra, was born, my sister was the most important person in my life. There is no secret I keep from her, and no advice I haven't sought from her. Even now, with both of us leading such busy lives, I feel a void if we don't talk at least once a day. I use my phone so much for work that I have an aversion to phone calls, but my sister is the one person who I genuinely feel the physical need to call. And just as she did when we were little, she tells me stories to help me fall asleep. More than anyone else, she has the gift of giving me a sense of peace, making me feel at home, and bringing me joy. Time spent with her is as vital as the air I breathe. I will never be able to thank her enough for the love she has given me and for being a constant role model throughout my life. Arianna is, without a doubt, the best person I have ever met on this earth.

But back to the day our mother lost the house—and a few years off her life in the process. That day, my sister and I had one goal: to organize a nighttime party. We built a makeshift fort in our room, filling it with toys, dolls, snacks, and drinks. When we finished, we looked at each other. What was missing? Light. But it had to be a dim light, otherwise Mamma would know we were still awake. We eventually came up with a solution: a candle. It was Arianna who found it, but I was the one who lit it.

It was only four in the afternoon, so we had to wait for nightfall to have our party. To kill time, we went to another room to watch cartoons. We left the lit candle behind.

How much time went by? I'll never know. All I remember is that, in the middle of an episode of *Candy Candy*, we heard a deafening crash from our bedroom. The three of us—my sister, mother and I—ran to see what had happened. Opening the door, we were nearly engulfed by flames. There it was: the panda burning along with all our toys. The noise we'd heard was the shutter collapsing.

In no time at all, the fire consumed the entire apartment. We fled with nothing but a single bag hastily packed with pajamas, two pairs of pants, and a T-shirt. All of a sudden, we were out on the street, alone and homeless. My mother had to start from scratch. A gargantuan task. Looking back, I sometimes joke that this experience is what gave me the courage many years later to rebuild a political house of my own after ours had gone up in smoke. After all, I'd already seen it done when I was four—why couldn't I succeed at thirty-five?

After selling the apartment, now reduced to a charred shell, my mother bought another one near my grandparents in the Garbatella neighborhood. A working-class district with public housing just outside the Aurelian Walls, it's nestled like a tiny jewel between Via Ostiense and Via Cristoforo Colombo, and had developed in the 1920s under the tufa rock that looms over the Basilica of Saint Paul.

Garbatella is my neighborhood not just because it's where I grew up and lived for many years, but because we can never be indifferent to the place that shapes us. We are unique in the world precisely because of where we come from.

Though the area gained widespread attention thanks to (or perhaps no thanks to) the TV series *I Cesaroni*, the first person to talk about it in cinema was the filmmaker and actor Nanni Moretti, who claims it as his favorite neighborhood in the movie *Dear Diary*. And how right he was.

Today it is a sought-after area, offering the charm of a made-to-measure hamlet despite being near the heart of Rome. It's far removed from the metropolitan beehives built in the 1970s, products of a collectivist culture that treated humans like battery hens. However, I didn't live in that magical, secret part of Garbatella, but rather a few hundred yards away—in the more modern section near the Lazio regional government building. Yet even there, the sense of belonging was palpable. It felt like living in a village within the city.

As a child, my life was divided between school, the church community, and the small house where my grandparents lived. They were authority figures for my sister and me, offering daily guidance. They were still young, around fifty years old, and they cared for us like a second set of parents.

My Nonno Gianni always reminded me of the adventure writer Emilio Salgari. Although my grandfather had never traveled outside Italy, never flown on a plane, he loved weaving tales of adventure set in the most far-flung places—whether real or imagined. Born in Messina, Sicily, he had come to Rome after World War I to work at what was then the Ministry of the Military Navy. Nonno Gianni was endlessly fun, always finding ways to spark competition between my sister and me, crowning the loser as the "Regina della monnezza" (the queen of trash). He was the only true father figure we ever had, and he died when Arianna and I had just reached adulthood. To us, he was a man of great strength, though his health had been declining for years. Two heart attacks, followed by a stroke and then dialysis, took their toll. He often argued with my Nonna Maria, who would force him to drink quarts of water daily, as prescribed by his doctor. He was on a strict diet and smoking was forbidden—yet he couldn't resist sneaking out to indulge in *cotolette fritte*, fried veal cutlets.

When we were little, my sister and I were fortunate enough to know our great-grandmother, Nonna Nena, who lived to the age of ninety-two. Nonna Nena (whose real name was Maddalena) had endured the loss of her son Angelino, who had died of meningitis at the age of five and was widowed early in life, when her daughter (my Nonna Maria) was just twelve. Like so many others in the first half of the twentieth century, Nonna Nena had faced much bereavement and hardship. Her struggles led to her daughter (my grandmother) being sent to a convent school, where she received a strict and disciplined education—the stories of which were her favorite topic of conversation. Nonna Maria never forgot her little brother. Throughout her life, she brought flowers to the cemetery and would light a candle for him. When she no longer had the strength to go to the Verano Monumental Cemetery, she asked us to carry on the tradition. Now that she is no longer with us, we continue to honor her wishes.

My grandparents lived in an apartment building with designated homes for ministry employees. I still remember how proud my grandfather was when he finally paid off the mortgage. At last, that tiny home was all his. It was a two-room apartment, just under five hundred square feet, and it was where my mother had grown up. The kitchen doubled as the dining room, and it was the heart of our domestic life. No one living inside those walls ever saw a sofa. There was a single table, and that is where we ate, did our homework, played, or watched TV. My mother was always working, so my sister and I spent our afternoons after school in that all-purpose living room. There was a narrow hallway with a convertible bed that we slept in whenever our mother chose to go out for the evening, in an attempt to live her own life (as much as that was possible). As my grandmother would say, we were tucked in "one with her head on top, one with her feet on top." Which means that I spent many nights in a hallway with my sister's feet stuck in my face. When I grew older, I was finally rewarded: a cot in the kitchen, all to myself. It was a significant upgrade.

Nonna Maria was a homemaker, and she treated caring for the home like a mission, organized according to a meticulous schedule and following procedures to a tee. To clean a house that size, she'd start at dawn and work until dusk. Not even the dog was spared—he was locked in the bathroom while she did her chores, then had to suffer the indignity of having his teeth brushed with a toothbrush.

That small dog with his bright smile was a poodle named Charlie. My sister and I were in charge of taking him for a walk every afternoon for years, earning us the neighborhood nickname of "Charlie's owners."

Whenever I see the vast mountain of toys my daughter leaves strewn around the house, I think back to an old shoebox where I kept my favorite toy: building blocks. Today, my daughter has enough blocks to construct the third lane of Rome's Great Ring Road, whereas Arianna and I could barely re-create our grandmother's kitchen to scale with our blocks. I'm not sure which way of growing up is better. Or perhaps I do know, but I'm afraid to admit it.

Arianna and I were remarkably independent. We even traveled by plane alone as young as the ages of eight, nine, and ten years old, to spend a few weeks' vacation with our father in the Canary Islands. The flight attendants would tie red envelopes with the necessary documents around our necks, and we would board the plane that would take us to Madrid for a stopover. One time we were stranded because the airport staff member who was supposed to meet us never showed up. We found ourselves lost in the seemingly enormous terminal. While I was in a daze, Arianna took my hand and somehow got us onto the correct flight. I'll never understand how she managed it. Our parents argued bitterly about that misadventure.

* * *

It may be hard to believe, but until I was fourteen, I was quite introverted. As a child, I always wore a sullen expression—the same one I have today when I prepare to answer the journalist Lilli Gruber's questions. To anyone who mocks my brazen and grumpy demeanor, I can show them a kindergarten photo where I look exactly the same.

I've always been on the defensive. A friend of my mother recently told me I was the kind of child who couldn't tolerate fairy tales, disliked being teased, and observed adults with mistrust and a raised eyebrow. When asked, "What kind of kid were you?" the answer is always the same: "A serious one." That description still lingers in my mind today.

I had a difficult temperament, and making friends never came easily to me. I was a textbook Capricorn—not shy or distrustful, but fiercely and stubbornly protective of my personal space. In other words, I was not an exuberant child, something I see even more clearly now as I watch my daughter laughing, chatting, and befriending everyone she meets. I, on the other hand, spent most of my time with my sister and a small circle of others. At school, I would stand my ground when provoked. I remember snapping at a classmate who refused to talk to any kid who didn't have a father. Yes, I was prickly, quick to retort, and my looks certainly didn't help my social life.

My grandmother wasn't a trained nutritionist by any stretch. To give you a rough idea, she was the kind of person who believed that a bit of extra weight was a sign of good health. Every night, dinner included milk and cookies. As a result, by the time I was nine years old, I weighed over 140 pounds. It's official: my grandmother wrecked my metabolism. And yet, to the very end, whenever I visited her, she'd offered me a snack. "Come on," she'd say, "you're too skinny, eat something."

I always looked skinny to her, even when I was the size of a blimp. "You're too thin. Are you eating? What are you eating?" Whenever I traveled abroad, her biggest concern was always the same: "Be honest, what did they feed you?" During a two-week school trip to Berlin, my grandmother constantly called me to ask, "What are they feeding you there? Furstels? All they eat are furstels there!" (I think she meant to say "wurstel," sausages.)

Though I made fun of her for it, I knew it was a completely normal reaction for anyone who had experienced wartime hunger. It had shaped her obsession with full stomachs.

My mother was also a member of this "anti-beauty conspiracy." For practical reasons, she kept our hair short in that unflattering 1980s hairdo that looked like a banana boat. Not even Charlize Theron could pull off that look, let alone me. My oversized head earned me the nickname "capocciona," (big head) from my grandmother. You get the picture. I could pretend that my grandmother dubbed me that due to my great intelligence . . . but no, that wasn't the case. To make matters worse, they sent us out into the world wearing tracksuits. Unsurprisingly, I wasn't considered attractive. And children, as we all know, aren't exactly politically correct when it comes to teasing someone because they're fat, poorly dressed, or whose family situations aren't the norm.

My mother was constantly working, continually inventing different professions. At one point, she thought she could be a writer and ended up writing 140 romance stories. Her extraordinary intelligence made her eclectic, but she lacked the luck to make it work—there was just never enough money. It was an unfortunate combination of circumstances that led her to be absent-minded and forced limitations on our lives—and for a child, that can really leave its mark. I still remember one Fat Tuesday celebration at school when I was the only one without a mask. My teacher quickly fashioned a daisy mask out of paper for me. My sister didn't fare much better: our mother bought her a space pirate outfit that wasn't the ideal choice for a girl. Arianna loves to tell the story of the time when Nonna Maria was asked to contribute to a buffet for some party or other (I can't really remember which one now). She gave my sister 5,000 lire, and Arianna went to the café, bought five pastries, and arrived at the party with a small paper bag. Meanwhile, everyone else had brought trays heaving with goodies and homemade cakes. To save the day, the teachers took the five pastries and mixed them in with the food on one of the other trays. My sister was so traumatized by that day that now, whenever she organizes a party for her own children, she starts baking cakes like there's no tomorrow, preparing enough sandwiches to feed the whole school.

But let me be clear: we were happy children. Despite my occasional bad temper and my father's absence, I was never sad because I had a family that gave me all the love I needed. I say this because—although I defend the nuclear family and the sanctity of marriage—I believe that the state should incentivize the most solid form of union to protect the children. I have witnessed how, even in a family where one of the two parents is missing, it is possible to grow up perfectly happy, thanks to the selflessness of those who shoulder that responsibility.

Inside my family, I had everything I needed. It was outside that family circle that I did not find that same acceptance.

I have talked about this in Parliament, during a debate on the Zan **draft** law. This was proposed as a measure to protect homosexuals from discrimination, but it is actually a dangerous tool, conceived to impose gender doctrine from as early as elementary school.

Our parliamentary colleague, Alessandro Zan, backed the draft law because he had been bullied as a child for being homosexual. But I was bullied, too—and I'm heterosexual. Bullying, for all sorts of reasons, is a universal experience, to a greater or lesser extent. This is why it is almost impossible to resolve the matter by making a long list of specific hate crimes, as if one type of insult or humiliation is worse than another. The Italian constitution already condemns discrimination in all of its forms, be it sex, race, language, religion, political opinion, personal and social status. To my mind, this definition already covers everything, including homosexuality. Drawing up a more specific list means entering dangerous **territory** because it inevitably means excluding anyone not explicitly protected by specific laws. Doing so creates a precarious mechanism, leading to endless and problematic hierarchies. Is it worse to offend a woman or someone who is gay? Someone who is gay or black? Someone who is black or disabled? Discrimination is discrimination. Period. No form of discrimination is more or less serious than another.

I found being bullied extremely tough, but I must admit that it shaped me and drove me to change so I wouldn't be such an easy target.

I remember everything clearly. One day, I was at the beach, and I was in my bathing suit, of course. Some kids were playing volleyball, and I asked to join them, but was rebuffed as they shouted back at me: "No, fatso! You *can't* play!" And they threw the ball so hard it hit me in the face. In that moment, I wanted to die. But Arianna, as always, was at my side. Unlike me, she was popular, pretty, and fun. Despite being forced to drag around a lumpy potato (yours truly), she was happy to argue with anybody to defend me.

Now that time has passed, I'm grateful to those idiots—they were the first to teach me that enemies can be useful. They spur you on to overcome challenges, to push past your limits, and to correct your mistakes. Of course, Plutarch explains it much better when he says, "a sensible man will receive profit even from his enemies.... But since friendship has nowadays become very mealy-mouthed in freedom of speech, voluble in flattery and silent in rebuke, we can only hear the truth from our enemies." It's also thanks to those kids that I developed a resilient personality to tackle both hardships and fears. I decided to go on a diet and lost twenty-two pounds in three months. I was going to play volleyball, all right, that was for sure. And I did, before the end of the season.

I learned the hard way that healthy eating habits are crucial for young people, not just for their health but also for their social lives. Whether we are accepted has a lot to do with our bodies. Though it might seem superficial, it's just a fact.

During my tenure as Minister of Youth, I turned this personal insight into political action. I commissioned a study on the subject that revealed the shocking prevalence of eating disorders, with over 300,000 "ProAna" websites. These are communities and personal blogs that promote anorexia, where young people share tips on how to keep their parents from discovering they are fasting, and even how to avoid being hungry, spreading seriously unpleasant practices and self-harm. Yet, there were no resources widely available to challenge these disorders. Not a single website for families that tells you how to recognize the warning signs or who to turn to for help.

I credit my strong character with saving me from falling into the spiral of eating disorders. Until I was thirty years old, I didn't think to blame my father for my problems as a child, believing his abandonment had no impact on me. But eventually, I looked inward and realized I was lying to myself. And denying the truth is never good for you. You must always have the courage to face the truth, even when you're wrong. Of course, mistakes are inevitable, but you must be self-aware and take responsibility for them.

We now live in a society where some may lead you to believe you can shift blame onto others. But that's not how the world works. Each of us has a role to play, for better or worse. Italy will change only when we understand that we are all part of the whole. We must learn that we cannot fix Italy from the outside, as if we aren't a fundamental part of it. To quote Michael Jackson, if you want to change, start with the man in the mirror.

Everything I've done wrong in my life, everything that made me angry, that I didn't like or didn't understand... I strive to understand the reasons behind all these things. I need to be honest with myself if I truly want to know who I am.

For a long time, I refused to admit to myself that my relationship with my father was a problem. Then, while watching the silliest American romcom (*The Perks of Being a Wallflower*), I had an epiphany. In the movie, the main character blunders into a succession of humiliations and miserable men. There's endless weeping. She can't figure out why she gets hung up on men who are objectively terrible. Finally, her male friend tells her the eye-opening truth: "*We accept the love we think we deserve.*"

I realized that all that my father had done was deeply significant. It wasn't just his abandonment of our home—after all, many fathers still remain a part of their children's lives after a separation. No, what hurt the most was his indifference to us. His lack of love is what scarred me.

Which is exactly why, at the age of eleven, I decided I never wanted to see him again.

It was my own choice, but I must admit that he didn't seem especially bothered by it. Until then, we'd see him for a few weeks every summer. Then we broke off all contact for several years. After sailing around the world, my father settled on one of the tiniest islands in the Canaries, La Gomera. Measuring just 14 miles across, it features the primordial landscape that is typical of volcanic islands: black sandy beaches, alien rock formations, and a prehistoric forest. When my sister and I were little, we didn't appreciate just how beautiful the island was: we were too focused on our games and the near total freedom we had to roam around the place. All the islanders knew each other, and there was no mass tourism to speak of back then, so us kids could run around from dawn 'til dusk.

We lived in the capital, San Sebastián, and spent a lot of time in the big restaurant our father had opened there. I remember one terrifying incident when Arianna and I swam to the nearby rocks on a wild beach. As we swam, the tide rose, trapping us in the water and crushing us against the rocks. Escaping was a Herculean task and we emerged covered in cuts and bruises.

We were lively girls and our father tolerated our . . . shall we say, less than discreet antics. We often played pranks on him, and there were a few times we pushed him too far. Looking back, he was right to lose his temper. Once, we were sailing on a boat and my sister threw a huge rock into the water while I hid. She shouted to my father, "Papa, Papa! Giorgia's fallen into the water!" Terrified, he dove into the sea to look for me, nearly drowning . . . until I popped out of my hiding place, laughing hysterically with Arianna.

The last summer we visited, my father thought it was a good idea to leave for a week. He left us behind with his partner, who—understandably—wasn't jumping for joy at the prospect. When he returned, instead of apologizing to her or us, he gave us a talk that I have never forgotten. It was the death knell for our relationship. I don't wish to repeat his words, but suffice to say he made it clear we were not his priority when it came to love. He insisted we had to behave accordingly whenever we stayed with him.

That marked the end. Or perhaps, the real and final end was two years later when he sent me a telegram for my thirteenth birthday. It was signed *Happy birthday. Franco.* "Papa" was evidently too personal.

The constant need to meet high standards, especially in male-dominated environments, along with my fear of disappointing those who believe in me, likely stem from the lack of my father's love.

I grew up convinced that I didn't deserve anything. My reaction was to strive relentlessly to prove otherwise. Because it boils down to this: what happens is one thing, and how we deal with it is another. And how we deal with it makes all the difference. Life is less what happens to us because of someone else's actions, and more about how we choose to react. Our courage to face up to situations defines us. In short, I discovered I was an unwitting stoicist.

Each day, I grapple with fear—fear of inadequacy, of falling short in the eyes of others. But this fear is also my strength; it drives me to keep studying and learning, to strive for the highest marks in every subject, even when I'm starting from scratch. This fear fuels my attention to detail, my stubbornness, my commitment, my willingness to make sacrifices. Competing with men (not with women), seeking their approval, friendship, and the esteem of my fellow fighters who are now my fellow party members, of all the men I respect and have met throughout my life . . . all of it is the result of that wound.

If this is who I am today, it is thanks to my father—for better or worse.

When he died a few years ago, I felt nothing. Writing those words is still painful. When I heard the news, I was furious that I felt nothing. I realized then just how deep the black hole was that I had buried my pain in—the pain of not being loved enough.

Baptism by Fire

At the age of fifteen and a half, I never imagined that knocking on the reinforced door of the Youth Front section in Garbatella would lead me to my second family—a family far larger than the one I was born into.

As fate would have it, the section was right around the corner from my house, though I had hardly ever walked down that street. I had to look it up in the street directory after calling the central office of the Italian Social Movement (Movimento Sociale Italiano, or MSI) on Via della Scrofa to ask which section was closest to my home. Via Guendalina Borghese, number 8: that was where it all began. But even more significant than the address was the date that triggered my decision: July 19, 1992—the day judge and magistrate Paolo Borsellino was assassinated.

These were tense, dark months. The political class was under justified scrutiny, and the Mani Pulite (Clean Hands) investigation was already unraveling the foundations of the main parties of what would soon be relics of the First Republic. Partly out of natural curiosity and partly because my mother watched the news, I started paying attention too. I had even attended a Youth Front demonstration some time before, dragged along by a schoolmate. It featured a performance where young people dressed as prominent political figures of the time, clad in prison uniforms, to symbolize how the First Republic had built its fortune by stealing from future generations. Despite these themes, the atmosphere was surprisingly festive, almost lighthearted. I felt at ease, and began to take more interest in a world that would soon become my own. The Italian Social Movement, untouched by the corruption and theft being laid bare in that era, emerged as a compelling key player amid the chaos of that turbulent transition.

I could still hear the haunting words of Rosaria Costa, the 22-year-old widow of Vito Schifani, one of the security officers killed in the Capaci massacre alongside Judge Giovanni Falcone, his wife, and two colleagues. It was impossible to be indifferent to Rosaria's simple request for "justice, now," to her fearless words to the men of the mafia, whom she knew were among the crowd before her. "I want you to know that you can be forgiven. I forgive you," she said, "but you will have to get down on your knees, if you have the courage to change." Then, in July, Judge Paolo Borsellino, a close friend and colleague of Falcone's and known as the mafia hunter, was also murdered, along with five other officers, outside his mother's house in Palermo. I can vividly recall sitting in the living room on a sweltering summer day, watching the news and the horrifying footage of that devastation. I can still feel the overwhelming anger and emotion—it was like a switch had flipped. I couldn't bear feeling powerless any longer. I couldn't just sit back and watch. I had to act. For me, action meant joining those I saw as a genuine alternative and role model. So, more out of instinct than calculated decision, I turned to the Youth Front and the Italian Social Movement.

At fifteen, you don't yet have the tools to fully understand the different ideologies driving politics. Choosing a side is a matter of instinct or an intangible sense of belonging. I opened the phone book, found the number for the MSI headquarters, and called. Determined to sign up, I followed their directions and knocked on the door of the Garbatella section, which had only recently reopened after being attacked by the extra-parliamentary Left.

My first impression wasn't what I had expected. A young man opened the door and introduced himself, saying, "Hi, I'm Marta." (I later found out his name was Alessandro.) "Hi, I'd like to join," I said. He looked at me with a puzzled expression and invited me to follow him.

We crossed through a large first room, the meeting hall, where a tall man (appropriately nicknamed "The Tall One"—Marco Marsilio, now president of the Abruzzo region for Brothers of Italy, Fratelli d'Italia or FDI) was speaking to a group of men seated before him. As soon as they saw me, the room fell silent, and everyone turned to size me up as I passed. I definitely felt uncomfortable.

We continued down a long corridor with peeling walls. I glimpsed a small, shabby bathroom and a room crammed with rolled-up posters, buckets of glue, and scattered flyers. Finally, the tour ended in a makeshift office, where the section secretary, Peo, greeted me. He had long hair, a beard, and a leather jacket adorned with a Ramones pin. "Have I ended up in a community center by mistake?" I wondered. We exchanged phone numbers, writing them on a protest flyer that we tore in half—a keepsake we both still have. Peo, whose real name is Andrea De Priamo (now our group leader in the Capitoline Assembly) still swears that I was wearing a pink tracksuit that day. Journalists loved that detail so much that it has become something of an urban legend. Let me set the record straight, once and for all: I have never owned, let alone worn, a pink tracksuit. That day, I was wearing a more modest outfit: a blue sweater, blue pants, and a red-and-white checked shirt. Imagine showing up at the Youth Front in a pink tracksuit! I may have been young, but I did have some common sense.

At one of the first meetings I attended, something simple yet powerful struck me. Near the end, a guy asked, "Does anyone need a ride home?" That small gesture made me realize that this was a place of brotherhood. Everyone looked out for one another. It was like a family—one in which everyone belonged to everyone else.

We were portrayed as villains—even violent—but the reality was very different. The Youth Front was a welcoming environment. It excluded no one, providing a home to many who might not have found a social outlet elsewhere. Of course, every Youth Front section worth its salt had its own "eccentric," though, in truth, we all had our quirks. Reflecting on it now, I realize that many of us who embraced political activism came from unique or challenging family situations—some had separated parents or faced other difficult circumstances. The young people most committed to political engagement were searching for a sense of belonging, a place to find their purpose in life.

This is similar to other communities, like church communities, volunteer organizations, or associations. Spaces with strong idealistic foundations tend to attract individuals who share a vision and want to walk that same path.

Being a part of something significant builds confidence, and that was what many of those young people were seeking. It was true for me as well. Finding a point of reference made me feel useful. Belonging to a minority group—one that had to constantly defend itself yet knew how to go on the offensive—gave me a certain pride, even a sense of superiority. I never enjoyed following the crowd or the dominant mindset. Instead, I found more satisfaction in standing by the underdog and proving that the dismissed or misunderstood could be right. Unpopular positions were always the ones that felt most natural to me. For instance, I never saw smoking weed as rebellious; if everyone was doing it, true nonconformity meant saying no. That was my stance long before my political involvement. Later, I found that same stance reflected in one of the Youth Front's most memorable slogans: "Weed? That's for the rabbits."

It was in that summer of 1992 that my enduring battle began. Now, I continue the fight in the halls of Parliament, but back then it was on the streets of Rome—my first initiatives, first demonstrations, and first time handing out flyers in front of schools.

My baptism by fire came almost immediately with a nighttime poster run. For us, putting up posters was more than an activity—it was a genuine ritual. We prepared meticulously for days, rolling the posters for quicker application, fine-tuning the glue's consistency, and mapping out the routes. Teams were formed, with each member assigned a role. Speed, synchronization, and discretion were essential to avoid encounters with the police or harmless clashes with our opponents. I felt at ease with the process, and from that day onward, I did many more poster runs. Over time, I specialized in smaller flyers, much better suited to my size and hands. Armed with a brush and roll, while others put up posters, I would dash around and place flyers in the most unlikely places. Poster runs were like scuba diving: the first rule is to never lose sight of your team. And we never did. Wherever you were, if there was a problem, all the teams converged to help.

That's how I met the Fare Fronte group in those early days. "Fare Fronte" means to stick together. These were university students led by Marco Scurria, known as "Il Noto" (The Known One), who became their leader for several years and later served as our MEP (Member of the European Parliament).

Unlike our peers, who were preoccupied with fashion, nightclubs, or shopping along Via del Corso, we devoted our time to political activism. It was an all-consuming passion. When you dream of changing the world, there's no room for anything else. With an entire nation to save, personal desires become an unforgivable indulgence.

Thus, activism seeped into every part of life—at school, in the afternoons, and on weekends. If you went out at night, it was with fellow activists, and inevitably, the conversations circled back to politics. Our ideas and values touched everything we did. Even the little money we had was funneled into self-funding. Youth sections received no party funds; we were actually the ones financing the section by occasionally contributing 10,000 lire from our own pockets so we could buy glue or print posters. Membership fees and small events brought in a bit more, but it was just small change.

To support myself while staying committed to activism, I worked evenings and Sundays. I took on jobs as a babysitter, a wardrobe attendant, a vendor at a music stand at the Porta Portese market, and a bartender (at The Piper, a nightclub in Rome, where I invented a cocktail called "Giorgia"—a mix of five types of alcohol—absolutely dreadful!).

I was also lucky to work at the Tina Pika club, where many famous comedians got their start, among them Enrico Brignano, Antonio Giuliani, and the *Mamma mia che impressione* troupe. They were already hilarious back then at the beginning of their careers. I had my own comedic moments there: I once presented the wrong cake to a birthday VIP, and accidentally drizzled ketchup on a panna cotta instead of berry sauce.

I began spending time at the Colle Oppio section, the flagship for the Garbatella section. Led by Fabio Rampelli (now Deputy President of the Chamber of Deputies for Brothers of Italy), it had a rich history.

The place had a powerful atmosphere. Originally a Roman ruin, it was occupied after World War II by Istrian and Dalmatian refugees. In recent years, the former Mayor of Rome, Virginia Raggi, cleared the building with a total disregard for its historical and social significance. We'd had many Left-leaning mayors in Rome, but none had ever dreamed of such an action. Only someone with no understanding of political culture could ignore history that way. After this stunt by the Five Star Movement (Cinque Stelle, or M5S) mayor, what's become of that space? It's been closed—for two years now. Of course, it is now uninhabitable—a sort of cave without even a bathroom. I still remember the long walk to the nearest café a quarter of a mile away, just to use the facilities.

Back then, Colle Oppio was a bastion of culture, political activism, and respect for the law, despite being a park that has struggled with drug dealing, crime, and vagrancy for many decades. We considered Colle Oppio our home: each year, we mobilized to clean up the park. We were like a light shining on the area in the evenings. And each year we organized a small event called the Festa dei Rioni for the whole neighborhood. We set it up entirely by ourselves, hand-painting the graphics because we didn't have the money to print them. The festival featured concerts, debates, book readings, and theater. It was the precursor to the Atreju demonstrations, whose first editions also took place there.

I recently came across one cringeworthy photo from those days, in which I'm dressed as Samwise Gamgee, one of the hobbits from Tolkien's *The Lord of the Rings*. Sam has always been my favorite character—not noble like Aragorn, magic like Gandalf, strong like Gimli, or swift like Legolas. He's just a hobbit—a gardener by trade. And yet, without him,

Frodo would never have completed his mission. He knows his deeds won't be sung of in the future, so he chooses not to risk everything for mere glory.

Those books were already legendary to us back then, long before the movies turned them into a pop-cultural phenomenon. With one of our associations, we organized Fat Tuesday parties for local schoolchildren and all of us dressed up: some as hobbits, others as elves or dwarves. Of course, we also had a Sauron, an Aragorn, a Gollum, and a Gandalf among us.

One of our group, Giuseppe, was forced to play the part of Tom Bombadil. Instead of a leotard, the organizers had bought dark brown pantyhose for him to wear. I'll never forget the look on his face. In real life, Giuseppe was an architect and he was trying to build a professional reputation. Needless to say, he was very concerned about the performance he was forced to give.

There were at least thirty of us, and we brought to life a series of episodes from the books. The children could cross the park to view one performance after another. Of course, I and some of the others of short stature in the group were asked to be hobbits. Apart from myself, there were Franceschina, Andrea (nicknamed Gibba), and Frodo—who so resembled the character in looks and manners, that this was his actual nickname.

As part of the Front, we all had a nickname. In fact, I didn't discover some people's real names until many years later—and for some, I never did. It was almost like being in a secret society. We thought of ourselves as being pursued, sometimes justifiably, by certain factions of the Left and the authorities. Perhaps it was a holdover from the harshest years of political clashes among young people, but we avoided using real names as a form of protection. My own nickname was Calimera, though it never really caught on.

These code names often led to amusing conversations. While I was a student representative in Rome, I was asked one night at ten o'clock to call a meeting for the next day. Since there were no cell phones back then,

I had to call each of the kids at home. I worked my way down the list until I reached the home of a boy we'd nicknamed Pinotto. His mother answered with a startled tone, and as soon she said "Hello?" I realized I had no idea what her son's real name was. I stammered, "Hello, Signora, I . . . need . . . to talk to your son." "Which son?" she replied. "The one with the glasses, Signora," I replied.

A veteran Front member whom we always called Nocciolino (Peanut) still likes to tell this particular story, laughing every time. One day, his father answered the phone, handed it to him, looked him straight in the eye and said: "Listen, there's some guy on the phone claiming his name is Marta and he's asking for Nocciolino. Any idea what it's about?"

Laughter was a constant companion in our cave near the Domus Aurea. But mainly we engaged in endless debates, passionately dissecting nearly every facet of human knowledge. Some in our group even got too heated at times, arguing over trivial topics—like whether Tom Cruise's character in the *Last Samurai* made the right choice by wielding a katana against cannonballs. I distinctly remember the fierce debates: some argued that he chose the katana out of loyalty to tradition, while others argued he was simply stupid.

Every week, we gathered for what we liked to refer to as the "horn call," a tradition inspired by Boromir's mighty horn in *The Lord of the Rings*, which summoned the Fellowship to action. These meetings were moments to share and reflect on aphorisms, books, and newspaper articles. Our community poured immense energy into cultural growth. We were unafraid to ask tough questions or propose answers on any subject. Foreign politics and major international conflicts were topics of particular passion: the Israel-Palestinian conflict, the Iraq War, the broader situation in the Middle East, and the relationship between the United States and Europe. All these topics sparked debates that often grew intensely bitter.

People accuse us of being anti-Europe, but that's simply untrue. Just listen to the so-called alternative music of the time, like "Sulla strada," composed by the Italian musical group Compagnia dell'Anello (The Fellowship of the Ring, clearly inspired by Tolkien). That song speaks of a Europe of people and nations—a Europe rooted in civilization and solidarity, with the potential to act as a significant geopolitical force. Even then, we envisioned a Europe of free people, united by identity, shared values and shared challenges. We continue to defend this vision and build on it today. This model is a stark contrast to the current European Union, a nebulous entity in the hands of obscure bureaucrats who operate irrespective of national identities, or even of their own national governments.

When the Berlin Wall fell, it was a moment of much celebration in our world. For decades, many had turned a blind eye to communist oppression—or even lauded it, as the Italian Communist Party did. But we on the Right never forgot our brothers in Eastern Europe, who were crushed by its weight. Music, once again, bore witness to this memory. After Soviet tanks rolled into Hungary in 1956, Maestro Pier Francesco Pingitore, cofounder of the Il Bagaglino theater company, composed a song that became a generational anthem in Italy: "Avanti ragazzi di Buda" (Forward Youth of Budapest). In 2019, when Hungarian Prime Minister Viktor Orbán was a guest at Atreju, he thanked Italy and remarked: "The most beautiful song about the Hungarian Revolution of 1956 was written by Italians, and it begins with the words 'Avanti ragazzi di Buda . . .'"

Suddenly, the crowd rose to its feet and began singing. At first, the voices were soft, but then swelled in unison:

Avanti ragazzi di Buda
avanti ragazzi di Pest
studenti, braccianti, operai
il sole non sorge più ad est . . .

(Forward youth of Buda / forward youth of Pest / students, laborers, workers / the sun no longer rises in the East.)

There were thousands in the room, and to everyone present, it was a reminder of where they had come from. In the over two decades that Atreju has been running, I believe that this was the most moving moment of all.

Yet, the fall of the Berlin Wall was about more than these countries gaining their freedom. For us, it symbolized the promise of a united Europe, capable of claiming a leading role on the world stage. Whatever your perspective—whether you were pro-American or deeply critical of the United States, which was often subject to debate within the Italian Social Movement—there was one thing everyone agreed on: Europe was a giant in world history, and it needed to reclaim its rightful place. The Europe we envisioned then, and still do, remains a champion of the nations within it.

In short, we studied, analyzed, and constantly shared our ideas and opinions. Even now, when I hear people express their surprise with comments like, "Meloni is the studious type," I can't help but smile. For those of us who grew up like I did, politics has always been a serious and profound endeavor. Empty slogans and words spoken just to win votes have nothing to do with true politics. While it's impossible to know everything, it's equally impossible to speak about things you don't understand. Without knowledge, you risk becoming a tool in the hands of your adversaries.

But our focus on in-depth, often obsessive study wasn't the whole story. There was a deeply human dimension that transcended politics. Sharing the "revolution" meant sharing everything—starting from friendships. Many of my best friends today grew up with me in that same environment. Most of the people I've shared my life with come from there. It's also where most of the leaders of Brothers of Italy originated, as well as the people I turn to for advice—whether within or outside politics. They remain political activists, regardless of the path they took in life. Being the offspring of that political history doesn't require holding a seat in Parliament, or being an adviser. Anyone who carries that vision can help make those ideals reality and defend those principles, no matter their field of work. Many former activists have stayed connected over the years while pursuing entirely different paths. The bonds remain as they still meet, discuss, and exchange books and ideas.

* * *

It's true that the organization itself was highly hierarchical, but that hierarchy was built organically. Each member earned their place. Leadership at every level of the movement was based on merit—on what each individual had proven in terms of self-sacrifice, debate, growth, and courage. Above all, courage. Learning to be courageous was a cornerstone of our growth, both as activists and as individuals. A person taught to be courageous is unlikely to succumb to corruption when entrusted with public office or power. They have already stood at a crossroads, their own interests on one side and their principles on the other. Someone who has sacrificed for their own ideals and community is unlikely to bow before injustice or corruption. This is why I believe our world produced people of exceptional character. To us young folk, being engaged in politics in these contexts wasn't a means of personal advancement; it was a test of bravery and conviction. In the Front, no one pursued politics for opportunistic reasons or for personal gain. Quite the opposite; in those days, aspiring to a political career was considered a mark of disgrace.

I believe young people today are deprived of an education in courage. To me, courage should be a subject taught in schools. If it were, the textbook I would choose for the course would be *Gates of Fire* by Steven Pressfield. This historical novel recounts the Battle of Thermopylae, where three hundred Spartan soldiers, led by their King Leonidas, faced Xerxes's powerful Persian army, fully aware that none of them would survive. But for me, the book transcends history; it is a philosophical guide that defines bravery in all its forms—from raw audacity to the most noble kind, such as defending what and whom you love.

* * *

Being identified, as I was, as the face of the Right within the school system also brought its share of hostility from some teachers.

My early years of activism were spent as part of the student movement. As the Roman leader for schools, I oversaw all the activities in educational institutes throughout Rome during an exciting time of mobilization. To operate effectively, we adopted a pre-political tool of "unitary student coordination." This was not an organization tied to a specific party or ideology, but a broad-based association that allowed us to focus on our core message, especially regarding school reform. One of the most successful initiatives from this period was Antenati (Ancestors), founded in 1994. At a time when the Right was far from the majority, this group organized a march of over 20,000 people on Rome to oppose Minister Rosa Russo Jervolino's proposed reform (which was never implemented). The name "Antenati" was coined by Federico Mollicone, now a member of Parliament for Brothers of Italy, and someone who has always been creative with words. Using this playful goliardic term conveyed that we were fighting a school system stuck in the Jurassic era. *Jurassic Park* had just been released in cinemas and, like many other times before, we leveraged the wave of this pop culture phenomenon to get our message across more easily, while sidestepping the stigma our party name might have carried. At the time, attending assemblies with groups like Fare Fronte or Azione Studentesca (Student Action) often meant being forcibly removed—sometimes violently. The Left has always considered this a legitimate tool against right-wing organizations. Subtler forms of obstructionism also existed. For example, when you signed up to speak at an assembly, they wouldn't outright deny you the opportunity, but would schedule you last when there was no one left to listen. Let's just say that at a certain point I realized I would have to "earn" the right to speak.

I recall a fantastic article published in *Unità* at the time. It began: "Giorgia Meloni, president of Azione Studentesca, is always present at the assemblies. This time, too, she climbed on desks that had been turned into a platform and grabbed the microphone." Learning to navigate such challenging environments became an excellent training ground for me. Years later, at the age of twenty-nine—without ever having served as a representative in Parliament—I became vice president of the Chamber of Deputies. When I faced the assembly at Montecitorio (the seat of the Chamber of Deputies, the lower house of the Italian Parliament, and a name that is often used instead of Parliament in general), many assumed my lack of experience would make me an easy target. But after surviving countless student assemblies, adhering to parliamentary rules felt much simpler. I firmly believe that student political engagement is an extraordinary educational tool. It equips you with invaluable skills for success not just in politics, but also in life. It teaches courage, persuasiveness, and debate skills, and there's no room for shyness or hesitation.

In those years, I think I was one of the biggest experts on school reform because I was forced to study the planned reforms in depth so that I could offer a credible opinion.

From my second to fifth year of high school, I either occupied or self-managed the school with other students every year, spending nights in a sleeping bag—not to camp out or fool around, as some might think, but always with a deep sense of purpose. My time was mostly spent organizing debates and meetings. Yet, I was still a young student like everyone else, and during these occupations, I would sometimes pause and sing with others when someone brought out a guitar. That's how I fell in love with Augusto Daolio, the frontman for the band Nomadi. The lyrics of the song *Il paese delle favole* (The Land of Fairy Tales) defined many of these nights of sit-ins for me, and it remains one of the most wonderful tributes to youthful rebellion ever written:

"Don Quixote isn't happy but he works in a windmill / Ali Baba and the forty thieves have already won the elections / Hansel and Gretel have opened a chocolate factory / and Alice is searching for her wonders in the bottles. / . . . And you intellectuals have never talked about / how the wave ebbs and flows."

Of course, my role as a firebrand earned me low marks for behavior every year, which forced me to study hard enough to maintain a high grade average and remain unassailable—otherwise I risked getting squashed like a bug. I served as both class and school representative, which meant I was constantly busting everyone's you-know-whats. I became a sort of "defender of lost causes" for the students, and even appeared on TV as a student movement representative (watching those videos again, I think I look eerily like the hippie character played by Carlo Verdone in the comedy movie *Un sacco bello*). When it came time for my final high school exam, one of the teachers on the examining board—who wasn't exactly a fan of mine—decided it was payback time. Back then, students prepared two subjects for the oral exam: one chosen by the student, and one assigned by the board. In reality, most teachers allowed students to pick both, so I had prepared Italian and French for the oral because I loved the Decadent poets. But that's not how it went. The day before the exam, they switched my choice of Italian to German. German! I doubt that anyone else that year was tested on German. Sometimes I wonder if that's where my lingering dislike for Germany comes from.... I vividly remember being asked about Thomas Mann's *Death in Venice*.... I'm not sure how I managed, but I somehow muddled through the challenging German. Next, it was time to discuss my essay in Italian. I had written an essay about immigration, and the oral quickly morphed into a political trial. After about half an hour of relentless questioning, I couldn't hold back any longer: "Excuse me, but I need to remind you that you're testing my ideas, which isn't allowed. Your job is to evaluate my preparation." The teacher who had it in for me sneered and said, "Or else?" Having reached my limit, I replied: "Or else I'll lodge an appeal with the administrative court."

The examiners were clearly annoyed. The English teacher stepped in, trying to defuse the situation. In the end, despite that teacher's complaint, I was awarded the highest possible grade: 60/60— a result I had truly earned.

* * *

Those years were deeply significant to me personally, but they also held broader importance for our world. Many of the battles we fought during that time later became part of our collective heritage, extending well beyond the domain of the Right. For instance, we opposed the idea of teachers selecting specific textbooks for high school classes. We believed that teachers should limit themselves to defining the topics to be taught while allowing students to choose their own books. This stance was motivated partly by economic reasons, but also to prevent textbooks from becoming tools for political indoctrination. A particularly contentious issue was the school's fifth-year syllabus, which included the history of the twentieth century to the present. My group and I spent an entire summer combing through widely adopted texts, searching for surreal or tendentious sentences. We then collected them all in a booklet that sold like hotcakes across Italy. A lot of this work focused on the Foibe massacres, the horrific ethnic cleansing in which thousands of Italians were killed by Tito's Yugoslav Partisans at the end of World War II. We also highlighted the Julian-Dalmatian exodus that followed the persecution, during which hundreds of thousands of our fellow Italians were forced to leave everything they owned behind just to remain Italians and not fall under communist rule.

For decades, Italy turned a blind eye to these martyrs because acknowledging them meant admitting that Tito's Partisans were murderers. But we never ceased our efforts to ensure that the truth about these events was widely known. I have always detested those who manipulate history for political purposes—who reproach others for tragedies that occurred decades or even centuries ago, wielding them as tools for self-serving agendas. Yet, without the awareness of our past, we can't look ahead and cultivate a shared memory. A country that forgets its dead for partisan interests forfeits its claim to being called a country at all.

At the time, the history of our eastern border was conspicuously absent from school textbooks, as though the page had been torn out. In some ways, it might have been better not to mention it at all, given the shameful way it was handled when it was discussed. I still remember *Elementi di storia—XX secolo* by Augusto Camera and Renato Fabietti, one of the most widely used textbooks. It relegated the Foibe massacre to a supplemental section, which included only a photograph of the plaque at the foiba of Basovizza—one of the two sites that remained within Italian territory. Beneath the photograph was a shocking caption:

"After World War One it was used as a landfill, also for war material, and it was notorious as a place where people committed suicide. It was declared a national monument in 1992."

Our booklet sparked intense debate and forced teachers to be more mindful of the choices they made. It also compelled militant party historians to rein in their biases when producing educational materials. This was a huge political victory. The campaign's accompanying demonstration made waves: we entered a bookstore and stamped the pages of the most biased textbooks with the words: "Fake, do not buy." We didn't want the bookshop owner to be out of pocket, so we asked the few members of the National Alliance Party at the time to buy all the stamped copies. To this day, some claim that we burned those books, but that's a lie. We bought every last one of them. Misrepresentations like that don't surprise me—our world has always been mischaracterized by others.

Few people know, for instance, that right-wing youth have always been environmentalists. A prime example is Fare Verde (Making Green), a pioneering environmental association born from the Right. It was founded by Paolo Colli, nicknamed Poldo (the Italian name for Wimpy from *Popeye*) for his resemblance to Popeye's sandwich-eating friend. Poldo was a visionary who tackled diverse challenges, from battling ocean pollution caused by non-biodegradable Q-tips, to supporting international cooperation for development in Africa and the Balkans. Paolo died of leukemia in 2005, which many attributed to his exposure to depleted uranium while working with refugees from Kosovo. In winters, Paolo led us on beach cleanups when they were closed to the public, and in the summers, he'd take us camping in the woods to fight fires set by arsonists.

We miss Paolo. We miss his wisdom, his madness, his ability to turn everything upside down because he simply couldn't stand rigid patterns.

Our community was filled with visionaries—people who refused to look back, to be relegated to caricatures in the eyes of others. For us, politics was never about passively implementing an ideology. Even when our party was marginalized, politics meant actively building those ideas, turning them into building blocks that could change people's lives. Proof of this lies in the names chosen by our youth movements: from "Fare" Fronte (Stick Together) to "Azione" Giovani (Youth Action). The fact that today some political groups borrow names like "Azione," and imitate the grassroots membership drives we pioneered twenty-five years ago, tells you just how ahead of our time we were.

The story of Paolo Di Nella, one of the last members of the Youth Front to be killed during the violent 1970s, is emblematic of our struggles. In 1983, Paolo was attacked with an iron rod while hanging flyers on a wall with another activist, Daniela. He shouldn't have been allowed to hang flyers in the Roman neighborhood deemed the least "safe" for us. But Paolo was too involved in the campaign to expropriate Villa Chigi, which had been abandoned and neglected. He wanted it to be used for neighborhood services, hoping a youth community could be born there, a social space run by the young people in the neighborhood. Our challenge was to fight isolation by offering practical solutions to people's everyday problems. It was no coincidence that in these times headquarters were popping up in the most run-down outskirts of the capital.

And so the stubborn Paolo Di Nella had gone out to hang his flyers. His attackers bludgeoned him in the head once, and then ran off. Paolo got up, rinsed his head in a small street fountain, downplayed the incident to Daniela, and asked her to take him home. That night, he fell ill and was hospitalized. Within hours, Paolo slipped into a coma. For seven agonizing days, his community kept vigil at the Policlinico Umberto I hospital. But it wasn't enough. Paolo died on February 9, just hours after his twentieth birthday.

However, during that week of agony something unexpected happened: Sandro Pertini, then-President of the Republic, the partisan Socialist president, visited Paolo in the hospital. It was a historic event for our community and beyond.

During the period of political terrorism known as the Years of Lead, many—too many—of our activists were killed. Some simply for being in an Italian Social Movement headquarters, like the killings that occurred at the Italian Social Movement headquarters on Via Acca Larentia, or for writing an essay against the Red Brigades, like Sergio Ramelli in Milan. They died for no reason, they had committed no crime, and they were systematically forgotten. The few times their names were uttered, it was to justify the actions of their killers. The phrase "it's not a crime to kill a fascist" wasn't just scrawled on walls, it permeated the mindset. I'm saying this because it is a significant piece of our history, but also because I realize that the idea of justified violence against "an unacceptable enemy" has reared its dangerous head again in recent years, fueled by irresponsible politicians and would-be intellectuals.

President Pertini's visit to Paolo sent a profoundly different message. We could no longer accept the fact that young people's lives were being destroyed. Violence was no longer acceptable, nor was the cowardly silence of the Italian nation that had turned a blind eye for years.

* * *

What truly changed everything were the municipal elections in Rome in 1993. I had only recently arrived, and maybe at the time, like many others, I didn't grasp the importance of the shift that was unfolding. The run-off election for Mayor of Rome between Gianfranco Fini and Francesco Rutelli signaled that the dam had burst. The moment had finally come when you could compete to win, to govern, to lead our people. Now, ideas could be turned into action.

And maybe because we had never resigned ourselves to being mere spectators, we were ready. We knew we needed to broaden our horizons and adapt our tools to this new and long-anticipated phase. For us, parties—which for many represent the culmination of their political commitment—had always just been a means to an end. The realization of ideas is the ultimate goal.

This is why the "svolta di Fiuggi"—the transition from the Italian Social Movement to National Alliance (Alleanza Nazionale, or AN)—felt entirely natural to us. In fact, many of us suffered much more, years later, when the National Alliance became the People of Freedom (Popolo della Libertà, or PDL). Fiuggi had been a way of making our demands more compelling, while the PDL risked, and in some ways succeeded in, diluting and weakening that legacy.

For the youth movement, especially the Roman chapter, which had never thrived on nostalgia and had always been at the cutting edge—even within the Italian Social Movement—the transition to National Alliance was clearly the right path forward at that moment in history. It was more effective to making our ideas triumphant, of bringing to fruition what we had only imagined for so many years, cramped in the cubbyhole under the stairs of some party headquarters. Among other things, we had always rejected the "whiplash" of nostalgic folklore that played into the hands of our adversaries. In fact, we actively fought against it, knowing full well that nothing could be built on nostalgia alone. To truly do politics, you must tackle the issue of garnering consensus. Ideas must resonate with the man on the street, who exists outside ideological complexities but is searching for guidance. If your ideas fail to persuade anyone and remain confined to an elite circle, you are not defending those ideas. True defense comes from sharing them widely. The hardest and most exhilarating challenge, then as now, is convincing as many people as possible without betraying who you are.

A year after National Alliance was founded, the Youth Front underwent the same evolution. The glorious history of the Front came to a close, giving rise to Youth Action. The change of name had once again been anticipated in Rome, where university students had earlier transitioned from the grandiose-sounding "Fare Fronte per il contropotere studentesco" (Stick Together for Student Opposition) to a more sober "Azione Universitaria" (University Action). Once again, the movement adapted by opening itself up while holding steadfast to its core values. However, the tools, proposals, and battles used to defend and develop those values had to adapt to a rapidly changing society.

Each generation bears the responsibility for paving its part of the road along this journey. Those who attempt to engage in politics by merely imitating what other young people like them did twenty or thirty years earlier will never get far. We were determined to prove what our generation was capable of.

Until that point, we had banded together for survival and self-defense. But now the time had come to step forward and take action. The transition from the Youth Front to Youth Action marked exactly that: the beginning of a new chapter in history.

We've accomplished so much since then, and everything has changed. For better? Or for worse? I'm not sure. What I do know is that those years were unquestionably the best phase of my entire political engagement.

I AM A WOMAN

The Stronger Sex

Yes, I am a woman, but I must admit that I have never experienced discrimination in my political career.

To be clear, I've definitely had to deal with attitudes of mistrust, and I've often felt people observing me and thinking, "Let's see how *this* one copes." In addition to being a woman, I was young and had decided to embrace the Right. So, according to an odious and false radical chic bias, if we're not deemed "unpresentable," then we must be subpar. Yet, looking back now, overcoming the expectations of those before me proved less challenging than I had expected.

In time, I half-seriously, half-jokingly adopted the words of Charlotte Whitton, Mayor of Ottawa in the 1950s: "Whatever women do, they must do twice as well as men to be thought half as good. Luckily, this is not difficult." Perhaps this resonated because meritocracy has always been a cornerstone for us. Those who must fight to earn every inch of their space cannot afford to base their choices on last names, bank accounts, or the education someone could afford. For us, the saying "one is equal to one" really holds true. This is not to say, as the Five Star Movement might put it, that "one is worth as much as another because no one understands anything anyway," but rather in the sense that everyone starts from the same point. No favoritism, no bias—how far you go depends solely on what you can prove.

I'm sure that, over the years, some have wondered, deep down inside, "Where will we end up with a woman leading us?" But if they did, no one ever let it show. On the Right, being a woman has never been a barrier to achieving the highest roles. In fact, it was the Right in Italy that helped the largest number of women to emerge and secure prominent positions. Before becoming President of Brothers of Italy, I was elected to lead the youth movement of National Alliance, in the only true Congress in which that party has ever been celebrated. That's the key: I was elected. By contrast, those on the Left pay a lot of lip service to equal rights for women but often reduce the presence of women to being a concession by men. Matteo Renzi exemplified this when, as he launched his new Italia Viva Party (Italy Alive Party, talk about optimism . . .), he proclaimed it to be "the most feminist party in Italian history" because he had chosen Teresa Bellanova to lead it and Maria Elena Boschi as head of the Chamber of Deputies. That is not how things work for us. On the Right, whether you're a man or a woman, your position must be earned through your skills—not handed to you by someone already in power. And if women rise, it's not because some man made it happen.

That said, I did have some challenging moments. Moments when I, too, had to confront ridiculous stereotypes. One instance that stands out was when I announced I was expecting my daughter, Ginevra. For the first time, I genuinely believed people might think I was unfit for an important political role because of my growing belly. In those days, the Center-Right was searching for a mayoral candidate for Rome. At the time, the city was led by a marvelous commissioner, following the distressing scandal surrounding Ignazio Marino—the surgeon-turned-mayor whom the Democratic Party had once fervently supported for the Campidoglio (Capitol), only to abandon him with ruthless cynicism after his expenses scandal. It was early 2016. I had learned just two weeks earlier that Andrea and I were expecting a baby. On the afternoon of January 30, I participated in Family Day at the Circus Maximus in Rome—a massive and deeply moving rally.

In a mix of happiness and euphoria, and feeling embraced by the warmth of the people in attendance, I instinctively shared the news with a reporter who was interviewing me. She looked at me in disbelief, aware that I was giving her a scoop. "Really?" she asked. "Yes," I replied, "God willing, the next time I'm here, it'll be as a mom, too."

A few hours later, the news had spread, and a wave of controversy and vulgar sarcasm exploded, amplified—as always—by the tremendous power of the internet and social media. The insults soon followed, ferocious and relentless. I'm used to being insulted—sometimes to such a degree that I've become immune to the nastiness—but not this time. Reading comments that someone hoped I would miscarry was deeply hurtful. Not for me—I've never been intimidated by keyboard warriors—but for the defenseless life I was carrying, which had unwittingly triggered such hostility. In that moment, I felt as though I'd failed my very first mission as a mother. I can still vividly recall the comic actresses who regularly appeared on RAI TV, the fixtures on talk shows who couldn't resist recycling offensive, hackneyed lines. For those self-proclaimed progressive thinkers, those modern, liberal women, I had no right to announce my pregnancy at a pro-family event simply because I was unmarried. I have often heard similarly ridiculous claims: if you're unmarried, you shouldn't defend the traditional family. It's as absurd as saying that if you're young, you shouldn't address issues affecting the elderly, or if you're human, you shouldn't advocate for animal welfare. That said, there were several moments of solidarity from political leaders expressing their support. I particularly remember Roberta Pinotti, then–Minister of Defense for the Democratic Party (Partito Democractico, PD), who sent me a pair of baby booties, along with a heartfelt message, quoting Dante, that essentially said "don't bother with them, just look and move on" (*non ragioniam di lor, ma guarda e passa*).

* * *

Still, the controversy did not die down until Guido Bertolaso, former Head of the Civil Protection Department and the Center-Right's unofficial mayoral candidate for Rome, weighed in on television. He said aloud what many others were thinking but hadn't dared to express openly: "Meloni just wants to be a mom." In hindsight, I believe Guido's intentions were paternalistic, and that his words simply came out wrong—but at the time, it enraged me.

Just a few days after Family Day, fully aware of the risks that a pregnancy at my age could involve, I had announced my decision not to run for the Campidoglio, and removed my name from consideration as a candidate. Yet, Bertolaso's absurd comment about staying home with a baby bottle and a high chair, coupled with the chaotic handling of primaries and campaigns essentially run from under a temporary gazebo, made me change my mind. Ironically, Bertolaso had become a great motivator. And it wasn't the last time I chose to do something simply because I was told I couldn't.

I've never believed that a woman should enter politics solely to represent women. Politics is for everyone—for the common good. But in that instance, I must admit that my candidacy was driven by a desire to combat "female discrimination." If someone like me, with my privileges, was being told to step aside because I was expecting a baby, what chance did a pregnant young woman have with a temp job in a call center? My campaign for mayoral office became a battle in the name of women, their freedom from discrimination for being mothers. I wanted to prove that children are not a limitation—in fact, they help us overcome limitations. Motherhood gives us extraordinary strength. What better place to convey that message than in a city symbolized by a she-wolf nursing twins?

Of course, some difficult pregnancies require extra care and protection, and every woman has the right to decide freely how to approach motherhood. But, as I said at the time, no man has the right to dictate what a woman should or shouldn't do.

My decision wasn't meant to impose a standard; I wanted (and still want) it to be seen as a free choice. In a society where fewer and fewer children are born every year, I want motherhood to be valued, safeguarded, and protected, not seen as a problem or an inconvenience.

* * *

Luckily, during the months of my electoral campaign I was in great physical shape. Between ultrasounds, I visited neighborhoods across the city, my belly growing with each passing week. Sadly, it wasn't just my belly that expanded. Between electoral dinners and croissants offered at cafés, the result of the campaign was fifteen pounds gained in a single month. And like so many other mothers, it took me years to shed those pounds. This, too, became fodder for ridicule. I remember actress and director Asia Argento snapping a picture of me in a restaurant and posting it online with the English caption (who knows why she chose that language): *Back fat of the rich and shameless—#fascistspottedgrazing*. I wouldn't have responded if her words hadn't also insulted every woman struggling to lose pregnancy weight. So, I shared her post with my reply: "I'm sharing this post by Asia Argento regarding a picture that she secretly took of me (how brave of her) because, aside from her tiresome insults that don't concern me, I was struck by her reference to my 'back fat.' I share this to tell every woman who has recently given birth and doesn't sniff cocaine to lose weight to ignore any poor soul who mocks her body. Putting on a few pounds was worth it, a million times over."

To go back to the electoral campaign, I discovered neighborhoods that I, a proud Roman through and through, had never even heard of. I treasure those memories, like that of the young mother in Tor Sapienza who had just lost her job a few days before, but still gave me a blanket for Ginevra—a simple yet powerful gesture. And I'll never forget the thousands of letters and text messages I received on my cell phone from other women, all of them urging me to succeed—not just for myself, but for them as well.

While some Romans likely believed my pregnancy disqualified me from serving as mayor, I have never ever regretted venturing into the fray while carrying Ginevra in my womb. Ultimately, while I lost the election, I won as a woman and a mother. I like to think that my candidacy sent a message that was even acknowledged by my rival, Laura Boldrini. I remember the sincere affection she expressed—despite our bitter political disputes—as she stroked my baby bump and told me how symbolically important my candidacy was.

Yet, I still wonder why there is such a marked resistance in Italy compared to elsewhere when it comes to entrusting women with significant leadership roles. Why is it that handing a woman the fate of a company, a bank, a city, or nation is seen as so risky in Italy, so exotic, or even revolutionary? After all, we recognize women's ability to manage a family with children, and women already play essential roles in society. So why shouldn't those same qualities that we value in a household—seriousness, sensitivity, responsibility, pragmatism—work outside the home as well? In Italy, we often say, *buon padre di famiglia* (good family man)—but it is actually "good family women" who run the household.

So yes, I am convinced that increasing the presence of qualified women in leadership roles would revitalize the morality and efficiency of our governing class, which at times feels lackluster, apathetic, and lacking any regard for work ethic. However, the solution isn't just about numbers; equal opportunities must begin at the starting line. Relying on quotas at the finish line, where a simple calculation overlooks the value of individuals, will only result in mediocrity. As a party leader (and I have always been against fixed quotas and in favor of a return to a meritocracy) I want to choose only the best people, regardless of gender. But don't voice that to some would-be feminists, who will cry: "What's the problem? There are tons of mediocre men, so why do women always need to be perfect?" Well, if there are any mediocre men running the country, then we need to get rid of them, not put mediocre women at their side. The problem isn't the number of women in charge, but their level of power.

Competent women must be given a level playing field, where they aren't pushed around or faced with prejudice. When that day comes, we can finally appreciate the value that most women have to offer. Women are pragmatic and resilient, qualities born of a society in which we have to do double the work of any man in a single day, with no time to spare.

Since the birth of my daughter, I can't bear people who drone on for hours just to hear their own voices—all without ever finding a solution. I can't afford to waste my time on futile debates because every minute is precious, and I must admit, I've often lost my patience. Seneca's words to his pupil Lucilius come to mind: "Set yourself free for your own sake; gather and save your time, which till lately has been forced from you, or filched away, or has merely slipped from your hands. Make yourself believe the truth of my words . . . Nothing, Lucilius, is ours except time." How many times have I been tempted to interrupt everyone just to read these lines aloud? I often think, "Make yourself believe the truth of my words," as I watch others squander precious moments. Etched in stone, Seneca's wisdom continues: "[Men] never regard themselves as in debt when they have received some of that precious commodity—time! And yet time is the one loan which even a grateful recipient cannot repay." It seems that little has changed since ancient Rome to the present, especially when it comes to "men" talking to each other.

That's right, women are more down-to-earth, and—if I may add—also prouder and less susceptible to corruption or betrayal. Several studies have explored this phenomenon, offering different theories, but the fact remains that—when the male–female ratio is equal—women are statistically less likely than men to be involved in corruption. When a woman is truly committed to a cause, she is unwavering in her resolve—something that Italy could benefit from greatly today. It's yet another reason to reassure Italians that electing women is nothing to fear.

As for me, I received that trust from voters for the first time about twenty years ago. I had just turned twenty when I ran as candidate for the provincial council of Rome, representing the Garbatella constituency. It was what is known as a "plurinominal" body, meaning that each party fielded one candidate in each territory. Garbatella was one of the capital's most left-wing constituencies, and Fabio Rampelli, who first believed in me, took a chance by encouraging my candidacy. He thought an outsider with an irreverent, mold-breaking campaign was the only way to tackle such a steep challenge. The strategy was simple: introduce Meloni—a fresh face—and let her run a disruptive election campaign. With nothing to lose, we went all in.

Given the odds, I had no illusions about winning. Still, when I think back to those days, those hours, I recall how determined we were from the very start. No matter how impossible the challenge seemed, we always played to win. Looking back, I still cringe at the facial expressions they forced me to make for campaign posters, but those were formative times. Each and every day we came up with new initiatives—something brilliant and outright crazy—to grab the attention of the constituencies. Thanks to the tireless efforts of my community, the results surpassed my expectations: against all odds, I was elected.

For the first time, the Center-Right won control of the Province, led by a president from the National Alliance Party, Silvano Moffa. It was a historic victory: National Alliance secured eighteen councilors (*consiglieri*). I was seventeenth, aged just twenty-one. That campaign also marked the beginning of one of my most solid friendships—one that spans a lifetime, from the political battlefield to summer vacations. I'm speaking of Francesco Lollobrigida, known as "Lollo," now President of the Deputies of Brothers of Italy. Though sharp-minded and loyal, he wasn't exactly easy going, and initially, we disliked each other. Over time, we became like siblings—arguing often but always standing by each other. I have never had much patience for yes-men, bootlickers, or people who say one thing to your face and another behind your back. I believe you can judge a person's intelligence (and this particularly applies to leaders) by the people they choose to surround themselves with. I have always surrounded myself with those who tell me the truth—even when it hurts. Lollo is one of them. These are the people who truly love you, who make you feel secure just by standing by your side as the battle rages.

I must admit, my revolutionary spirit burned so bright that issues at the Provincial level seemed dusty and—let's face it—boring. Of course, the topics we discussed were practical and undeniably important: from road maintenance to waste management. My background as a student leader drew my attention to one particular issue: the condition of school buildings. In my view, the state of our education facilities lies at the heart of the challenges facing Italy's education system. A significant portion of its dysfunction stems from the dilapidated infrastructure. We wanted schools to serve as community hubs, akin to those in other leading Western democracies—institutions equipped with gyms, science labs, reading rooms, and dining halls. Places where kids could spend their mornings and afternoons beyond the classroom, engaging in sports and other extracurricular activities.

For five years, I attended a high school that didn't have a gym. Our building, like many others, wasn't even designed to be a school. We were lucky to sometimes have a volleyball net hanging sadly in the courtyard.

In short, I lived through the limitations of Italian schools. I've verified, touched, and immersed myself in the situation—that's always been my working method. Because to solve a problem, you have to dive in and fully understand it.

I began working for the Province in January 1999, and for the next four years, I commuted between various towns and cities, striving to provide solutions for the many issues facing the administrations. Being part of the majority party gave me the freedom and authority to intervene, and I felt truly happy when I could solve problems. Yet, whenever I returned to my seat in the council, I never hesitated to speak about broader issues, even those that had little to do with the immediate challenges of the Province.

That's how I ended up in a tent in the middle of a desert, wrapped in a woolen blanket, trying not to think about the endless sand around me, and dreading the moment I'd have to use the bathroom—a humble hut made of bricks and mud, with a hole in the ground teeming with gigantic cockroaches.

I was in Southern Algeria, near Western Sahara, where the Sahrawi people had been resisting since 1975. That year, Morocco staged the "Green March," a mass demonstration demanding that Western Sahara be handed over to it. The Sahrawi people, the region's native inhabitants, stood firm to protect their culture, ancient traditions, and dignity.

The story of the Sahrawi people is emblematic for understanding the complexities of international politics. After sixteen long years of conflict, in 1991, the United Nations finally intervened with a peace mission. Their white jeeps arrived, adorned with blue flags and carrying officials who promised to hold a referendum on self-determination. Enthusiasm, hope, and expectation filled the air. Yet, to this day, there has been no trace of that referendum.

At the time, my goal was to support the Sahrawis, who lived as refugees in the middle of the desert with virtually nothing. I managed to secure funds to purchase and install a solar-powered desalination unit—a device that transforms water from the earth's deepest veins into drinking water. For the makeshift refugee camp, this was an invaluable tool.

I spent ten unforgettable days in that camp together with my fellow councilors, and the memory of a people with an unshakeable sense of belonging is still etched in my mind. It was there that I truly learned what it means to love one's land—to feel an inseparable bond with it and decide to defend it at all costs. Someone once wrote that we are offered the chance to love and serve a specific place to honor it, and that we are given the opportunity to undertake an extraordinary act to prove, against all cynicism, that Paradise is not everywhere—and not just anything, but something. From the Saharawi people, I learned that even a fistful of sand can become our little piece of heaven. As is the case for the people of postcolonial regions, the Saharawis' plight is shaped by complex dynamics, the kind that the international community often finds intractable. Yet, I firmly believe that seeking a peaceful, long-term solution for this area would send a profound message. It would come to the aid of a moderate Islamic people who have rejected terrorism and extremism as a means of drawing a spotlight to their cause. Instead, they have entrusted their fate to international bodies. The Saharawis chose diplomacy, but the sad truth is that their choice is yet to be rewarded.

In the company of the proud women of this forgotten people, I sipped tea in the desert, poured from teapots with slender spouts and served in small glasses. The tradition requires drinking three glasses with varying amounts of sugar: one as bitter as life, one as sweet as love, and one as gentle as death.

* * *

This experience in the desert remains the most curious of my years as a provincial councilor. I was always busy trying to understand how the administrative machinery worked while simultaneously seeking meaning for the battles of my youth.

I am a woman and I don't want to be treated like some vulnerable species, like the panda, for instance.

During my time as a councilor, I also remember clashing with structures supposedly designed to protect women but which I found—and still find—grotesque and counterproductive: the so-called "Commissione delle Elette" (Board of Elected Women). In addition to the standard boards covering various topics, this one focused solely on "equal opportunity" and was exclusively for women, regardless of their party.

The effect was infantilizing—like being confined to a children's playroom, all of us there forced to talk about our problems, while the men next door were engaged in "real" politics. I quit the "Commissione delle Elette" after only a couple of meetings. The real challenge for women, in my view, lies in competing in the game played by all the "adults"—not creating a separate one where we merely feel safe because we've been isolated in a comfortable space that we perceive is ours. Perhaps it is a reaction to this tendency—this inferiority complex that leads many women to compete primarily with each other—that I have always preferred competing with men.

I am a woman, and I have never had the physical presence that might be expected of someone leading young right-wing activists, most of whom are men. As I said before, I've never felt discriminated against, but I've always understood that a leader must be the strongest, the bravest, and the person most capable of guiding a community through challenges.

Being a petite blonde woman might have been perceived as an obstacle or a weakness, but I never let this stop me. I simply had to prove I had more courage—and I realized that sometimes a bit of madness proved useful.

A strong, loud voice has been one of my assets. It compensated for my appearance and made me easy to recognize. Giuseppe Conte, during the phone call where he tried to persuade me to participate in some useless States-General meeting at Villa Pamphilj, after the first wave of the COVID-19 pandemic, admitted that he envied my voice. His own voice, softer and hoarser, often made it harder for him to impose himself.

* * *

Politics is made up of seasons, paths, and leaps. For me, the leap that mattered most—on a national level—was the one I took in 2004, aged twenty-seven, at the National Alliance youth movement meeting in Viterbo. After several days of heated debates between the supporters of two candidates, it was just a fistful of votes that made the difference. I was elected President of Youth Action, defeating Carlo Fidanza, now head representative for Brothers of Italy in the European Parliament. Carlo was—and is—a formidable opponent, with great rhetoric skill and shrewdness. He is one of the few people I know who studies as rigorously as I do. After winning the election (somehow), the first thing I did was ask him to lend me a hand. He agreed, and we continue to work together to this day. To be honest, many of the people involved in that meeting have since become executives of and representatives in Parliament for Brothers of Italy. It's fascinating to think that those who once beat each other up—politically and beyond—are now united on the same team. Giovanni Donzelli is one of the people I could and still can count on the most; Mauro Rotelli is our communications go-to and was then the head of the event that had hosted the meeting; "terrible" Andrea Delmastro and the patient Marcello Gemmato; Salvatore Deidda, whom everyone called Sasso; Augusta Montaruli and Carolina Varchi, two of our brightest parliamentarians; the Venetian Ciro Maschio; the excellent Mayor of Catania, Salvo Pogliese; and two of the key figures in Brothers of Italy's most recent victories, Francesco Acquaroli, President of the Marche Region, our second president of a Region after Marsilio (of fundamental importance in Viterbo as well), and Emanuele Prisco, who managed his campaign. There are also lesser-known names, the people who never sought the limelight, like Roberto Mele, the current treasurer of Brothers of Italy. Though not in the spotlight, many owe him a great deal.

* * *

Just two years after that meeting, Gianfranco Fini helped me become Vice President of the Chamber.

The run-up to this unexpected appointment to one of the highest posts of the state began in 2002 at the National Alliance meeting in Bologna.

At the time, I had just become one of the four commissioners for Youth Action. Despite trying to flee from that event, I was scheduled to speak on Saturday—the assembly's most important day. My speech was slotted between Francesco Storace and Ignazio La Russa, on a massive stage, in front of the entire party elite, with my face projected on two giant screens before a crowd of five thousand people. It was a whole new dimension, and I was petrified.

Still, I managed to keep control of the situation. I steadied my nerves, memorized my speech, and delivered it successfully. Unsurprisingly, I concluded with a quote from the *The Lord of the Rings*:

"It is not our part to master all the tides of the world, but to do what is in us for the succour of those years wherein we are set, uprooting the evil in the fields that we know, so that those who live after may have clean earth to till."

Fini stood up to congratulate me—a small gesture that everyone noticed. The next day, in the final report, he even went so far as to quote something I had said.

I first encountered Fini during my candidacy for the Province of Rome, but it was little more than a formal introduction. I got to know him better after I was elected President of Youth Action—a role for which he would have preferred Carlo Fidanza.

To faithfully recount the genesis of our relationship, I must mention another instance after the episode in Bologna, where Fini had no choice but to take notice of me. It was in Rome, at the Atreju Festival, where he became the first victim of the first of many pranks we would play on festival guests.

It was 2005, and Fini was serving as Minister of Foreign Affairs. True to his belief in youth questions from the young people in the audience. I must give him credit—he never criticized this approach. Having himself been secretary of the Youth Front, Fini respected our independence and even our irreverence. As questions were fired at him—most of them polemical on all types of human knowledge—one university leader, Cristian, stood up (we called him Hobbit):

"Given that the topic is people's self-determination, now that we've been elected, can something be done for the Christian minority of the Kaziri in Turkmenistan?" Immediately afterward, a bald man with a long red beard stood up, clasped his hands together, and pleaded for help in a petulant, exotic accent: "Much help needed, President, help Kaziri."

Fini, with his usual aplomb, crossed his legs and began to answer the question: "I am aware of the situation, the discrimination . . ." At this point, Simone, another university leader, got up and interrupted, "We're students, sir, please forgive us for such a harmless prank." At first, Fini was at a loss for words, then good-humoredly stood up to shake the hand of the faux Kaziri, correcting him with a smile, "It's Kazaro—with one 'z,' not two."

That was just the beginning. Fini may have been our first victim, but many others followed. Berlusconi, for instance, was reminded of the cruelty of a fictional dictator in Laos named Pai Mei (a name borrowed from the movie *Kill Bill*). At the time, the Cavaliere always carried a black book on communism under his arm. Then there was a lot of talk about the prank on Walter Veltroni, who attended one of our events in 2007 while serving as Mayor of Rome. We asked him about alleged blight in the "Pinarelli district." Unfazed, Veltroni began listing all the measures being taken to address issues in the city's peripheries. At a certain point, I interrupted, "Walter . . . there is no Pinarelli district in Rome." This time, we'd borrowed the name from a film starring Tomas Milian, *Crime in Formula One*. The mayor did not take the joke well: "Oh, so you just wanted to play games. . . . I think I know Rome well!" In 2009, we convinced Massimo D'Alema to sign a petition to name a park after "Friederich Kemp," the alleged sole victim of the Fall of the Berlin Wall. The backstory? A piece of the wall had supposedly fallen on this fictional martyr's head, making him a symbol of European unity. Surprisingly, D'Alema got a good laugh out of it. In 2013, we targeted another mayor of the capital, Ignazio Marino. He was introduced to the supposed 1960 Olympic rowing champion Daniele Oscherz advocating for the Olympics to return to Rome. That prank marked the end of an era, as by then, most people knew to anticipate our antics—they came ready for us. But these frat-house pranks never truly disappeared from Atreju.

* * *

Atreju began with Youth Action in 1998, under the leadership of Basilio Catanoso, who is now a member of Brothers of Italy. Some mispronounce it as "Atreggiu" or "Atruia," while others assumed it was the name of a Sardinian shepherd. Clearly, not everyone has read *The Neverending Story* by Michael Ende. Its protagonist is named Atreju, a courageous young hero fighting the encroaching Nothing. The name symbolizes the fight against nihilism, perfectly capturing our vision. For over twenty-two years, the Atreju celebration has been a vital cornerstone for the right-wing world. Throughout upheaval, collapse, and reconstruction, Atreju is there without fail, every September. It has stood firm as a reminder of identity and unity, even during times of great uncertainty and torment. We like to call it a "nonpartisan" event, in the sense that it's not linked to one party.

In fact, we've never featured symbols of specific movements at Atreju, which is now one of the main international and national political events. Not because we wanted to hide, but because the scope of Atreju is much broader than those of a single party. True, organizing it has ruined nearly all the summers of my life, keeping me on the phone nonstop to plan every detail and organize all the stands. It's also true that, at times, I hated it. But Atreju also brought me some of the most profound moments of my entire political life.

One such moment was meeting Thomas and Kate, the young parents of little Alfie Evans, a British child with a severe neurodegenerative disease. Alfie died at just two years old after the hospital where he was treated decided to stop life support. His parents had opposed the decision and a long legal fight ensued. They demanded that their son be transferred to the Bambino Gesù di Roma to continue receiving palliative care. Along with Angelino Alfano, the then–Minister of Foreign Affairs, and Marco Minniti, at the time Minister of the Interior, we managed to grant Alfie Italian citizenship, hoping to ease the transfer process. Unfortunately, British judges sided with the British physicians, and nothing could be done. So, in 2018, we awarded the *Premio Atreju* to that young couple, who had just experienced the most devastating of deaths, to honor their courage not only for fighting for their child, but also for upholding the universal principle that life is *always* sacred—even when the life of little Alfie was deemed "futile" by British judges. Oh, how wrong they were. The truth is, in his short life, Alfie had left a profound impact on the world, far greater than many who live long and healthy lives.

I asked myself, years later, why Pope Francis never stepped in to reconnect Alfie's life support, and was instead so concerned with a defaulting community center where rave parties were organized.

Atreju has always epitomized who we truly are: curious people who seek answers to complex problems and reject the arrogance of power. We are unafraid of debate, secure in our strong sense of identity. It is not for nothing that we were the first to organize debates between representatives of opposing political parties. For example, no one had ever invited politicians from the Right to the Festa dell'Unità—and they still find it difficult to do so. In contrast, no major political figure has ever declined an invitation to Atreju, except for Matteo Renzi, whom we invited repeatedly, three or four years in a row during the era of his meetings called Leopolda, before he became Prime Minister.

On the other hand, in 2006, Fausto Bertinotti's participation in a debate with Gianfranco Fini made history. His decision created such an uproar that it sparked a debate within what was then the Communist Refoundation Party (Partito della Rifondazione Comunista, or PRC).

For us, however, it was normal to listen respectfully to an adversary's views. This was evident with Bertinotti, with whom I still maintain a sincere friendship to this day. While the audience may not have shared his ideas, they recognized the depth with which he had introduced them. I believe Bertinotti himself was taken aback, given the political climate of the time, but he was applauded by our audience. I vividly recall at the end of our encounter when I asked both Fini and Bertinotti to share a movie, a book, and a song that symbolized something meaningful to them, Bertinotti recited a poem by Ibsen, and a very powerful song by Jacques Brel, "Amsterdam." Fini, on the other hand, told us that his favorite movie was *To Kill a Mockingbird*—not exactly an epic movie, considering the audience preferred movies like *Braveheart*. However, what Fini really meant to say was that his favorite movie was *Being There* (the film titles in Italian are somewhat similar, *Oltre la siepe*, and *Oltre il giardino*, respectively). Sandro Curzi, seated in the first row, noticed the mix-up and corrected him. Fini also revealed his favorite song: "My Way" by Frank Sinatra. Looking back, the lyrics—*I did it my way*—might have been a warning we should have heeded.

* * *

Over the years, a large number of Leftist politicians have attended Atreju: from Bersani to Gentiloni, from Veltroni to Rutelli, from Violante to D'Alema, from Turco to Boldrini, and from Fico to Zingaretti. Before becoming Secretary of the Democratic Party, Zingaretti even expressed his pleasure at being on our stage, partly because he hadn't yet been invited to the Festa dell'Unità during the Renzi era. Each year, we invite the most prominent figures of that political season—those we respect, oppose, or find controversial and want to better understand. For instance, when Steve Bannon, a guest at Atreju, was arrested in October 2022, the Italian Left celebrated gleefully, declaring that "my guru" was a criminal. Setting aside the legal issues—details of which remain unclear—let me say this: if the accusations against Bannon I read in the newspapers constitute a crime, then I fear no NGO is safe. Like countless others, we invited Bannon out of curiosity. Around here, we've never had any gurus, especially not foreign ones. Wouldn't it be great if the Left displayed the same level of independence?

Or does anyone want to claim that Giuseppe Conte, who attended Atreju the following year in 2019, is also one of my "gurus"?

In truth, Conte was the only guest in Atreju's twenty-two-year history who tested our audience's ability not to heckle. The sacred rule of Atreju is that all guests are treated with respect. The problem with Conte was the timing: we had invited him in June when he was leading the coalition government of the Five Star Movement and the League. By September, however—the month Atreju takes place—Conte was leading the new Five-Star-Democratic Party government after a dramatic agreement between the two parties. Just a week before the event, when the new government had finally been seated, Brothers of Italy launched a protest against the umpteenth backroom political dealings. The Italian public's response was surprising. The situation was, to put it mildly, embarrassing and incendiary. Conte was brave to come to Atreju.

Maybe he had anticipated the potential for protests, calculating that any such outburst would reflect poorly on us rather than him. It was true. We managed to keep the audience eerily quiet, almost motionless—no whistles, no heckles. As we exited, Rocco Casalino quipped with a smile: "And I was hoping for at least a little protest." I replied, "Rocco, my dear, I've been organizing this event since before you set foot in the *Big Brother* house." And that, too, was true.

We wanted to organize evening entertainment at Atreju, but initially, it was practically impossible. No artists were willing to come. Advised by agents and record labels, they preferred to pay a penalty rather than expose themselves. While we could find alternative musical groups, they weren't enough to draw the large crowds we had envisioned. So, we came up with the idea of an "Eighties" night, inviting artists who had made their mark during that era: Pupo, Sabrina Salerno, i Righeira, Ivana Spagna, Jerry Calà, and Alan Sorrenti. The evening was a success, and word quickly spread—Atreju became a cool place to be. Mario Biondi was the first big name to join us, and after him, many others followed: from Max Pezzali to Max Gazzè, from Zero Assoluto to Irene Grandi. Davide Van De Sfroos also performed, and I'm proud to know his songs by heart, even though they're sung in *laghee*, the dialect spoken around Lake Como. His concert was a personal treat for me—the only one I allowed myself in all those years. Because, let's be honest, I was never able to fully enjoy the Atreju days, our guests, or the shows. I was always swamped by a million tasks, obsessed with ensuring everything was under control. Only in the most recent editions have I been able to delegate responsibilities to others, freeing myself to spend more time with our guests. I must say, the team has done an excellent job in managing the event.

* * *

"I've decided to nominate you for the Chamber."

In the spring of 2006, during a national assembly of National Alliance, Fini stopped me in the hallway and, without changing his expression, said those seven words then walked away. Although it was a long-standing tradition for youth movement leaders to be nominated for Parliament, I had never asked anyone for anything. Yet, perhaps thanks to the support of the Kaziro people, I had earned the secretary's respect. I was nominated and elected.

On my first day at Montecitorio, I arrived wearing a suit and a blouse, all dolled up for the occasion and accompanied by the members of my political party.

The reporters already recognized me, thanks to "Sette," the weekly supplement of *Corriere della Sera*, which had featured me on the cover of a special issue on young candidates. Like any newcomer, I attracted curiosity. As soon as the photographers spotted me, they crowded around, calling, "Hey Gio, give us a smile!" or "Meloni, look over here!"

Suddenly, in what he thought was a playful gesture, Federico Mollicone decided to lift me up—literally. He grabbed me and hoisted me into the air. Stiff as a board, I instinctively kicked at him, forcing him to let me go. I tumbled to the ground, much to the photographers' delight. Although they didn't manage to capture my picture on the floor—I'd gotten up too fast for them—there's still a widely circulated photo of me wearing only one shoe, with my sunglasses askew on my head.

Ten minutes later, I entered the chamber for the first time. It was one of the most exhilarating moments of my life. I looked around at the wooden chairs, red velvet, and the Italian flag hanging up above, and thought, "Okay, now you're in for it." Little did I know just how true that would be.

A few days later, Fini summoned me to the Farnesina. Those were his final days as Minister of Foreign Affairs, and I arrived feeling a bit apprehensive. I knocked on the door and he invited me in, a somber look on his face. The large room was filled with boxes, since he was packing up his things. "I didn't think I'd have to go this far with you . . ." he began. I stiffened. What could I possibly have done? My mind raced, but it came up empty. Meanwhile, his face grew even more serious. "Listen," he said in a flat tone, "I've decided you're going to be vice president of the Chamber."

Several long seconds of silence passed. I was incredulous. His face remained a gray mask. Suddenly, he broke into a huge smile. I thought, "This is a joke. He's getting back at me for Atreju." But after a moment of confusion, I answered honestly, channeling Bartleby, the diligent scrivener in Melville's story: "Thank you, but I would prefer not to."

And I meant it. I didn't feel ready to preside over the chamber. Despite years of activism and overcoming numerous challenges, I was still a newly elected representative. How could I possibly take on the responsibility of silencing someone like D'Alema in the Chamber, for instance? And, truthfully, I only had a vague idea of how Parliament functioned. But for Fini, these were minor details.

He had just one big problem: convincing the colonels of the party, who also aspired to that post, to agree. I could be of use to him to quell the disputes.

The discussion between the two of us, in that room at the Farnesina, lasted only a few minutes. He regained his serious demeanor and told me he had made his decision—I couldn't say no. As I was about to leave, he added, almost absent-mindedly, "I'm going to ask you one favor. You need to hire Patrizia Scurti to work with you. She's been by my side all these years, and she's an excellent worker, but I can no longer keep her with me. In a few days, I won't have the same kind of staff I do now." I agreed, of course, but privately thought that he might be handing me a charity case. Looking back now, between becoming vice president of the Chamber and having Patrizia by my side, the latter was the far better news. Fifteen years have passed, and Patrizia is still with me. I jokingly call her my boss because every aspect of my life goes through her. I've grown attached to the idea that she sees me as a kind of daughter. In a world where everyone asks what I can do for them, Patrizia stands out—she only thinks of what she can do for me. She is my harbor, my protector, my source of tranquility. Her nickname is Wolf, after the character in *Pulp Fiction* who introduces himself with the words, "I solve problems." There isn't a single issue she can't handle or problem she can't fix. What brings her the most joy is being able to say, "Already done." She always wears a smile on her face, even though most people are terrified of her. She is never wrong, and sometimes her perfectionism makes you feel terribly fallible. The only challenge is remembering to "deprogram" her—if you don't, you might find yourself in a series of mishaps. For example, I often go on diets. Whenever I do, Patrizia informs everyone around me about what I'm allowed to eat. Once, I was finally leaving for my vacation, boarded the intercontinental flight and, as soon as I sat down, the steward says: "Did you order a light meal?" Instinctively, I said no—then it hit me. I hadn't told Patti I was dropping the diet while on vacation.

Nothing escapes her notice. She is far more than an assistant, and maybe even more than a mother and friend combined. Every day, I thank God and Gianfranco Fini for placing her at my side.

That afternoon, after my meeting with Fini, I headed to the Colle Oppio section. When I arrived, the kids there greeted me with applause—the news had made it into the press. I felt like I was on the verge of a nervous breakdown.

From the outset, I felt that my work as a member of Parliament was far greater than me. Managing an entire chamber filled with individuals with decades of parliamentary experience felt completely out of scale compared to what I believed I was capable of.

But there was no room for hesitation—Fini had made his decision. My response was to face it head-on: I sought parliamentary rules and video cassettes of past sessions, immersing myself in intense study. I quickly recognized the trap: the chamber is not to be trusted. If they sense any weakness in you, they will exploit it.

My first session was relatively straightforward. During the vote for the President of the Republic, all I had to do was recite the words that began and ended the procedure. But the routine daily sessions were a different story—where anything could happen.

There was the representative who thought his speech could stretch on all afternoon, and if I tried to cut him off, he would take it as a personal affront. Then there was one who spoke on topics he knew nothing about, spouting one absurdity after another that infuriated his adversaries into a pandemonium of shouts and whistles. There were those who brought out protest signs, others donned T-shirts with slogans. Some talked too loudly, and others fell asleep mid-session, only to wake with a start, mishear a point, and launch into an argument, sometimes losing their temper completely in a hissy fit. In those cases, clerks had to step in—literally lifting an individual up and carrying him outside the hemicycle.

The first time I ascended to the highest bench, I prayed no one would notice me. I walked quietly, head down. But from the section where the National Alliance members were seated, a long roar of applause erupted.

I was stunned—and, honestly, embarrassed. The elder statesmen of the Republic must have seen me as a bizarre creature. Francesco Cossiga once called me, perhaps to put me at ease, and said, "Did you know that there was a President of the Chamber who was even younger than you? Enrico De Nicola—thirty-seven." I quickly clarified that I was just the vice president and only twenty-nine.

In those early weeks, I remember some people staring at me, the looks in their eyes clearly saying, "We're going to destroy you." My position as a member of the opposition party made my role even more difficult. Accusations of bias were a constant threat. I realized that if I wanted to succeed as vice president, I would have to set aside my identity as a *"combatant"* and assume the role of impartial judge. As a member of Parliament, I could argue as passionately as I wanted, but as vice president I had to remain composed, and defend my adversaries when necessary, obviously within the framework of the rules.

In the end, my obsessive and somewhat desperate study of codes and codicils paid off.

In one of the very first sessions, I made it clear that I wasn't going to be anyone's punching bag. Amid a typical clash between the president and the groups, I firmly responded to Dario Franceschini, then head of the Democratic Party, who was criticizing my management of the chamber. Quoting the relevant article by heart, I replied, "President Franceschini, you should know that according to article etc. etc." From the National Alliance section, where everyone had been holding their breaths, thunderous applause broke out with shouts of "Bravaaa!" My adversaries, taken aback, could only murmur "Well, well, well. We never expected that from Meloni."

Of course, over the next two years, I did stumble a couple of times. The person who came to my rescue was the representative of the Democratic Party, Roberto Giachetti, a sort of Rain Man—in other words, someone who knew all the rules of Parliament. Roberto was smart, funny, and ruthless when he needed to be. Most importantly, he has always been free. Perhaps it was this independence—or maybe the fact that he had a soft spot for me—that led him to help me out on more than one occasion. From these moments, my strongest friendship with a political adversary in Parliament was born. Of course, Roberto, you could have nipped my political rise in the bud. . . . But you did not and never have.

The Open Sea

I don't know why, but throughout my life, just as I am settling into a position and finally starting to feel comfortable, that position has been taken away from me, only to be replaced with an even more challenging one. So, just as I had grown accustomed to presiding over the chamber at Montecitorio, after about two years the legislature came to an end.

It was January 2008, and the Prodi II government, after a prolonged period of instability, was brought down by a vote of no-confidence in the Senate. Following the initial round of consultations driven by Giorgio Napolitano, then-President of the Republic, the message from the four leaders of the former House of Freedoms (Casa delle Libertà, or CDL)—Berlusconi, Fini, Bossi, and Casini—was clear: they wanted early elections. The Center-Right coalition unanimously decided to approach the elections with Berlusconi as their candidate for Prime Minister. In the meetings held at the Quirinale (the official residence of the President of the Italian Republic), Napolitano recognized there was no viable alternative. Italy had no choice but to return to the polls.

But the surprises didn't end there. During those weeks, an unexpected twist emerged. A few months earlier, Berlusconi had floated the idea of creating a new party to unite the various factions of the Center-Right, a vision famously articulated in his "step-stool speech." Initially, the proposal was met with indifference and then firmly rejected by Gianfranco

Fini. Many of us, deeply proud of our symbol and community identity, breathed a sigh of relief when we heard National Alliance's leader deliver the unequivocal words, "There is no way that National Alliance will dissolve and merge into Berlusconi's new party." Yet, two months later, we had joined the People of Freedom (Popolo della Libertà, or PDL).

I remember the day the announcement was made with absolute clarity. It was during a regional party assembly in Rome, held at the Hotel Plaza on Via del Corso. Fini was there, wrapping up the event as usual with an excellent speech that outlined the political situation and National Alliance's role. Everything appeared perfectly normal. Once the meeting ended, I began walking back toward Montecitorio to get my car—a walk that takes no more than seven minutes. Before I even got there, I got a text message: "Fini just announced the creation of the unified party." I froze. "That's impossible, it's not true. I was there! He never said that!" But it *was* true—and he hadn't told us. He had kept the decision a secret, and we later found out he had decided days earlier.

Thus began my phase in the People of Freedom Party, marked by a mix of surprise and apprehension, and—admittedly—a fair amount of frustration. From that period, what stands out the most is the fear of failing to keep the youth movement united during the transition, as well as the challenges of integrating our members. Some still wore army fatigues, while others were a world apart, ambitious young professionals in blue suits and high heels—figures we had always observed with a certain irony. And yet, once again, Youth Action rose to the challenge.

The decision to unite the two parties proved to be a resounding success in terms of public support. In the elections of April 13–14, 2008, the People of Freedom Party achieved remarkable results, securing 38 percent of the vote—a figure exceeding the combined support that National Alliance and Brothers of Italy had garnered in earlier elections.

National Alliance elected its largest-ever group of parliamentarians, and I was among them, reelected to Montecitorio.

A few weeks later, as speculation about ministerial appointments dominated the news, I was summoned once more by Fini. He told me, "I've considered you for a government position . . ." My immediate thought was, "Here we go again. . . . I've just gotten the hang of Parliament, and now I have to move into government?" I tried to wriggle out of it, thanking him for his confidence while suggesting that I might be more effective by remaining in my current role. But, as before, I couldn't sway him.

A few hours later, from the Quirinale, Silvio Berlusconi announced the list of ministers for his fourth government. My name was among them—listed as a minister without a portfolio (i.e., with the full status of minister, but without a ministry). And so, at just thirty-one years old, I became the youngest minister in the history of Italy.

In the years that followed, especially during moments of tension as the leader of a party allied with but distinct from Berlusconi's, I was frequently accused of being "ungrateful" to the Cavaliere for making me a minister. While I hold firm to the belief that a good politician must remain loyal to individuals, they must also be unwaveringly faithful to their principles. For this reason, the story is not entirely accurate.

When I became Minister of Youth, Berlusconi barely knew me; to him, I was just another member of National Alliance. I have always maintained an honest and loyal relationship with him and continue to hold him in high regard. Yet, my story comes from a world he never truly understood. To Berlusconi, I have always been an anthropological outlier—difficult to fully accept, both as an individual and as a representative of a different political culture. We were loyal allies, but often distant in our fundamental views of what politics should be.

It was six in the evening, with the swearing-in ceremony scheduled for noon the next day. Confused and, as usual, slightly anxious, I spent the evening with Giovanbattista Fazzolari. Known as Spugna to old friends and Fazzo to me, Giovanbattista is the most intelligent and levelheaded person I'd ever had the good fortune to know. Today, he's a senator for Brothers of Italy, but to me, he has always been so much more. I cannot recall a single challenging moment in my life when he wasn't by my side. With his ever-calm demeanor, sharp wit to lighten any situation, and answers to any question, Fazzo has been a constant companion throughout my journey. Our connection is so strong that we forget which one of us originally came up with a particular idea. We complete each other, often joking that we saved the other from our own worst instincts. With Fazzo, I can talk about anything, share everything, and trust that he will never judge me—and he'll always tell me the truth. The right-wing movement is lucky to have him among its ranks, and I've been even luckier to have him in my life.

In the end, I slept poorly. But the next day, the journalists didn't notice the bags under my eyes—they were too busy judging my outfit. That's often how it is for women: you can become a cabinet minister, yet people are far more interested in what you're wearing than the policies you're proposing. This phenomenon, unfortunately, was even more pronounced during Berlusconi's fourth government.

The truth is, I had recently indulged in a moment of weakness and vanity, purchasing an elegant two-piece suit by a famous Italian designer. I was probably the only one who loved its iridescent fabric (maybe with the exception of Platinette, a famous cross-dresser on Italian TV in the 1990s and 2000s). When I bought it, I couldn't have imagined it would become my attire for such a solemn occasion as my swearing in as minister. In any case, it seemed the perfect time to show it off.

It wasn't. For the photographers, I became an easy target. Gossip magazines feasted on photos of yours truly entering and exiting the Quirinale, gleefully comparing me to car reflectors with legs. This went on and on for weeks.

As if that weren't enough, in the official photograph of female ministers, someone decided to line us up by height, like in elementary school pictures in the 1950s.

The result? Not only was I the shortest, but I also stood out for having the weirdest outfit. Flanked by Mara Carfagna, Stefania Prestigiacomo, and Mariastella Gelmini, I was the ugly duckling. Someone had even made a fantastic photomontage, swapping me with Kermit the Frog from *The Muppets*. I use the word "fantastic" because I adore the Muppets. Still, I didn't let it get to me. Others had it worse. I remember a photomontage where someone had edited Maria Elena Boschi to appear as if she was wearing a thong during her swearing in. I'm sure she was less amused. What's most telling about these incidents aren't the photomontages themselves—it's the fact that so many people believed them. Similarly, I spent years battling the fallout of a viral video from the founding of the People of Freedom Party In it, you can hear Berlusconi summoning me to the front with the words, "Where's the little one?" (*piccola* in Italian, as he probably couldn't remember my name). However, due to audio distortion, it sounded like he said "*zoccola*"—a slang term meaning "whore." To this day, I struggle to comprehend how anyone in their right mind could believe I would accept such an insult with a smile in front of millions of people. These episodes offer a glimpse into a pervasive cultural bias: the reflexive association of any woman in power with reductive and sexualized narratives. It's a conditioned response—a deeply ingrained subculture—that we are still far from defeating.

* * *

The Ministry of Youth Policies was a recently created, portfolio-less ministry. At first glance, one might assume that leading such a ministry—deemed insignificant, with no spending power—would be easier. After all, it ranked so low in the state protocol, it was practically an afterthought. But that's not how it works. Large ministries benefit from established structures that could function even without a minister (in some cases, one might say that's a blessing!). They have well-defined responsibilities and a team of tried and tested staff that the new minister inherits.

A portfolio-less ministry, however, is a completely different story. It lacks structure and personnel, leaving the minister—and their vision—squarely at the center. For me, the challenge was even greater because I had to build everything from scratch. My predecessor, Giovanna Melandri, had served as Minister of Youth while also overseeing the Sports portfolio. Once those two areas were split again, the slate was wiped clean.

But we did it—me and a group of visionaries. Patrizia, my steadfast companion, was always at my side. Giovanbattista led the political secretariat, while Nicola Procaccini served as spokesperson. Nicola, now a Member of the European Parliament for Brothers of Italy, is the most skilled person I know when it comes to giving things depth and meaning. We collaborated closely for years, so when he decided to run for mayor in his hometown of Terracina—and could therefore no longer work with me—it felt like the ground had opened up beneath my feet.

"I can't manage without him," I thought. But I also worried whether Nicola, brilliant as he was, had the practical nature required to be a successful mayor. I was wrong. Not only did he prove to be a beloved, capable, and compassionate mayor, but when political squabbles cut his first term short, he was reelected with overwhelming support.

Today, years later, I'm glad he made that choice.

At the ministry, our first move was to change the name—from the Ministry of Youth Policies to the Ministry of Youth. If you ask enlightened and intelligent people like Gad Lerner, who pride themselves in finding fascist undertones in everything I do, they'll tell you the change was one of the many supposed throwbacks to Italy's past. For those who aren't blinded by ideological delusions, the truth is much simpler. I believed—and still believe—that treating "youth policies," like "women's policies," as niche or sectoral issues is a flawed approach. When framed this way, they're nothing more than token gestures.

The real challenge lies in integrating the needs of young people and women into the broader political agenda, giving them full legitimacy in all major decisions. For example, I don't see female unemployment as a "women's issue" but as a national one. Similarly, addressing youth concerns means pushing politics to focus on the future—not just on the next election cycle but on the decades to come. It means confronting the pervasive "presentism" that has turned one of the world's most visionary civilizations into a country adept at handing out short-term bonuses like candy.

This is why, as minister, I proposed adding a "generational impact assessment" to the constitution—a mechanism to evaluate the future costs and benefits of every government decision. Had this been implemented, it would have exposed how often we've taken more from younger generations than we've given back. For four years, we worked with this mindset. With a small but dedicated team, a clear vision, and plenty of courage, we transformed the Ministry of Youth into an agile, dynamic entity capable of maneuvering among the bureaucratic battleships of larger ministries. Our agility was perhaps symbolic of my own preference for traveling by scooter rather than using a government car. I still remember the disappointed faces of the security personnel when I told them I'd declined the privilege of an official car. I'd rather get around on my own, using my own means of transport.

This wasn't just about a cost-cutting gesture in line with our battle against political waste—it was a statement of independence. I refused to let the system entrap me or make me dependent on its privileges. Of the many loudmouthed politicians who built their careers on antiestablishment rhetoric, only to double their salaries and staff once in office, I believe I remain the only minister who served for four years without ever using a state-funded car.

We poured our energy into those offices, often working thirteen-hour days, and the results spoke for themselves. I'll never forget Giulio Tremonti, the notoriously frugal Minister of the Economy, glaring at me and asking how I'd managed to find the €300 million needed for our "Right to the Future" initiative, which focused on youth employment and stability. "It's all about speed, Giulio. You're all just so slow," I quipped. In truth, we identified overlooked budget items that no one had ever claimed, proving that navigating bureaucracy required knowing where the real levers of power lay—and how to ensure they didn't waste your time.

Every now and then, I meet someone who thanks me for what they were able to achieve because of those resources. Recently, a young couple said, "Did you know we have a house thanks to you?" They had secured a mortgage using our state-backed fund for young people without steady jobs to buy their first home. It was a solution to a glaring contradiction: on the one hand, the modern labor market demands flexibility; on the other, banks demand permanent contracts to issue loans. That's untenable. So, we created a state guarantee for mortgages aimed at young people on flexible contracts. This wasn't just another scheme for the state to prop up the banking system; in fact, the Associazione Bancaria Italiana (the trade association of Italian banks) initially opposed it. Sadly, after the Center-Right government fell and the Left took over, the program was modified to benefit banks more than the people it was designed to help.

I know the struggle firsthand. Like many young Italians, I left my family home at a late age. While I was financially independent by the age of twenty—contributing to the family budget—I resisted paying rent. Rome's exorbitant real estate prices made it impractical, and I firmly believed it made more sense to invest in a mortgage than in rent.

Like anyone who has experienced economic instability, I carry a constant fear of what tomorrow might bring. This fear drives me to ensure I'm prepared for whatever challenges may arise. My relationship with my home reflects this mindset with a deeply ingrained Italian tradition: for many Italians, your first home is not just an economic refuge but a profound symbol of sacrifice. It represents the culmination of a lifetime of hard work—often spanning multiple generations. A home is the final gift parents leave to their children, a tangible legacy that embodies everything a family has built. The home you live in is not an asset that generates income; it isn't comparable to a business or an investment designed for profit. Your home is indispensable for your family's sustenance. This cultural value is precisely why we in Brothers of Italy consider the primary home sacred. It should not be taxed, foreclosed, or seized.

I was fortunate to realize my dream of owning a house in my thirties—a privilege that many in my generation have not had. My little apartment, just over four hundred square feet near Garbatella, might have cost more than it was worth, but it brought me immense joy. I bought it during a time when scandals about homes for the powerful were making headlines: politicians buying properties for peanuts or receiving extravagant political favors. During an appearance on the radio show *Un giorno da pecora*, they asked me how much I'd paid for mine. When I told them, they burst out laughing: "How did you allow them to do that? Onorevole Meloni, you're the only politician who lets a common citizen get the better of them!"

Still, I adored that apartment. It had a small, quiet balcony that was sun-drenched at lunchtime, where I often sat with my legs crossed at the table, listening to my favorite songs. It was my sole sanctuary. The apartment reflected the Capricorn in me: everything was kept in perfect order, to keep the stress at bay. I've always believed it's best to shape a space to bring peace to your mind rather than force your mind to adapt to chaos. Sometimes I joke that I should have invented the game *Tetris*. That apartment was minimalist, entirely white, with only the essentials of decor—no unnecessary decorative frills or those dreadful "pocket emptiers" that encourage clutter. It resembled a house you'd see in a design magazine, the kind of place that makes people say: "No one actually lives here." My closet was arranged by color (though "color" might not be the right word; let's just say I was the forerunner to *Fifty Shades of Grey*), and the knives in the flatware drawer alternated blade to handle to stay perfectly aligned. Yes, I know, it's not normal.

This penchant for order might explain why I never lived with my partner until after Ginevra was born. Even when I was pregnant, I lived alone. Andrea was working in Milan at the time, so we only spent weekends together.

I loved that apartment also because it was so small. That little nest reminded me of the words etched on the facade of Ariosto's home: *Parva, sed apta mihi*—small, but suited to me. As a young woman, I often dreamed of having a place of my own, though I was convinced it would be nearly impossible to achieve. Back then, I juggled up to five jobs at a time just to scrape together 100 euros a month. My constant question was: *Will I ever earn enough to afford a mortgage?* In my dreams, I always imagine a small house. I used to linger in front of the tiny model homes displayed in furniture stores, enchanted and fascinated by how everything could fit into one hundred square feet. That two-room apartment in Garbatella was everything I had envisioned. The day I signed the papers to make it mine remains one of the happiest days of my life.

In those first years, while serving as Minister, I would return home in the evenings and thank God for giving me a sanctuary—a space of my own where I could shut out the rest of the world. My days were filled with avoiding traps, solving problems, discussing, debating, fighting. But when I shut the door behind me, I felt safe. Finally at peace. Finally free. It's at moments like those—when the sun sets and you stand at the threshold of your home—that you fully understand the value of walls and boundaries.

I lived in that tiny jewel box for eight years. I finally moved out just two weeks before Ginevra's due date, at nine months pregnant and weighing almost 180 pounds. The moving van also served to move me.

I cried when I went back alone to collect a few last things. The house was so empty that my footsteps echoed, and I knew it would be my final time on that little terrace. I left behind not just a piece of my life, but a piece of myself.

* * *

There were many initiatives I'm proud of during my time as minister. One that comes to mind is the *forfettino*: the extension of a 15 percent flat rate tax to all young entrepreneurs under the age of thirty-five. Securing the measure was no small feat, especially with the formidable Guilio Tremonti. In the end, Giulio preferred approving the expense to enduring hours of my persistence. Countless young people took advantage of that scheme, though few realize it was the fruit of our hard work.

Education was another cornerstone of our efforts, and we envisioned young people as active participants, not just passive beneficiaries. If you want a child to truly grasp something, have it explained by their peers. One of our key projects began with the subject of the fight against the mafia, rooted in the teachings of the Magistrate Paolo Borsellino, who believed that "if even young people refuse to consent to its existence, then even the mysterious and all-powerful mafia will vanish like a nightmare."

We distributed the booklet *Il profumo della libertà* in every high school for two years, filled with testimonies from those who had worked alongside Falcone and Borsellino. Schools were encouraged to organize student assemblies on the topic. In city suburbs, we partnered with artists to create murals on crimefighting in spaces assigned by the town administrations. Our "Red Nose" initiative also made waves. We trained young people to work in nightclubs to promote the message "Don't drink and drive." We also encouraged them to be designated drivers for those who'd had too much to drink. I can't know for sure, but I like to think this initiative may have saved some lives.

Looking back, I can't help but compare the immense resources, the energy, and the sacrifices we devoted to the fight against COVID-19 to protect the elderly, with the almost nonexistent attention we devote to combating road accidents. Drug and alcohol use, a leading cause of these tragedies, kill thousands of young people every year. Yet, society seems resigned to this carnage, as if it were inevitable. Worse still, we continue to normalize—or even glamorize—this culture of getting wasted. It drives me crazy when people credit drugs for the brilliance of musicians like Kurt Cobain, Jimi Hendrix, Janis Joplin, or Amy Winehouse. What utter nonsense. Drugs didn't create their talent. If anything, they amplified their inner turmoil, leading to Kurt Cobain shooting himself in the mouth while alone at home. Drugs killed Hendrix, the greatest guitarist of all time, who choked to death on his own vomit. And drugs also killed two extraordinary and iconic women, Joplin and Winehouse, who both died of an overdose. And all of them taken early, in an eerie coincidence, at the age of twenty-seven.

* * *

In another ironic twist of fate, during my time in government—a period in which my friends jokingly referred to me as "a would-be patriot in Risorgimento style"—Italy celebrated the 150th anniversary of its Unification. It was a unique opportunity to express our patriotism, and we seized it with enthusiasm. After decades, we finally had an excuse to proudly display our flag in every size and form. As Minister of Youth, I took particular pride in the celebrations, especially since few people realize how much of Italy's Unification was driven by the passion and sacrifice of young people. This is a paradox, considering how often young Italians are sidelined, dismissed as inadequate, foolish, spoiled by their mamas and lacking ideals. In Italy, you're always "too young" to do anything. To this day, despite a proposed constitutional amendment to lower the voting age for the Senate to eighteen instead of twenty-five, a person cannot be elected Senator before the age of forty. By that logic, neither Jesus nor Alexander the Great would have qualified, and Paolo Borsellino became a magistrate at an age when he couldn't have served in Parliament. I have always believed that if someone is mature enough to vote for their representatives, then they are mature enough to represent their country.

This conviction is reinforced by the history of the Italian national anthem, *Canto degli Italiani*, written by the twenty-year-old patriot, writer, and poet Goffredo Mameli, a notable figure of the Risorgimento. Mameli was wounded on Janiculum Hill while defending the Roman Republic; when his leg began to bleed profusely, he reportedly declared, "Cut it off, for I don't care, all I want is to be able to continue to live, sing, and fight." Even after his leg was amputated, he succumbed to his wounds at the age of twenty-one. There are many other such stories. The Sicilian Rosalino Pilo devoted his whole life to the dream of uniting the island of Sicily with Italy. He died from a bullet to the head just as Garibaldi's Expedition of the Thousand was nearing its goal. In the Expedition of the Thousand, young men from every corner of Italy set sail on two ships, the *Piemonte* and the *Lombardo*, determined to create a united Italy despite opposition from foreign powers and the usual ineptitude of fellow Italians. Among the Thousand was a lone woman: Rosalia Montmasson. Garibaldi famously declared, "There will be no wives, mothers, or volunteer women on board," aware of the risks they faced. But Montmasson was undeterred, with a history of defying authority, even going so far as to have a waiver signed against her father's wishes so she could marry the man of her choosing. Tales of heroes and heroines, revolutionaries, patriots—tales of identity, service, and freedom. Yet, so many of our young people today are unaware of them. These figures, with their extraordinary sacrifices, overshadow the romanticized image of other revolutionaries often celebrated on red T-shirts—the Argentine who died in Bolivia comes to mind.

To bring these stories to light, we collected them in a series titled *Gioventù Ribelle* (Young Rebels). Through exhibitions, plays, books, and other events, the Ministry of Youth sought to share the legacy of these young patriots. Beyond the confines of our role, I take pride in the contributions of the National Alliance delegation in government to celebrate this anniversary. At the time, not everyone—even within the Center-Right—shared our belief in the importance of a united Italy. This was especially true of the recent work done by Matteo Salvini, known as the Lega Nord per l'Indipendenza della Padania (Northern League for the Independence of Padania). I recall bitter clashes with Umberto Bossi—who liked to refer to me, perhaps disdainfully, as "la Romanina," that little girl from Rome—regarding our proposal to establish March 17 as a national holiday to commemorate the Unification of Italy. Historically, our country has preferred to celebrate moments of division rather than those of unity. In the end, we were given half of what we'd asked for. To reach a compromise, Berlusconi declared March 17 a solemn celebration, but not a national holiday.

As I fought against those who are now my principal allies—though with different protagonists and ideas—I found myself unexpectedly supported by Giorgio Napolitano, then-President of the Italian Republic. I had first met him in 2006 on an MTV show, where the format paired a novice candidate with a seasoned politician. When we met again a few months later, I as vice president of the Chamber and he as President of the Italian Republic, he smiled and said, "That TV show brought us both luck." Nonetheless, the Unification of Italy celebration was the only time in his presidency that we were on the same page.

* * *

Another significant, even "formative" moment came during the 2008 Beijing Olympics. Unlike the Five Star Movement and some key figures of the Left currently in government, I have never harbored any sympathy for the Chinese Communist regime. Hosting the Olympics there struck me as absurd—bringing resources and visibility to a country without demanding important progress on human rights or the long-standing oppression of Tibet.

When Federico Garimberti of ANSA (Italy's leading news agency) interviewed me, I said, "Our national team needs to send a strong signal, even by boycotting the opening ceremony, given how human rights in China have been swept aside." The next day, headlines in all the major newspapers screamed: "Olimpiadi, bufera sulla Meloni" (Olympics, Storm Brewing over Meloni).

The controversy lasted for days, but I've never regretted my stance. What I did learn, however, was how sensitive Italians are about sports—and how, in government, you represent an entire nation and must carefully weigh your words. Still, I believe leadership means staying true to your principles and to all the battles you've fought to get to the highest levels. With experience, I've learned that while the substance of your convictions matters, form is essential to defending them. You can say what you want, but you have to know *how* to say it.

Those years in government were a valuable but exhausting experience over three and a half years. I was very young and unfamiliar with the political pitfalls I'd have to navigate. Learning quickly wasn't easy, and I often stumbled, especially when the government's actions clashed with my values in ways that were hard for me to digest or were even embarrassing.

Founding Brothers of Italy has been a great source of pride because now I answer only for decisions I've consciously made. Back then, as a member of a party where decisions were out of my hands and where I sometimes felt uneasy, I dreaded the sight of a distant camera and the inevitable questions from reporters. I was uneasy not just because of the facts that were being discussed, but also because I was part of a team that was always under attack. I knew that by being disloyal to my colleagues,

I would play right into the hands of my adversaries. It was a difficult balancing act, and I have never been good at tightrope walking.

At the start of the legislature, I fell into my first journalist's trap, revealing my naivety to the world. One late June day, I was at the beach taking a break from work. I was walking along the water's edge when my cell phone rang: it was Fabrizio Roncone from the *Corriere della Sera*. At the time, I didn't realize he was one of Italy's most incisive political journalists.

A few hours earlier, wiretaps of phone calls between aspiring actresses and Berlusconi had surfaced, suggesting these young women were seeking "references."

Roncone flattered me—"you're so good, you're really serious"—and I let my guard down. I didn't realize where he was leading me.

It takes years to learn how to handle journalists. Nowadays, my first question is always, "What headline are you going to pin on me?" before I decide whether I want to be interviewed. Back then, I spoke freely on the phone with Roncone, stating what I thought—and still do: that "references" are the product of a society that does not reward merit, that the women involved saddened me, and that, as a woman on the Right, I disapproved of Berlusconi's behavior. I even threw in a comment against Rutelli, tied to a controversy about a TV series.

I hung up, convinced I'd done well after all. Then I relaxed on the beach, enjoying the sun on one of the longest days of the year.

The next morning, at the crack of dawn, I got a phone call from Ignazio La Russa, head of the National Alliance delegation. Half-asleep, I answered drowsily. He was very awake, and said in a firm voice: "What were you thinking? Berlusconi is out of his mind." I leaped out of bed like a cat, and opened my front door. In those days, there were no iPads or smartphones to read the news on; I still had newspapers delivered to my home and they were left on my doormat every morning. During my time in government, there were days when I dreaded opening the door and reading the headlines. Who knew what I'd have to deal with that day!

To make a long story short: I opened the door to find the *Corriere della Sera*. At the top of page five was my interview. Headline: *Questo Silvio non mi piace* (This Is a Silvio I Don't Like).

At dawn, Berlusconi had phoned La Russa in a fury: "That girl has busted my balls." What followed were tense hours of mediation, explanations, and clarifications, but in the end, I stayed in my post. I had learned a crucial lesson: skilled journalists are not your friends. Over the years, I've built respectful relationships with many in the media, but I've never let my guard down again.

* * *

The growing emphasis on image—particularly at a time when appearance heavily influenced popularity in politics—was something I found difficult to reconcile with my background as an activist in the trenches of politics. I had grown up believing that the way a politician looked was irrelevant. Yet, I suddenly found myself in an era where "casting" was used to select candidates. The term *velinismo*—a reference to the use of attractive young women as "decorative features" for TV shows—was often used to criticize this trend, but the truth is that it applied to men as well.

Personally, I have never liked the limelight. It may seem paradoxical to describe me as shy, but I am truly reserved. If I walk into a store and notice people staring at me, I leave. If I'm in a restaurant and realize that conversations stop as people look at me, I feel anxious. What makes me especially nervous is when someone secretly takes a photo of me with their cell phone. I can't help but assume that if someone takes a picture of you without asking, it's not for a good reason. When I catch someone doing this, I often approach them and ask, "Did you get my good side?" Over the years, I've grown somewhat accustomed to these situations, but at the beginning, they were really hard.

That said, I've never gotten used to the paparazzi. I guard my private life fiercely, and I firmly believe that there must be a boundary between legitimate curiosity about a public figure and treating them like a contestant on *Big Brother*, subjected to 24/7 surveillance—even in the bathroom. I've had clashes with the paparazzi, especially when they attempted to take pictures of me with Ginevra. What infuriates me most is the refusal to acknowledge that not everything can or should be sold. You can't monetize everything. Among other things, my family fell victim to a stalker—so this isn't just a matter of privacy but of safety.

Over time, I learned to choose destinations where I was less likely to encounter paparazzi who specialized in photographing the jet set and the high life. For years, I've preferred to visit a beach that's a few miles south of Capalbio. I'm referring to the delightful Focene, in Coccia di Morto—a location that even inspired movies like *Come un gatto in tangenziale*. Focene is named after the Tiber River, which flows into the sea there, creating an area known for its crystal-clear waters. My friend Marco Mezzaroma jokes that letting Ginevra swim in that water is like giving her an "eleventh mandatory vaccine" from the Ministry of Health. But I love the place—not only for its unpretentious charm but also because it has become a gathering spot for my oldest friends. Whenever I manage to escape for a few hours, I know I can always count on good company and cheerful faces there.

* * *

The final months of my tenure as Minister of Youth were among the most difficult of my entire political career. These difficulties culminated with Gianfranco Fini's fateful decision—one that risked consigning the glorious history of the Italian Right to oblivion. At the time, I couldn't fully grasp the implications, but as my mandate as Minister of Youth was coming to an end, I found myself becoming politically mature, preparing to shoulder the responsibility of preserving our community's legacy alongside other fearless companions.

To this day, I struggle to understand why Gianfranco Fini made the choices he did. How could a man who had dedicated his entire life to strengthening the Italian Right—using his skill and insight to pull it from the margins of the constitutional framework to become a vital force of government—undo that legacy in just a few months? It baffles me. How could someone who entered politics to challenge the arrogance of the Left and then follow its self-seeking advice, not realize that the Left was using him against his own people?

I know him well enough to imagine that he too, deep down, cannot fully explain his actions.

I clearly remember those dramatic days. The rift between Fini and Berlusconi had grown irreparable on a personal level, long before it became political. Their clash was raw and unrestrained. At the pivotal national meeting of the People of Freedom, Fini stood up, pointed his finger at Berlusconi, and delivered the now-infamous line: "What are you going to do, kick me out?" The fallout left our community in turmoil, torn between loyalty to its ideals and its historic leaders. It was not a decision to be made lightly. For me, the decision was especially agonizing; my friendship with Fini had meant sleepless nights, wrestling with which betrayal would be worse: abandoning our principles or walking away from someone I deeply respected and owed so much.

I tried to reason with him. I assured him that we were ready to follow him if he sought to break away from the People of Freedom Party to rebuild a right-wing party. But not if his actions played into the Left's hands—undermining a government that, for all its flaws, still represented the national interest. My efforts failed. The sirens of the Left—singing from the highest institutions in Italy—had cast their spell on him.

I know those sirens well. I still hear them today, their voices sweet and seductive, trying to lure me into conflicts with my Center-Right allies. To my fellow members of parliament who attempt this strategy: it won't work on me.

For most of us, following Fini became impossible. In the end, we were left politically orphaned within a PDL that could no longer represent us. At the time, it felt like the end. But as it often happens, it was actually a new beginning. I often associate this turbulent period for the Italian

Right with the words of Lao Tzu: "What the caterpillar calls the end of the world, the rest of the world calls a butterfly." Everyone fears change, but it is a mistake to shy away from new challenges, especially when you are confident in your identity.

Our movement may never reconcile with Fini or the choices he made. But that chapter taught us a critical lesson: the Right—our community, our history—can endure anything and anyone. People once said that without Gianfranco, the Italian Right wouldn't exist, just as they now claim that without Meloni, Brothers of Italy wouldn't exist. It isn't true. No matter the circumstances, there will always be someone ready to rise to the challenge, discover a strength within them they didn't know they had, ready to shoulder the weight of our shared cause.

* * *

Looking back, my life has been one relentless challenge. I've defied expectations in a country where gerontocracy reigns supreme: the first woman to lead a right-wing youth movement, the youngest minister in the history of the Republic, the first woman to head a political party, and now, the first Italian woman to lead a major European political family, the ECR (European Conservatives and Reformists) group. In dedicating myself to these roles, I've poured so much of myself into my work that sometimes it feels like Meloni has consumed Giorgia. I often wonder, "What do you really want to do? If you could wish for anything, what would it be?" And I find I can't answer. I've forgotten what it means to pursue personal happiness.

A doctor once warned me that the accumulated stress was putting me at risk of burnout—a full-on breakdown. He handed me a prescription. But instead of listing an antianxiety drug with dosage instructions, it simply read: "Dance."

The diagnosis and the treatment were correct. I needed—and still need—to reclaim a sense of lightness, a quality that my character and circumstances have often denied me.

I've had to learn everything quickly, facing challenges head-on, relying on discipline and focus. Yet, while discipline has been my driving force, it has also been my cage. The paradox of my life is that in striving for freedom to be the woman I want to be and make the choices I want to make, I've sacrificed nearly every other kind of freedom.

Perhaps that's why I've never truly learned to dance. But sometimes, on quiet Sunday mornings, dressed in my pajamas, I turn on some music, raise the volume, and dance with Ginevra.

I AM A MOTHER

When a Mother Is Born

I discovered I was expecting Ginevra on my thirty-ninth birthday. A few years ago, I took a fertility test and the doctor told me that the chances of having another child were slim.

"I suspect the situation was similar when you conceived Ginevra," he added, "so you should think of your daughter as a Godsend."

All children are a gift, but learning you're going to be a mother on your birthday gives the word "gift" a profoundly different meaning.

I found out just as I was heading out with Andrea to join my friends, who had organized a surprise dinner to celebrate my birthday. Calling it a "surprise" might not be the right word; after ten years of the same ritual, you come to expect it. The real surprise would be if they stopped doing it. It's my fault, though—just the thought of organizing my own birthday party where I'd be the center of attention makes me break out in hives. So, I've always refused to arrange events like these. My loved ones all know that I know, but that's never stopped them. For my last birthday, my sister laughed and remarked, "Should I add you to the secret chat about your surprise party?" Arianna was the first one I'd told the news that night in the restaurant restroom. She is always the first to know everything. I'll never forget her reaction: emotional, with the same look she had years earlier when she shared her own life-changing news with me. That's Arianna: whether it's good or bad, she feels everything I experience as though it were happening to her. I waited for the right moment to tell Andrea. When the time came, I handed him a small package containing a pair of baby booties. His speechless, emotional reaction remains one of the most touching moments of my life.

I gave birth at San Camillo Hospital in Rome, which offers an excellent service to families called "rooming-in," where mothers can keep their newborns in the same hospital room. It's a wonderful example of public health, and I recommend it to all expectant Roman mothers. Of course, the announcement of Ginevra's birth came with its own fake news. When I posted on social media, "My daughter Ginevra is born," someone deliberately distorted the words and posted "My daughter was born in Ginevra,"—which, in Italian, also means Geneva. What followed was a flood of mockery and insults. "Meloni claims to be a patriot, but then she goes to Switzerland to give birth." It's a good thing I called her Ginevra. Who knows what people would have said if I'd chosen the name Luna, meaning "moon," a trendy name for girls these days?

Motherhood was never one of the big goals of my life. I'd always believed that children were the product of deep love—if you find the right person, then that is how you strengthen your relationship. Looking back, I regret how shortsighted that belief was. Children *are* love, in its purest form, but you don't fully grasp this until you experience it yourself. I wish I'd understood that sooner. I wish I'd become a mother earlier and more than once. Sometimes, Ginevra asks with that innocence so typical of children, "Mama, I want a real baby girl," and I feel a pang of guilt. Guilt for not being able to fulfill her wish. Guilt for not giving her the kind of sibling bond I share with Arianna. Guilt for prioritizing things of secondary importance and for running out of time to embrace what is life's most amazing mission. Our society deceives us, convincing us that youth and fertility are endless. It encourages us to delay life's essential decisions until you tragically discover, too late, that time is finite. I firmly believe in the importance of raising awareness about fertility and encouraging women to monitor it early on. I know such a campaign might provoke backlash from some feminists, who may see it is a violation of their self-determination or a return to outdated stereotypes that women are only of use when they become mothers. But I believe the opposite is true. Freedom begins with knowledge. To make truly informed choices, women need to understand their biological realities. Freedom, above all, is rooted in awareness.

Motherhood, of course, turned my life upside down, filling it with moments of pure joy—and others where I felt like banging my head against the wall.

As members of parliament, we are privileged in many ways, particularly economically. But there's a flip side to this privilege. No law or union safeguards your rights to live as "normal" human beings. The pace of work is relentless, your days are unpredictable, there are no set hours and—most importantly—you can't afford to be anything less than alert, not matter how exhausted you are. When you've endured sleepless nights for months, rocking a baby who refuses to sleep, only to face cameras and reporters the next morning, there are times you feel like you just won't make it. Some nights, I broke down in tears—that kind of hysterical weeping that happens when your body and mind reach their limit. Yet, oddly enough, I've never been as informed as I was during those first months of Ginevra's life. Late at night, while hoping she'd fall asleep, I'd watch TV—the news and even a few series. Then came the US presidential elections, culminating in Donald Trump's unexpected victory. I watched every single debate, listened to all the comments, and memorized the results of all the swing states. But the real challenge came during the day, when I needed to be just as sharp and efficient in my own debates. That was the period of the constitutional referendum called by Renzi—a critical moment for the nation's future. I had to ensure that the voice of Brothers of Italy was heard loud and clear.

So, I'll be honest and tell you it was really hard, but I never gave up. I did everything in my power to balance my roles. I breastfed Ginevra every four hours until she was weaned, taking her with me to the Chamber of Deputies every day and traveling with her across Italy whenever work required it. I continued breastfeeding her until she was a year and three months old because, luckily, my body still produced milk, and I knew there was nothing better for her immune system than her mother's milk.

Things are much easier now. Ginevra sleeps through the night, and it's my cats, Micia and Martina, who wake me up at dawn, demanding cuddles. Funnily enough, I used to be a dog person, but with so little free time, I've converted to being a proud "cat lady."

They say that it's not the amount of time you spend with your kids that matters, but the quality of that time. I like to believe it's true. When I'm home, I make a conscious effort to invent something new—a game of sorts—to play with Gigì (the only nickname that someone named Ginevra Giambruno could have). I've set strict rules for myself when it comes to spending time with my daughter. Andrea and I alternate taking her to school in the mornings, and one of my biggest regrets is that I can rarely be there to pick her up at the end of the day. To be honest, even dropping her off isn't always easy. A while ago, I was invited to do an interview on Radio24. "How about from 8:30 to 8:45?" they suggested. "I can't," I replied, "that's when I take Ginevra to school." They suggested 8:45 to 8:55 instead, the very end of the show. True to Murphy's Law—that anything that can wrong will go wrong—that very morning, Ginevra had a meltdown at the school gates. She refused to go inside and kept pleading, "I want to stay with you." Meanwhile, the phone was ringing—the station was calling about the live interview. I tried to stall but time was running out. I had to beg the teachers for help, and they gently wrestled Ginevra from my leg while I stood there swaying, trying to focus on speaking about the Recovery Fund. As I talked, I could see my daughter walking into the school in tears. I will never forget that scene. I felt truly awful.

I try to keep one day—either Saturday or Sunday—completely free to spend with her. Every night, I do everything I possibly can to get home before she goes to bed. I don't want her to fall asleep before our bedtime ritual. I read her books or sometimes invent fairy tales on the spot. After reading countless fantasy novels, it's easy for me to conjure up kingdoms, dragons, and warrior princesses. And I always end the ritual by singing "La canzone di Marinella" by Fabrizio De André. You might wonder why

I chose such a melancholy song, but when I first sang it to her, she was too young to understand the lyrics. She became attached to it after hearing the rendition by Caterina on *X Factor*. Now, if I try to sing it, she stops me and says, "Mama, put the lady who sings it on—you can't sing." Recently, as she listened to the song, she said, "I want to go to Marinella's house with you." So, I held her hand and said, "If you close your eyes, you can visit Marinella's house in your dreams. Think about her and you can fly to her house. But hold my hand—I don't want to get lost." She closed her eyes and squeezed my hand, but after a minute she opened them again. "Can we go tomorrow?" That's children for you—one moment they're sweet, and the next, they're heartless.

* * *

Because of my commitment to spending time with her, I avoid attending dinners or evening events. I record TV appearances in the late afternoon and have sacrificed those rare evenings with friends that allowed me to unwind from my duties. Election campaigns are the problem. Each day, you're in a different region, and if you insist on returning to Rome every night, the pace becomes brutal. Before Ginevra was born, I would leave with a suitcase and have no idea when I'd be back. Weeks on the road, sleeping in a different place every night, was the norm. Since she was born, the time I spend in transit has multiplied. Cars, planes, trains, ferries, steamboats, trolley cars, rack railways—you name it, I've used it. The only exception is scooters. I've never liked them, especially after the Five-Star-Democratic Party government thought it was a brilliant idea to spend hundreds of millions of euros encouraging their use at the height of the pandemic. Now, I often race off when an event has ended to catch the last plane. If someone stops me to ask for an extra selfie, I tell them, "It wouldn't make sense for me to promise to take care of your family if I can't even take care of mine." People respect that. After all, consistency matters. I've met people who talk endlessly about family but only see their kids three days a year.

In Italy, the electoral campaign never seems to end. As soon as you finish in one region, it's time to start on the next. Then there are the European elections, political elections, administrative elections, referenda—there's always something. No matter how hard you try to cover every corner of the country and honor the efforts of local organizers, there's always a place that gets left out. Unfortunately, only saints like Padre Pio are blessed with the gift of ubiquity. Looking at the typical electoral campaign schedule, you can't help but wonder if the person who planned it has any grasp of the laws of physics and the space-time continuum. The itinerary might call for a rally in the morning, two more in the afternoon, another in the evening—all in three different regions. Remarkably, I somehow manage to follow these absurd schedules, though often at the expense of basic needs like eating, drinking, or fixing my makeup. And after all this effort, my mother's supportive evening critique often comes like this: "Sweetheart, I saw you on the news today. You're good, but you need to put on some makeup—you look like a toad."

Once, during one of these whirlwind election tours, I arrived in a small town where my staff immediately began rushing me around. Apparently, the townspeople had been waiting an hour for me. Talk about anxiety.... As soon as I stepped out of the car, I was whisked to the stage, where the mayoral candidate, party executives, and maybe even a few random passersby had already started speaking. They quickly handed me the mic, and it was my turn. I cracked a few jokes to break the ice and began my speech. But when the time came to announce the name of the mayoral candidate—zilch. I couldn't remember his name. Although I knew him quite well, my mind went completely blank. I tried to stall, improvising as I scanned the area out of the corner of my eye for any clue—a placard maybe. Desperately, I even pretended to fix my hair so I could glance behind me at a hypothetical sign. But there was nothing! Not a scrap or single flyer on the table. So, I kept talking. I rambled for an hour, hoping some corner of my brain would eventually supply the candidate's name. The sun set, and dinnertime rolled around.... Finally, I gave up. And as I continued to talk, filling the silence with whatever came to mind,

I discreetly picked up my cell phone and texted the person next to me: "What the hell is the candidate's name?" A moment later, he slid me a card with the person's name. At last, I could wrap up my speech with a triumphant: "Vote for him!"

* * *

I consider events organized in local areas—rallies in town squares, gatherings in cities, and other scheduled in-person events—to be absolutely essential. Meeting a candidate face-to-face creates a much stronger, more genuine impression. Seeing places and experiencing the realities of those who live there is crucial to understanding their lives. I've never believed that politics can be conducted solely from behind a screen, and history has proven me right. Those who rely exclusively on television or online platforms often build their influence on shaky ground, as fragile as a house of cards.

Rallies are where I feel most at ease, for two reasons. First, I thrive on the energy and enthusiasm of the crowd. Second, I prefer to improvise when I speak, and rallies give me the freedom to take my time and fully develop my message. I've never read a speech—except for those delivered in English. Reading from a script strips away the empathy, the energy, the frankness. I come from a political tradition of great orators, where no leader has ever relied on a script. The best example is Giorgio Almirante, who on January 16, 1971, delivered an impromptu speech lasting over nine hours in the Chamber. He spoke against the Special Statute of Trentino Alto-Adige, a measure that, even today, we see gave preferential treatment to the German-speaking population while disadvantaging Italian speakers. Striving to live up to this "school" is another way of showing that we haven't forgotten where we come from. That said, I do prepare texts on occasion—specifically for occasions with strict time limits. Pinuccio Tatarella, another great figure of the Italian Right, used to say that the shorter the speech, the more important it is to prepare. When time is limited, you must know exactly what to say. For example, when I take the floor in Parliament to declare my vote, I'm allotted no more than ten minutes. In such cases, I prepare an outline—not to read word for word, but to ensure I stay within the allotted time. A ten-minute speech typically translates to three pages, and I know that if I dwell too long on one point, I'll have to cut something else. Having a draft helps me take my message to its logical conclusion, underscoring my most important points.

Rallies are different: when I prepare a speech for a rally, I jot down keywords of the points I want to address. There, I have the luxury of speaking for as long as I want—and I never talk for less than thirty minutes. I admire those who can do ten rallies a day, speaking for just three minutes at each, getting their applause, and moving on. I've never been able to do that. It's almost like I have the mindset of a stage actor: I start from the belief that, even though the audience didn't have to pay to attend, they still made sacrifices to be there. Maybe they closed their store early, left their kids with grandparents, or took a break from their studies. They gave me their time, they placed their trust in me, so they deserve my full effort in return. Whether just ten people or two thousand have shown up doesn't change how I feel. I'm responsible for making sure they leave satisfied. In short, if you come to hear me speak, don't expect to leave quickly.

I write everything down by hand—it's my way of fixing things in my mind. I've been doing this since I was a student. Back then, to avoid having to study too much in the afternoon, I forced myself to pay close attention in class, jotting down what the professor said in real time.

I have a particular fondness for pens, especially fountain pens or ones with colored ink, and I will only write on graph paper. I always print my handwriting because, no matter the content, the final text must be neat and tidy. I'm not a fan of reading on a computer, and if I'm reading from a printed page, it must be justified, and the page must end with a period. Those who work with me also know that I want Segoe font size 12. I think that Sheldon Cooper, the character with idiosyncratic behavior in the series *The Big Bang Theory*, would be proud of me.

I always carry three notebooks with me. The first, a white one, is for noting down "things to say." The second is for recording "things I've recently said." The third is my "to-do list." I save all the small sheets of paper I write on, organizing them by topic. Each sheet is written in two different colors: this helps me to remember what they say and quickly locate specific notes later. My office is home to an "encyclopedia of sheets," all available for reference. Every now and then, I smile at the thought of some poor soul who, after my death, will write a book about my political ideas. I imagine them frazzled and overwhelmed as they sift through all the colored sheets of paper.

* * *

The obsession with keeping everything under control extends to many other aspects of my life. For instance, despite what many might think, I've never relied on a spin doctor. Instead, I've worked with the same people for years, honing my work on a daily basis. Take Giovanna, for example. Known as "fearsome," she's in charge of press relations and has been with me since my Youth Action days. Back then, she was a dedicated activist who aspired to become a journalist. We started working together years ago and haven't stopped since. We grew up together, learning in the field—through mistakes, debates, defeats, and victories. Sure, I could have hired someone with more experience, but I chose instead to rely on the bond forged between people who share the same ideas and fight the same battles. Skills can be learned, but sincerity and devotion—born from deep conviction—cannot. There's also Paolo, the most fastidious and dependable member of the team, currently responsible for preparing notes for TV appearances and electoral campaigns. Paolo was a dedicated activist, and now, with his wife expecting their third child, I honestly don't know how he does it. Even with kids crying, playing, and jumping around him, he manages to focus, working late into the night or on weekends when necessary. Then there's Tommaso, our social media manager, who works with Alberto and their small team of university students. They're young, passionate, and hardworking, and they always bring fresh perspectives on how Italians are feeling. Though they are self-taught, I trust them with my life. Yet, none of them—nor anyone else—could ever convince me to be someone I'm not or do something that doesn't align with my values. Over the years, many professionals have approached me with advice on how I should present myself in public, especially on TV—what I should wear, how I should do my makeup. But I won't do it. I refuse to wear clothes that don't feel like me. Those who work with me know it's futile to try to persuade me to do something that doesn't sit right in my heart. If I'm asked to promote an event on TV that I don't believe in, even if you put me in front of a prompter with all the words in capital letters, I wouldn't be able to do it. My brain simply freezes if what I'm being asked to say hasn't first passed through my heart.

It's not necessarily a strength. This part of my personality has, at times, prevented me from addressing some of my shortcomings. For instance, the way I gesticulate like an octopus when I speak, or how, when I'm deep in thought or concentrating, I frown and end up looking angry. Or the fact that I'm so emotional that my passion sometimes gets the better of me, and I start shouting. And then there's the way I talk too fast. I still remember the desperate expression on the face of a sign language interpreter at a rally, sweating profusely as they struggled to keep up with my pace. Now, whenever I know a sign language interpreter is present, I make sure to apologize in advance.

Could I smooth out these flaws? Probably. No doubt, it would improve my public image. But would that really be me? In the end, I believe a public persona cannot be fake. Over time, you can't hide who you truly are, for better or for worse. And even if you could, it wouldn't be right. People need to believe in you for who you genuinely are, not for who you pretend to be. Eventually, the facade will crumble, and people will see through the bluff. I've seen politicians who were meticulously crafted, with one face and soul in public, but the complete opposite as soon as the spotlight is turned off. They never lasted.

* * *

That said, I've picked up a few tricks over the years. Take television, for example. In the beginning, I was so nervous about being on TV that it's a wonder I even managed to dress properly. Now, with more experience, I've learned how to handle the medium. I even pay attention to details that might seem secondary. If I know I'll be on a particular show, I visualize the studio set and what "costume" I should wear so I don't look out of place. I learned this the hard way: once, when I was on *Porta a Porta*, I wore a white shirt. The armchair they had me sit in was also white, and I ended up looking like the invisible man.

I have written "details that, in theory, might seem secondary" because I've had to come to terms with the fact that they're not. On TV, appearances often matter more than the substance of what you're saying. People see you long before they hear you. So, after spending hours preparing, memorizing figures and data to sound competent and persuasive, the message you get at the end of the event is inevitably something like: "I saw you on TV—your hair looked great that way!"

I know. This is a society based on image, but it still drives me crazy. That's why I much prefer radio to television. On the radio, there's no room for frills, flashy visuals, or colors. Everything relies on imagination, and what you express comes straight from your soul, stripped of any superficial trappings.

* * *

Still, I'll always be thankful for TV. It played a crucial role in my rise to popularity, and by extension, the success of Brothers of Italy. And, of course, it was in a TV studio that I first met Andrea.

He was so incredibly good-looking, and he caught my attention during one of my early appearances on Paolo Del Debbio's show. While I was on set, he stood to one side of the studio, wearing headphones and managing the timing. I found myself stealing glances at him, hoping he wouldn't notice, though he never exchanged a glance with me. He only spoke to me once: during an ad break, I'd grabbed a banana to stave off my hunger, and as the break ended, I awkwardly held the banana peel, looking around for help. He walked over with an air of amused condescension and took the peel out of my hand. "Give me that. The last thing we need is to go live with you holding a banana peel." At that moment, I thought, "Cute, but brutal."

I didn't see him again on that show. Many months later, I was in Milan as a guest on *Mattino Cinque*, the iconic Mediaset program. I got there at dawn, still half-asleep, and headed straight to makeup, pleading with them to work some magic on my puffy face. And then, suddenly, there he was. He walked into the makeup room wearing a white shirt, came right over to me, and started joking around. "Well, I guess he can be friendly, too," I thought. After the show, I returned to Rome, but he'd left an impression on me. So, with the kind of straightforwardness women are known for, I found a way to get his number and texted him something casual. He didn't let the opportunity pass him by.

That was the beginning of the most beautiful love story I've ever experienced. A couple of months later, he took me to Paris for my birthday. He had made dinner reservations at the most luxurious and expensive restaurant in the city, right across from Notre Dame Cathedral. I'm convinced he emptied his bank account just to let me live that fairy tale. I still remember the panicked look on his face when the maître d' handed him the wine list. He took the large book and flipped straight to the last pages, likely searching for a bottle that wouldn't require a mortgage. In a decided tone, he said, "This one is fine." The gentleman looked at him with compassion. It didn't take long for me to let my guard down, and we spent the entire evening laughing. There we were, giggling in this refined place, surrounded by bejeweled women who looked down their noses at us.

Andrea is intelligent, confident, and exceptional at what he does. These qualities make him one of those rare men who aren't threatened by having a successful woman by their side. He has never had an issue with my role as "boss," maybe because he understands the vulnerability I reserve for the people I love. His character is not an easy one, but neither is mine. We've managed to blend our pragmatism with love and determination. When we shut the world and all its storms out of our home, our story still feels like a fairy tale.

Though he's a complete stranger to the world I've spent most of my life in, Andrea has the ability to keep me grounded, tethered to reality and what's normal. And that's what makes him truly unique.

Andrea is an amazing father, and I am incredibly proud of the bond he shares with Ginevra. During the weeks when he's working in Milan, Gigì often says to me: "Mama, I miss Papa. Can't we go to Milan?" She loves going to Milan, where Flavio and Elio—her paternal grandparents—along with her Aunt Ilaria, Uncle Paolo, and her little cousin Ascanio spoil her ever so much. We all struggle with the distance that separates us, and this was especially true during COVID-19. For someone like me, who dreamed of having a big family as a child, now having one but rarely being able to see everyone together feels like a cruel twist of fate. Andrea and Ginevra's relationship is filled with laughter, playfulness, and a level of complicity that children usually reserve for their peers. It often leaves me feeling like the stereotypical party pooper mom, chasing after them with a jacket to put on while they throw snowballs at each other. But seeing their joy makes me deeply happy. Only God knows how much I longed to feel as happy as Ginevra does today. Of all the comments I've heard that make me feel like a proud mother, the one that stands out most came from her pediatrician. During an exam, I asked her, "How is she?" The reply was simple: "She's a happy child."

I'm not entirely sure what happiness is. I've been chasing it my whole life and still don't think I've ever fully caught it. I've come to believe that Giacomo Leopardi, one of Italy's greatest poets, was right when he wrote the poem "Saturday Night in the Village": happiness is mostly the anticipation of something that you think will make you happy. Yet Gigì has reminded me that you can also catch glimpses of happiness, just for an instant. When something unexpected happens in a flash, your heart bursts with joy. One such moment happened after an afternoon the two of us spent together while Andrea was away in Milan. Ginevra suddenly came over and kissed me. She doesn't do that often—probably because I kiss her so much, she doesn't get the chance to take the initiative. Surprised, I asked, "Why did you kiss me?" She replied, "Mama, I'm so very happy when we're together." There it was—happiness. A simple moment. When you become a mother, you experience all the ups and downs. And among these, you can feel happiness and fear at a level you've never felt before. Not a single night goes by that I don't want to gently touch her as she's falling asleep, and I thank God for another day of health and happiness for her. But I never fall asleep without revisiting in my mind all the tragic "what-ifs" that could have happened to her during the day. At first, I thought I was being crazy. Then I spoke to nearly every mother I knew, and I discovered that we're all the same. Even though women don't always stand in solidarity with one another, mothers certainly do. It's solidarity of a kind that's only felt by veterans who have survived the same battles. Whenever something terrible happens to a child—or even to an adult—I instinctively think of their mother and her pain. I weep for children who are not mine, pray for children I have never known, and try each day to do something to ease the fears, struggles, and suffering of every mother. This isn't unique to me. It's simply what we, as mothers, do.

I've spent a lot of time reflecting on the difference between parenting in our generation and in our parents'. We seem to spend our days figuring out how to entertain our kids, how to introduce them to new experiences, as if they must have everything and experience it all immediately. We cater to their desires. Our parents didn't. We had to do what they wanted us to do and adapt to their expectations. Perhaps the biggest difference lies in the fact that our parents were, on average, younger than us. They were more focused on their own goals, their desire to live fully, and their expectations for themselves. We, on the other hand, often became parents after we had already explored much of life, and now channel all our emotions and expectations into our children. But this dynamic comes with a paradox. If our parents were younger, how did they maintain their authority and uphold a clear hierarchy in their relationship with their children—something we can only dream of today? And when, in

December, we pile more gifts under the tree than Santa Claus could possibly carry on his sleigh, are we making our kids happy or simply spoiling them? When we say "yes" too often, are we doing something good for them or complicating their lives by creating a bubble where everything seems possible, only for them to discover too late that real life doesn't work that way? Is it better to give them an easy "yes" today, or teach them the value of hard-won achievements tomorrow? There's probably no definite answer to these questions because parenting involves constant on-the-job training, with no universal guidebook to rely on. Here, again, my pediatrician came to my aid: "You'll hear lots of conflicting advice on how to raise your daughter. Always trust your instinct. No one knows what's best for a child as much as their mother does."

* * *

So, Andrea and I decided to trust our instincts—and to trust in love. For me, it wasn't a given that I'd be able to let myself be loved or to love beyond the boundaries of our community. When your life is entirely devoted to political activism, as mine has been since I was a child, it's easy to end up with nothing outside that sphere. For many of us, that's exactly what happened. I remember during campaigns, someone might say, "Make a list of your friends to contact." Some didn't want to admit that they hadn't made any friends outside the movement. They'd end up making phone calls reminiscent of Carlo Verdone's in *Un sacco bello*, desperately grasping for connections. In the movie, Verdone calls all his friends, trying to find someone willing to go to Kraków with him: "Hello, Amedeo? Hi, it's Enzo. . . . Not Renzo, Enzo. We met two, three months ago, no, at the army barracks—we were in line together. . . . I was just wondering what your plans are for the summer."

Love, friendships, social contexts, and work—they all intersect. That's why I can't help but smile when a reporter thinks they've uncovered a scoop by noting that two members of Brothers of Italy are related, as though their personal relationship preceded their political engagement instead of the other way around. Some think they can discredit me by calling Lollobrigida "Meloni's brother-in-law," implying that his position as one of the party's frontline leaders is solely because he's my sister's partner. What these "professionals" fail to mention is that Lollo, as we affectionately call him, was already provincial councilor when he met Arianna. A little fact-checking might help them present the situation as it truly is, rather than twisting it into what they'd like it to be.

My sister has perhaps been the biggest victim of this ruthless game of fact-twisting. Every so often, she appears in the papers labeled as one of the "most favored," simply because she works for Brothers of Italy's regional group. Never mind that she started working at the Region as a party activist over two decades ago, when I was still unknown to the general public. Never mind that, of all those who started working with her, she's the only one, at the age of forty-five, still in a precarious position. She has consistently refused to participate in any competitions for a permanent role precisely because, if she were to win, people would claim it was thanks to me. None of that matters, as long as they can slap a sensational headline on the front page. Every time I've read one of these articles, I've thought that, in Italy, there's an ingrained effort to prove there's no point in being honest or respectable. If someone wants to tear you down, they'll find a way to do it. Yet, they won't make us change. In the end, the most important thing is being able to look yourself in the eye. So long as you can do that, no one can force you to bow your head. This mentality ties into a broader problem with certain forms of anti-political sentiment. When the goal is to paint all politicians as bad, it becomes impossible to distinguish those who are genuinely trying to do their best from those who treat public office as a lifelong competition to collect rewards.

* * *

I've been a victim of this thinking on several occasions. For instance, the self-proclaimed moral crusaders in the Five-Star Movement love to undermine my work by publishing attendance statistics from parliamentary voting sessions. They've repeatedly claimed that I'm earning three salaries because I supposedly hold three positions simultaneously: a member of the Italian Parliament, a member of the European Parliament, and a city councilor of Rome. But you don't need to be a Member of Parliament to understand the rules governing these roles. The law doesn't accept ignorance as a mitigating factor, and even the most foolish person in the world could do a bit of research and discover the truth. In Italy, it's illegal to collect more than one salary for certain public positions, and in some cases, it's impossible to hold multiple posts at the same time. This means that you cannot serve as both a member of the Italian Parliament and the European Parliament simultaneously. That's why, when I was elected to the European Parliament, I had to choose between the two roles, and I decided to remain in Italy. On the other hand, you can hold the roles of Member of Parliament and city councilor at the same time, but in that case, you're not allowed to collect two salaries. I waived my salary as a councilor for the city of Rome. Incidentally, I attend more council meetings than the Mayor of Rome, Virginia Raggi. So, I'd venture to say it's a good thing that I do my job in Rome without any cost to the public.

My attendance at voting sessions is a different matter. While it's true that I'm present for 40 percent of the votes, you'd have to be as politically naive as a Five-Star member to think that this is an accurate measure of a Member of Parliament's effectiveness. To make it clear, evaluating an MP's competence solely based on voting attendance is like judging a chef's talent by the number of hours they spend at the stove.

To date, my attendance record is comparable to that of other party secretaries. But even if that weren't the case, this metric alone doesn't determine whether the Italians who voted for Brothers of Italy made the right choice. A good MP isn't defined by how often they press a button—often following the advice of a colleague who worked on the measure in committee—but by their productivity. A Member of Parliament is good if they work on solving problems. If it were up to me, I would base salaries on this measure. By counting the amendments, motions, questions, and proposals approved with my name on then, you'd find that I rank among the most productive members at Montecitorio—among the very top of all 630 members. Let me also add that voting in the Chamber takes place in a small window: during forty-eight hours in a week, starting on Tuesday afternoon through to Thursday at noon. Attendance is calculated based on these hours, but the rest of the week isn't factored in. By this logic, I could work for forty-eight hours, do nothing the other five days, and still receive a full salary with a perfect attendance record. That's why, on Mondays or Fridays, the Chamber is often deserted. In contrast, you'll likely find me there—unless I'm away for work—because I go to Montecitorio every single day to carry out the endless tasks required by my role as a party secretary.

My responsibilities go far beyond rallies, parliamentary work, television appearances, interviews, and traveling across Italy. I aim to do all these things to the best of my ability—and more. A party secretary draws up and decides on policies in collaboration with other members and specific department heads. They create the electoral program and oversee the individual proposals for each measure to ensure they align with the general guidelines. They dedicate a great deal of their time to meetings with union representatives, associations, and others who deal with real-world challenges every day. For me, a good politician listens to find out what problems exist, and works on solving them. As someone who has shaped Brothers of Italy as a "productivist" party, I believe the most valuable task force consists of people who live and breathe the real economy daily. If there's one thing I know, it's that wealth isn't created by the state—it's created by businesses and workers. At most, the state can redistribute a portion of that wealth, but it must also empower those who create it to do so in the best possible way. That's why open communication with entrepreneurs, professionals, workers, volunteers, and representatives of civil society is fundamental to us.

Then there's the organizational side. A party is a complex structure, and as its leader, I am like the CEO of a big company. I must understand how this intricate machine works. For it to function effectively, there need to be rules and strict adherence to them. Any time a cog in the system gets stuck, the responsibility falls on the person in the driver's seat.

Since Brothers of Italy was founded, we've had to fight for every inch of progress with our sweat and blood. Failure is not an option for us. This is why our movement is a true meritocracy: everyone must know how to do their job well, with no shortcuts and no limits. This is what we do every day. I get mad when I hear people say, "Meloni's good, but she's on her own." That couldn't be farther from the truth. Yes, I am the face and name representing this community, but without that community, I would be nothing. To quote Mowgli from *The Jungle Book*: "For the strength of the Pack is the Wolf, and the strength of the Wolf is the Pack."

The Things That Count

In the eyes of the dominant single-minded way of thinking, I am a bigot—an unacceptable obscurantist, prowling around, ready to pounce on anyone who champions progress. To be clear, by "progress" I mean the ideas surrounding gender theory, surrogacy, and abortion beyond the permitted term.

That's right, I do absolutely oppose these practices. But not because I'm resistant to "progress." The exact opposite is true: I stand against barbarity. And my stance isn't rooted in religious dogma. Again, quite the opposite. Of course, I believe in God, but my fight has never been about upholding Church doctrine or garnering support from the faithful—that is, if a cohesive Catholic voter movement still exists in Italy after the demise of the Christian Democratic Party. I fight these battles because I strongly believe in them, out of a conviction of secular common sense. I ask uncomfortable questions and seek practical answers. All too often, the so-called solutions to these same issues by proponents of political correctness are devoid of common sense. If taking a newborn puppy away from its mother is wrong—and it is—how can it be right to do so with a human child? How does it make sense to condemn the sale of women's bodies while celebrating the sale of their children? How can Italian judges terminate the parental rights of biological parents—against their will—because they are deemed "too old" to care for their child? Yet, all the while, they turn a blind eye to two men over fifty who go abroad to pay for a child? Similarly, judges determined that Eluana Englaro's father was free to remove the feeding tube that kept her alive because "no one knows better than a parent what's best for their children." Why, then, were the parents of Charlie Gard or Alfie Evans denied the same rights when judges intervened to remove these children from life support? Did these children not have the same right, with physicians going so far as to turn to the courts, taking the decision away from their families? Why must the culture of death always prevail? And why do we rightly fight the battle to stop animal testing, but label experiments on human embryos as progress? Why does Europe, which weaponizes secularism against Christian symbols, tolerate whole neighborhoods under Islamic sharia law? And why is respect for every minority on the planet sacred, yet the plight of persecuted Christians goes ignored?

None of my opponents have ever answered questions like these. Perhaps that's why I, along with those who share my vision, have been portrayed as terrible people. It's a way of avoiding a comparison of the two groups. The Left, the so-called do-gooders, use this tactic often: when they lack convincing arguments, they dismiss their opponents as unworthy, so they can sidestep the actual issues. I, however, am always willing to engage in public discussion on these topics, relying on pure and rational reasoning.

I recall being invited to the World Meeting of Families, an event organized by several associations to discuss the state of family-related topics in Italy. For this, I became the target of every insult under the sun. I remember the protests in Verona: feminists shouting at me, picket lines attempting to block our entry, and debates over whether it was appropriate for the Italian government to endorse the initiative. That's right. Because the same government that had, over the years, supported the most horrific things—from works portraying Jesus Christ on the Cross immersed in a glass of urine, or the Virgin Mary crying tears of sperm, and which remained silent when schools organized activities in which six-year-old children swapped clothing, with girls putting on boys' clothing and vice versa, in order to explain gender theory—this government was now being shamed for putting up signs for a meeting that focused on how to support natural families founded on marriage; how to assist women in avoiding workplace discrimination so they don't have to choose between bringing a child into the world and having a job; and addressing the commodification of humans by the hands of science, instead of the opposite.

The most glaring paradox of all is this: according to the high priests of "one thought fits all," people must be free to do whatever they want. Free to deprive a child of its mother or father, free to decide the fate of another person's life, free to abort in the ninth month of pregnancy, or to take a pill at home as if ending pregnancy were no different from curing a common headache. Free to declare yourself a woman even if you are not, a man even if you are not, free to take drugs and decide how to die. But you are not free to say that you disagree with all this. The supporters of the most extreme freedoms are also the fiercest censors of dissenting views.

There is nothing monstrous or unacceptable about defending families founded on marriage. And let me add: I don't believe that other types of civil unions should face discrimination. People are, of course, free to love whomever they choose. But love has nothing to do with the law. A country's laws do not regulate feelings—that would be absurd. Rather, the state incentivizes what it deems beneficial to society. Our founding fathers, far from being a bunch of narrow-minded bigots, enshrined *favor familiae* in the constitution—legislation dedicated to stimulating the stable union between a man and woman, supported by benefits. Why? For a reason that transcends personal emotions: families built on the marriage of a man and a woman are advantageous to the state. First, they serve as societal safety nets, taking on responsibilities that institutions cannot bear alone. Second, marriage between a man and a woman often leads to children, and society needs children. The Italian population is declining at an alarming rate. That's not an opinion, it's a fact. Consider this: 2020 (annus horribilis) marked the lowest birth rate since the Unification of Italy in 1861! And if that weren't enough, the COVID-19 pandemic caused the highest death toll since World War II. Nearly twice as many deaths as births. Italians simply aren't having enough children. I reject the Left's assertion that we can do without Italians, replacing them with immigrants freshly arrived from other parts of the world. As the French philosopher Rémi Brague, a great conservative thinker for our modern age, astutely remarked: "An epidemic kills, a drop in the birthrate makes it impossible to be born. The result is the same."

The decline in birth rates is the greatest challenge facing the West today. It threatens not only our very social fabric but also our economic fabric. To sustain our welfare system, we need population turnover. Aging communities, rising average ages—this all means that our system of social protection cannot survive if the number of elderly people continues to grow while the number of children shrinks. Without reversing this trend, the state will have more and more people to support, and fewer working people to support them. Encouraging people to have children must be a priority, and this is why we should strengthen family-friendly policies, instead of criticizing them, blinded by ideological dogma.

I know what some of you are thinking as you read these lines: "You talk a lot about families founded on marriage, while you yourself are not married." That's true. Personally, if I were to marry, it would be in a church. In my view, if you commit to doing everything necessary to safeguard your marriage—"in good times and in bad, in sickness and in health, all the days of your life"—it makes sense to do so before the eyes of God. But that is a personal choice. If you choose to marry before the state instead, you know it will still reward your commitment to stability. You can also decide not to marry, as I have done so far, fully aware that I am forgoing certain benefits. The point is that I do not expect the state to extend the same privileges to me as it does for those who formalize their commitment in writing.

The real problem is that we live in a society where the connection between rights and duties has vanished. Every desire becomes a right, even when it's based on nothing more than a whim, while any sense of responsibility has all but disappeared. I advocate for a society where every choice corresponds to specific consequences, where freedom is paired with responsibility. Instead, here in Italy, selfishness often transforms into a political program. "I want to give birth to a child at seventy." "I want to be a mother even though I'm a man." "I want a 'reddito di cittadinanza' (a basic income provided by the state social welfare program) even though I'm fit to work." "I want to become an Italian citizen, even though I've just arrived in this country." The list of such demands grows endlessly, with many of them becoming political claims—and, in some cases, Italian laws.

* * *

Today, the family—the backbone of society and foundation of individual identity—is under attack. It is under attack, just like everything that defines us, because globalist ideology seeks to dismantle identity itself. Have you noticed how all the pillars of identity, everything that distinguishes us, are being eroded? Family and country, gender identity and religion—these are treated as relics of the past, archaic concepts to be overcome. But my role, as someone who identifies as a conservative, is to defend these principles. Roger Scruton, one of the greatest conservative thinkers of our time, put it like this: "The real reason people are conservatives is that they are attached to the things that they love, and want to preserve them from abuse and decay." Scruton passed away in early 2020 (that infamous year again!).

Most of us, when we were young, probably sang "Imagine" by John Lennon, one of the most iconic songs in music history. We felt his words were revolutionary, and that resonating in this pioneer of globalism's lyrics was the dream of a world that was finally just, finally good. But let's pause and think for a moment: is it truly a dream to imagine a world without borders, without distinctions, devoid of centuries of culture and tradition? A world where we are all not equal in rights, but just made the same? Is this really what we should hope for—to abandon the uniqueness of the human experience, to give up the central role of the individual? To become nothing more than interchangeable parts in a global assembly line, mere numbers devoid of consciousness, roots, and the civilization that defines us? Civilization shaped not just by triumphs, but by the suffering that enabled each hard-won conquest? Isn't the world Lennon sang about with poetic optimism, and which today's do-gooders pursue with far less poetry, actually a precursor to a homogenized society? A society where we are rendered so weak that we can no longer defend our rights? A world where we are at the mercy of major economic powers—the architects of bold globalism—who hoard power and wealth in the hands of a select few, at the expense of millions of people under their control?

We are all the same—consumers of the same product, all slaves. "Produce, consume, die," warned the singer Giovanni Lindo Ferretti with his band CCCP Fedeli alla linea (Loyal to the Line). In response to Lennon's famous song Lindo Ferretti wrote "L'imbrunire" (Dusk). His ode begins, "I dream of drawbridges and buttresses/small homelands of the living" (Sogno ponti levatoi e mura a protezione / piccole patrie sempre sul chi vive). Words like these would surely shock the sensibilities of those do-gooders. In the words of Marcello Veneziani, if there is one enemy against which the "global idiot" wages unrelenting war, then it is the wall: "The appeal to tear down walls and build bridges has become an obsession and it concerns not only people and territorial borders, but also the sexes and the natural borders, cultures and behaviors, religions and belonging, and even the human kingdom and the animal kingdom. . . . Without walls there is no home, no temple, no safety. Without walls there is no decency, intimacy, protection from the cold, from the darkness, from the unknown. Without walls there is no sense of measure, recognition of the limit and of one's own limits. Without walls there is no beauty, no strength, no foundation for the city, no erection of civilization. . . . Walls are the bastions of civilization, of charity hospitals, libraries of culture, they are the partitions of art, the moment of prayer."

The relentless campaign against natural boundaries is rooted in ignorance: limits are not a form of violence, that is sheer madness. Alberto Angela made this point well during a 2017 monologue on RAI television, using simple and effective words to explain how "a wall does not just unite a people, it unites many people throughout the ages."

* * *

So no, the world that John Lennon envisioned is not my utopia. My utopia is one where more and more people find the courage to say out loud what, deep in their heart, they continue to believe but are too afraid to express for fear of being labeled unacceptable. Because these ideas are far from unacceptable. Often, they are even common sense. Yet, today, it is necessary to defend them. "Fires will be kindled to testify that two and two make four. Swords will be drawn to prove that leaves are green in summer," wrote G. K. Chesterton. Tolkien is very clear when, in *The Two Towers*, Faramir says: "War must be, while we defend our lives against a destroyer who would devour all; but I do not love the bright sword for its sharpness, nor the arrow for its swiftness, nor the warrior for his glory. I love only that which they defend: the city of the Men of Númenor; and I would have her loved for her memory, her ancientry, her beauty, and her present wisdom." (Yes, I know, two quotes back-to-back may not be the standard approach for making my point, but in this case, it's impossible to choose between them.)

Now, let's talk about Italian law number 194. I will say this until I'm blue in the face: I have never sought to abolish the law that legalizes abortion. What I do insist on, however, is its full enforcement—especially the section that pertains to prevention. Law number 194 was conceived to put an end to illegal abortions, but it also treats abortion as an *extrema ratio*—a last resort. Its goal was to help women avoid being placed in a situation where an abortion is even necessary. Unfortunately, the ideological zeal of a certain Left—unsurprisingly—ensured that the preventive aspects of the law are ignored. For me, it's self-evident that our institutions should stand by women who choose to keep their children.

Throughout my political career, I have consistently advocated for alternatives to ensure that abortion is not the only option available. I have proposed financial support to help mothers carry their pregnancies to term, even when they wish to put up their children for adoption. I have called for psychological support and the strengthening of pro-life centers.

Yet, every time I raised these proposals, swords were drawn in the name of a "woman's right to self-determination." And each time, as always, no one answered my questions. What kind of self-determination is it if abortion is presented as the only solution? True self-determination means the ability to decide freely, without pressure or bias, and with full awareness of all the different opinions. Today, this freedom is not guaranteed. Protecting women from unsafe, back-alley abortions is one thing, but it's something completely different to frame abortion as a victory, as something to encourage, incentivize, or trivialize. Abortion can be painful—for body and soul—and we cannot pretend otherwise. We cannot dismiss the idea that women who choose to have an abortion might one day regret it. I have met many such women. We cannot call it a "civilizational conquest" to allow women to perform abortions alone at home with a pill, enduring contractions and hemorrhaging, just to sustain the notion that abortion should be easy. I envy those in this debate who claim to be truth-bearers—those who tell you without hesitation that an embryo is not a life, or that life only begins from the fourteenth week of pregnancy. I cannot claim such certainty. But I do know this: when I saw my daughter, Ginevra, during an ultrasound, it was *her* heart that was beating. And I know that from the moment of conception, each of us carries a unique and unrepeatable genetic code—forever. This reality, whether you like it or not, carries something sacrosanct. And what is sacrosanct cannot be treated with arrogance or superficiality.

What kind of civilization spends more money and resources finding the easiest way to dispose of human life than it does protecting it? Are these ideas truly unacceptable? I don't believe so. What is unacceptable, however, are policies that are financially tied to the multinationals of abortion, as is the case with Democratic US presidents and Planned Parenthood. These entities have suggested the legalization of practices such as partial-birth abortion—a procedure so horrific that the former US President George W. Bush worked tirelessly to outlaw it, while Hillary Clinton, during her presidential campaign, fought just as hard to have it reinstated. If you are sensitive, you may want to skip the next lines, as they describe something deeply disturbing. A partial-birth abortion involves deliberately delivering a living fetus vaginally, only to suction its head while it is still in the uterus so that the procedure can be classified an abortion rather than homicide. I will fight against this practice with every ounce of my strength, no matter the cost.

I will also continue to fight against a society that claims to champion women, mothers, and children, but when push comes to shove, fails to make any real cultural progress. A society that refuses to acknowledge that children are an indispensable resource, and that those who bring them into the world are doing something that benefits all of us. This is why we need to breathe life into policies that allow women in the modern era to balance raising children with pursuing careers, without penalizing those who employ them. It's all too common to criticize businesses for hiring men over equally qualified women of childbearing age, citing a "fear" that women might go on maternity leave. But we rarely acknowledge that our welfare system offloads much of the financial burden for maternity leave onto the businesses themselves. In these challenging economic times, not every business can afford the cost. Similarly, we lament the fact that young people increasingly delay or forgo parenthood. But what we fail to recognize is that this decision is not born of selfishness. Having a child means that one of the two parents—usually the mother—must give up their salary, and they don't know for how long. It is incredibly difficult to get by in Italy with just one salary. So, it isn't selfishness that discourages young people from having children, but fear—the fear of instability, of never being able to buy a home, of never securing a decent retirement. In short, it is the fear of not being able to guarantee their child the best life possible. Ironically, it is often the very love for their unborn children that prevents young people from having them in the first place. For this reason, I have often called young people who choose to become parents "heroes."

These reflections are the root of many cross-party proposals we have supported, such as the family subsidy. When it comes to certain issues, it is crucial that we collaborate and stand united in our opinions and many of the demands that we have worked on over the years, especially with Brothers of Italy.

We have devised the expansion of nursery and preschool programs. This would extend hours until after store closing times and even include summer hours on a rotating basis—something already implemented in Italy's poorer towns. Additionally, we have also submitted dozens of proposals urging the state to cover the cost of substitutes during maternity leave, rather than placing the burden entirely on businesses. We have also recommended increasing maternity leave pay to 80 percent beyond the initial few months, as the current 30 percent is often impossible to live on. All these measures are designed to make women's employment easier and more sustainable. Of course, such policies are expensive, and there isn't that much money to go around. That's why we called for both Giuseppe Conte and Mario Draghi to prioritize the birth rate issue within the Recovery Plan. The demographic time bomb is not just an Italian problem—it affects all of Europe. Yet, I find it baffling that Europe, which has a plan for virtually everything—from Erasmus to Horizon research mobility—has never considered allocating resources to address this issue with a *Familiae* plan. Despite these discussions, some fundamental points continue to be overlooked. First, there's the argument from some quarters that incentivizing births or larger families would deter women from participating in the workforce. With the proper tools, motherhood and labor can move forward together, as many other countries have shown. France and countries in Northern Europe are in the lead, having implemented proper strategies to encourage motherhood. These nations now boast of women's employment rates and birth rates above the (low) European average. Second, female unemployment is a major barrier to Italy's economic growth. Data shows that if Italy were to close the employment gap between men and women, it would also significantly reduce the employment gap between Italy and the European average. By making it easier for women to work, we would not only boost productivity and wealth but also generate higher revenues for the Treasury. These funds could then be reinvested in social protection and incentives, creating a virtuous cycle of growth.

* * *

I sincerely hope that what I'm saying isn't misconstrued as outdated on the role of women. I hope that my words can offer a common ground for a reflection on what must be done to modernize Italy. The ideological dogma of some often prevents us from serious and conscientious debate on such critical issues. Too often, I find myself attacked or marginalized by certain members of the intelligentsia—not for the content of what I say, but because they feel it's more important to label me or force me into a preconceived stereotype. Everyone agrees that Italy's low birth rate is a problem. Yet, when someone like me from the Right raises the issue, I am dismissed as expressing nostalgia for Benito Mussolini's Social Policy for Mother and Child.

The same can be said for all topics labeled as ethical that I actually prefer to call "nonnegotiable values," especially when it concerns the sanctity of life. This principle has shaped Europe into the civilization it is today, and made Italy a pioneer of that civilization. After all, it was the Grand Duke of Tuscany who, in 1786, became the first to abolish capital punishment on the continent. Why are we against the death penalty if life is not sacred? Even today, in other parts of the world, serial killers are sent to the electric chair—people who, without question, are definitely unlikeable. Yet, we in Europe refuse, rightly so, to accept the notion that human life, no matter whose, can be extinguished by law at the hands of another person, like flipping a light switch. If we uphold this principle a value—and I believe it is—then certain issues must be handled with care.

Let's consider the hotly debated and complex matter of euthanasia. I can still remember the dramatic case of DJ Fabo, a young man bursting with life, left completely paralyzed by an accident. He fought for a long time for the right to die because he couldn't imagine enduring the rest of his life in that condition. I remember my mother calling me, furious, because she supported his request and found my opposition to euthanasia cruel. I also remember the countless times that I wondered, as I watched the young man's story unfold, how I would feel if I were in his place—or worse, if I were his mother, devastated every day by the sight of her son in that condition and willing to accept his death to end his suffering.

I am a human being, like everyone who supported Fabo's battle. But I am also a legislator, and my responsibility is to consider the impact of decisions that may seem humane and just when viewed through the lens of individual cases but lead to inhumane and unthinkable outcomes when applied universally. Because "all citizens . . . are equal before the law." Let me explain. If I were to enshrine into law the principle that any person who considers their life undignified—whether rightly or wrongly—should be free to end to it, then that principle would apply to everyone. But the concept of dignity is entirely subjective. Where would the limits lie? If someone like Fabo, paralyzed from head to toe, could request to end their life, would the same right extend to someone who "only" lost their legs? What about someone who is physically healthy but unhappy? Either I make decisions about my life, or I don't. There are no parameters to regulate this distinction. I'm not being philosophical here. I am speaking of the realities of what has happened in countries that have legalized euthanasia. These laws often begin with extreme cases, and then expand to include depressed minors who seek to end their lives. The role of a legislator requires grappling with these complex factors, and involves more than just following facts in the news—and that's the way it should be. We need people willing to take responsibility for difficult decisions that are not made based on momentary emotions. This involves asking painful, even agonizing questions, but that's the job of politics.

* * *

As I see it, not everything that is scientifically possible is humanely lawful. Is it lawful for a poor woman to be forced, out of financial necessity, to rent out her womb, endure an entire pregnancy as well as birth, only to sell her child? All so that someone can have a child with their own genetic makeup, despite it being biologically impossible for them due to their age or because the aspiring parents are two men? To me, the answer is no. This is yet another instance where we start with an emotionally compelling individual case—a person longing to experience the love and emotion of being a parent—and end up with a commodified reality: supermarkets for children, where you can select the child's hair color as if it were an item on a shelf. It either is or isn't lawful to buy a child, so once you declare it so, there will be a "store" that sells them, and you won't be able to stop the process.

Why aren't these questions being asked? Or are they simply being ignored to gain easy consensuses? This reflects another troubling aspect of a society that has lost control: the idea that everything is owed to you, combined with a tendency to prioritize the voices of those who are loud enough to claim their alleged rights, while neglecting those who cannot speak for themselves. All due to consensus. Those who vote win. But should the state protect the strongest rather than defending those who cannot advocate for themselves? To my mind, the answer is a clear no. This is why, for example, I oppose adoptions by homosexual couples—not because I'm homophobic. This is what people say about me to avoid having to answer the simple questions I ask.

In Italy, single people are not allowed to adopt a child, and adoption laws impose strict criteria on prospective couples. These include assessments of the couple's financial situation, relationship stability, and the age of the prospective parents. Yet, no one has ever accused these criteria of being "single-phobic," "poverty-phobic," or "ageist." The fact is, phobia has nothing to do with it. All these regulations are made to protect the most vulnerable: the child. A child cannot make their own decisions and depends on the state to act in their best interests. The underlying belief is that every child deserves the best possible situation—a father and a mother, a united family, and parents of a proper age to raise them. I am convinced that every child has the right to a mother and father. This does not mean that two men or two women cannot raise a child with love—many children grow up happily in single-parent families, myself included. I had a wonderful childhood, thanks to my mother's huge sacrifices. But when I see Ginevra playing with her father, I can't help but reflect on a happiness I never got to experience. Life can take certain things away from us, but we face our destinies and adapt. It's a different matter when the law deprives a child of something because others have decided that their wants take precedence over a child's rights. If I were debating this issue, my interlocutor might respond with something like: "Isn't it better for a child to be raised by someone who loves them, whether it's one person or two people of the same sex, rather than forcing that child to grow up in an institution?" The principle is correct, but the premise is flawed. For various reasons, these days, there are fewer children up for adoption than there are families eager to adopt them. This allows us to guarantee that the children only get the best—at least on paper.

I'm sorry if there are some gay people who don't agree with my position. However, I'm not in politics to chase consensus but to defend the ideas I believe in. I'm sorry that some choose to label me a "homophobe" because of this, especially because I believe I'm one of the least biased people on the planet. I don't say this to appease advocates of political correctness. I truly believe that anyone can love whomever they choose and live their sexuality in whatever way they see fit, as long as it does not harm others. My stance is not rooted in "intolerance" toward those who are different from me. On the contrary, it is precisely because I don't judge people based on the emotional choices they make. Rather, I'm intolerant of illogical ideas—for instance, the concept of gender as an endless spectrum, detached from the biological categories of male and female, and instead based on preferences, personality, or tendencies. This issue raises numerous questions that many pretend not to understand.

For some time now, there has been an effort to introduce gender theory into schools, under the guise of promoting a culture of tolerance. These initiatives are expected to start as early as elementary school. This is one of the objectives of the Zan law, which ostensibly aims to combat homophobia but, in practice, achieves the opposite. When the law was debated in Parliament, I posed a question to my colleagues that no one could answer: is it appropriate to explain homosexuality to six-year-old children in schools that have chosen not to teach sex education? And why is it that we don't teach sex education in schools? The reason is simple: it was decided that children of such a young age lack the maturity to process certain topics, and that these matters should be handled by families, who know their children better than anyone else. I still agree with this approach.

Again, we are all free to feel as we wish and to label ourselves however we choose. But when individual behaviors are transformed into norms that regulate the life of an entire community—principles meant to apply universally in the name of "protection"—we risk creating new injustices. When taken to extremes, gender theory could have far-reaching consequences, many of which would ultimately discriminate against women. Ironically, some of the most prominent supporters of these bizarre theories are feminists.

A man may feel like a woman, and a woman may feel like a man, but you cannot expect a country's laws to indulge such feelings. Doing so would lead to chaos, and, more importantly, undermine many of the hard-won rights for women. Consider just one example to help readers understand what I mean: transgender athletes in sports. In Australia, a male volleyball athlete who transitioned to female now competes on the national women's team. This athlete is 6'2" and weighs 220 pounds. Is this fair to athletes who are biologically women, who will never be able to compete with such strength? Martina Navratilova, a tennis champ who is both openly gay and a feminist, has rightly stated: "You can't just proclaim yourself a female and be able to compete against women." Navratilova goes on to say that it's cheating, and has allowed hundreds of athletes who changed gender to win what they could never have won in men's games, especially in sports where strength is required. Clearly, things have gotten out of hand.

And then there's this question: will we eventually establish quotas for every sexual orientation and gender identity? If so, would it not ultimately be unfair to women? As you know, I'm not a fan of the "female quota," but how would those on the Left feel if, while compiling electoral lists and struggling to meet gender parity requirements, I asked one of my male representatives to declare that he feels like a woman so I could replace a female candidate with him? And if we decide it's discriminatory to state that men do not have a uterus and cannot have children, does that mean laws and resources that favor mothers should also be extended to anyone who feels they have a uterus, even if medical science proves otherwise? My dear friends on the Left, make peace with yourselves, as you risk tying yourself in knots with your bizarre claims.

* * *

Allow me to be a little facetious: it almost seems as though some men, recognizing that the time for women has come, are rushing into this middle ground to claim space. But, jokes aside, if we decide to abolish genders entirely, it will be to the detriment of women—just as the world is finally beginning to understand their value. Hard-won breakthroughs will be erased. And for me, as someone who has never identified as a feminist but who has always been proud to be a woman, this does not seem like progress.

I am proud to have been born a woman and to have grown up in a family of women. I was never subjected to outdated notions of subordination for wives and daughters in relation to the men in the household. Obviously, that hasn't changed in my own family today, where there are no predefined roles that I see as relics of the past. To me, a family is a team. Its members share responsibilities based on time and ability, without stereotypes and abuses of power. It's like a puzzle: at first glance, the pieces might seem mismatched, but in the end, they fit perfectly. After all, the foundation of love and friendship is choice. When you feel forced to do something, it's a sign that something isn't working. I have said this time and time again to my best friend Milka, a beautiful woman with a proud presence and an infectious smile, who has accompanied me, listened to me, and put up with me for the past quarter century. We can go weeks without talking on the phone, but it doesn't matter. We both know what we mean to each other, and that is enough. That's true friendship.

I'm certainly not the stereotypical housewife, but when I'm at home, I don't mind doing household chores. In fact, I find some tasks, like tidying up, quite relaxing. I enjoy cooking, though I can't always say the same for those who have to eat what I cook! And when I cook, I don't necessarily expect Andrea to do the dishes—I'm happy to do them myself, as long as I can listen to some good music while I do. That said, if there's something I can't manage, Andrea is always ready to step in. This is something else that I love about him: Andrea will do anything. Andrea's mother has always been a big part of his life, but since he left home at a young age, he learned how to take care of himself early on. He even knows how to iron a shirt, and thank goodness for that because, at the ripe old age of forty, I still haven't figured out how to iron the sleeves on men's shirts.

Sharing my living space wasn't easy for me at first, as I was used to living alone, with only my cat, Martino, for company. For Andrea, I imagine it is even harder, considering how little closet space I left for his things. Still, we're doing pretty well. Of course, my obsession with keeping everything in its proper place can present a challenge. Whenever Andrea leaves something out—or puts it in a spot I hadn't intended—it feels like sacrilege. He loves to kick off his shoes and leave them wherever they land. Sometimes I wonder if I'm living with Carrie Bradshaw from *Sex and the City*, given the sheer number of shoes he has. When I'm home, I'm often trailing behind him and Ginevra, putting things back where they belong as soon as they're moved. I must seem like a frightening presence to them. And honestly, you might feel the same way if you rang the doorbell unannounced to be greeted by me in a sweatshirt with a stuffed bear on it, my hair in a mess and fastened with a clip, vacuum cleaner in hand. Jekyll and Hyde have nothing on us women when it comes to how quickly we can transform—from career professionals confidently striding in high heels to manual laborers in oversized fleece pajamas.

I must admit, I love doing the grocery shopping. Whether it's a quick trip to the supermarket or, even better, to the local market, I love it. Markets are where you find genuine, high-quality produce—and, in my view, it's the best opinion poll institute you could hope for. When I need to understand what people think, I spend time at the market. Of course, I shop, but more importantly, I listen. Whenever something politically significant happens in Italy, pundits on talk shows talk about "marketplace" reactions. But what they mean is the financial market. The only markets that truly reflect the people's voice are the ones held in squares across Italy's cities and towns. Maybe that's why I feel the need to surround myself with people, so I never forget where I came from. I trust the voices of ordinary citizens far more than the opinions aired on talk shows. Because of this connection, my adversaries mockingly call me a "carciofara" (artichoke seller) or "pesciarola" (fishmonger), but that doesn't bother me. In fact, I'm proud of it. I'd rather be called those names than resemble those who discuss Italians and their problems while sitting barefoot, sipping champagne. If I ever become like them, please cancel me. Like many Italians who voted for the Left in good faith, that option has lost its way.

The Left that once claimed to champion the voices of the marginalized and fight for the rights of the poorest is unrecognizable today. Now, from their newspaper columns or the mouths of their gurus, they accuse me of being "the queen of losers," that I'm too "close to the marginalized," as if proximity is an unforgivable sin. How can the former French President François Hollande call himself a socialist while mocking the poor by referring to them as "toothless"—as though it's not shameful to live in a society where so many can't afford dental care? Or the former US presidential candidate, Hillary Clinton, claiming to be a Democrat while labeling Donald Trump's Republican voters as "deplorables."

* * *

For some time now, this do-gooder Left has also set its sights on the world of gyms and sports, treating physical activity and taking care of your body as though it were a symptom of violence or backwardness. But I love gyms, and I believe sports are the healthiest activities young people can pursue. Surely, it's better than drinking, smoking pot, or wasting hours on video games.

I have long followed the "Icelandic model." In the 1990s, this small country in Northern Europe faced alarming statistics on youth alcohol and drug abuse, as well as suicides—among the worst in the world. The Icelandic government responded decisively, investing heavily in accessible sports for everyone, that could be practiced anywhere—even braving the cold and ice if necessary. The result was nothing short of a miracle, with Icelanders excelling in soccer, basketball, and other disciplines. But more importantly, the societal impact was profound, as the grim statistics of alcohol and drug abuse were replaced by medals, victories, and success stories. I believe that Italy should emulate this model. If I had the power, I would ensure that sports and physical activity became integral from nursery school, continuing into old age.

Sports changed my life. When I was young, I struggled with being overweight, I smoked, and I often felt stressed. Then I began exercising—regularly and with determination—and eventually, I realized I couldn't live without it. Sports have become my personal addiction. I do a variety of them, from biking to CrossFit, to Pilates, swimming, and my newest passion, the Mexican racket sport padel tennis. I don't just do this for my body but for my mind. When I'm forced to stop exercising, I feel like a pressure cooker ready to burst because I rely on the endorphins that physical activity releases and on the discipline that sports have taught me.

I always make time for training. When I'm traveling around Italy on the campaign trail, I choose hotels where I can go for a run early in the morning. The same goes for vacations. Even during lockdown—when we weren't allowed to go more than a few hundred feet from our homes—I didn't let that stop my habit of running, and I raced up and down the 150-foot slope outside my house. I must have looked like Forrest Gump. When the gyms were closed, a group of friends I've been training with for years got creative. We took to cycling on the sidewalk or running together outdoors. The gym is also one of the few places where I tolerate being insulted without reacting: "Daje a balè che me stai a scredità la palestra"

(Come on, you whale, you're making my gym look bad!") That's Fabrizio, my trainer. He'd call me "balena" (whale), even if I were skinny. It's his form of motivation. Antonio, my hairdresser, is worse. He's completely merciless whenever I let myself go. I remember once, after I'd gained a few pounds, I complained that he'd gone overboard with the highlights in my hair. He answered drily, with his usual surly smile, "I just wanted to see what Fat Barbie would look like." What can I say? It's important in life to have friends who test your resilience.

Another great thing about sports is that they foster a sense of belonging, the desire to be part of something bigger, and the drive to give it your all for victory. For a long time in Italy, sports were the only socially acceptable way to express national pride. For decades, waving the Italian flag was seen as an act of subversion or nostalgia—something only the youth on the Right had the courage to do at public events. The one exception was during national soccer games when everyone could embrace the tricolor. But in those moments, many Italians realized they didn't even own an Italian flag. Pietrangelo Buttafuoco, a talented and brilliant right-wing intellectual, captured it beautifully in an article for *Italianieuropei* a few years ago: "The national team is playing, it might win something, and a crowd of compatriots will throng the streets trying to find a flag. The only place they're sure to find one is in the headquarters of the Italian Social Movement. Hopefully without the flame in the middle. So borrowed flags and one single cry: 'Forza, Italia,' i.e. 'Go, Italy,' with a comma that's an omen."

Italy has come a long way in reclaiming its national identity. Today, nearly every political party references the red, white, and green in its symbols or rhetoric. And I'd like to believe that, in some small way, we played a role in this change. A few years ago, when I described Brothers of Italy as the party of patriots, some told me the term was outdated and incomprehensible. But listen to political debates today, and you'll find everyone vying to call themselves patriots. Matteo Renzi invoked patriotism to justify toppling the Conte government. Graziano Delrio, an important member of the Democratic Party, once said at a party congress: "We cannot let Meloni be the only using the word 'patriot.'" And even Nicola Fratoianni, a member of the radical Left, declared in Parliament, "*We* are the real patriots." There's plenty to say about what these people mean by patriotism, but that's not the point. The point, as Giorgio Almirante once said, is this: "When you see the truth you believe in emerge from your adversary's lips, you should rejoice, for that is a sign of victory."

I AM ON THE RIGHT

It All Began When Everything Was About to End

Rome, Via della Scrofa 39. The door is that of the historic headquarters of National Alliance and before that of the Italian Social Movement. And here I am again. It's a morning in November 2019. Inside me a small storm of feelings is brewing, ranging from anxiety to pride. This is the place I called—twenty-seven years ago!—asking where I could find the Youth Front headquarters closest to my home. Now, this is where we are relocating the Brothers of Italy headquarters.

Much of my life, much of my experience as a human being and as a person in politics, is connected to this building, to these rooms, even though—to be honest—I did not spend a lot of time in them. For years, as president of Youth Action, I had an office in this building, but we were relegated to another stairwell.

I walk up the steps of what is both our new home and our old one. I enter slowly, trying not to be seen. I arrive at my new office and I shut the door behind me. My heart is beating fast, but I have never been as clear-minded as I am at this moment. This same office once belonged to Gianfranco Fini, and, before him, to Pino Rauti and Giorgio Almirante. I stand there in silence and suddenly I realize just how immense the responsibility I have chosen to take on is. I have picked up the baton in a story lasting seven decades. I have chosen to bear the weight of the dreams and hopes of people who had found themselves with neither a party nor a leader, on my shoulders. It was a party that risked becoming lost, as if those millions of people, the ones who fight with me today and the ones who are no longer with us, were all right there. As if they were looking at me, in silence, asking me: "Are you up to the task?"

More than a decade before this moment, whenever I entered this room to talk to Gianfranco Fini, I would feel small. Maybe that's also why this space seemed bigger. I no longer feel small now, but neither am I reckless enough to be comfortable in my role. Will I be strong, courageous, just, capable of being remembered by those who will come after me as a leader who did her part on this noble journey?

Before my eyes I see a feature film, a plot filled with tragedies, betrayals, desires, victories, defeats, dreams. A whole world that never stopped believing, fighting. The story I am talking about is not just that of Brothers of Italy. It goes much farther back, and it is the story of many people.

This is another reason why we founded our party. We know we are the relay runners in a very long race, and we run in the hope that there will be others to pick up the baton when we are forced to stop.

Today, this hope is more solid. The polling data report percentages that the Italian Right has never had before, and it is the first time that a leader who comes from this political world ranks at the top for popularity among party leaders. In Parliament our numbers are relatively small, but in the public debate our opinion counts, it has clout, it shifts things. We have done a huge amount of work to reconstruct our credibility and earn this space for ourselves because no one has ever given us anything for free: when you're on the side that's considered the wrong one, you can't afford to make even the slightest mistake. Today, we can safely say that the Right exists, it grows, and it wins. And all those who hoped it would be overcome and marginalized will have to accept it. It is thanks to us if things went this way, in spite of the vultures circling above our heads.

If elections were held today, millions of people would be ready to confirm their confidence. And we're ready to take office so we can finally put our ideas and our policies to the test. Yet, there has been nothing easy about getting this far.

It all began when everything was about to end.

* * *

On November 12, 2011, after a year of constant attacks, Silvio Berlusconi resigned as Prime Minister. Many Italians will no doubt remember the panic over the spread. Exactly what does the word "spread" mean? Technically, it is the difference between German and Italian government bonds. Economically, it is one of the indicators used to measure a state's solvency, and thus its credibility in the markets. Politically, however, it has long been a tool used to support or penalize governments, depending on whether they are liked or disliked by the powers-that-be. But most importantly, why did the spread rise so dramatically in 2011? Certainly, the Italian government was weakened by various investigations, but the reason for that spike, easily verifiable, was that at a certain point, Deutsche Bank, a German bank, decided to sell off a significant amount of the Italian bonds it held within a few hours, creating panic and triggering emulation on the market. It was a German decision

It seemed that Italy was on the verge of defaulting and there were loud calls for the government to step down. Today, no one would have the chutzpah to say the reason for the spread was the inadequacy of the incumbent government or the Prime Minister's private life, which was instead what the media were saying in those days. Of course, because of his conduct in private—frankly lacking in scruples—Berlusconi had made himself vulnerable to his critics. However, the truth about that two-year period was another.

Berlusconi's Center-Right government had to be ousted. For the exact same reasons that still today make me feel proud to have been a part of it, regardless of its many limits. For that government the defense of the national interest was important; it rejected taking on a subordinate role with respect to France and Germany; it behaved like what it was, that is, the government of one of the founding nations of the European Union, one of the world's major economies, with a strategic geopolitical role that deserved to be valorized. In the eyes of those who believe that Italy's role should be that of a colony, a land of conquest in which lootings can be carried out freely, the Berlusconi government was guilty of wanting to continue to consider Italy a great nation. It was, therefore, an obstacle to be removed. Whenever one discusses the politics that in Italy managed to raise its head and show its pride, the Crisis of Sigonella is almost always mentioned, when Prime Minister Bettino Craxi, in 1985, gave the order to stand up to the American military—who, without coming to any agreement with the Italian authorities, had hijacked a plane with kidnappers on board, forcing it to land in Italy—to uphold the principle of territorial sovereignty. The Berlusconi government was guilty of several such situations, some of which even more serious in the eyes of certain foreign cliques. The 2008 Treaty of Benghazi comes to mind, with which Berlusconi and Gaddafi sanctioned a close alliance between Italy and Libya and healed the wounds of the colonial period. The treaty included cooperation between the two countries to stop the trafficking of illegal immigrants, it mentioned Italian investments in Libya, and, above all, it incorporated special accords in regard to energy supplies. I remember Berlusconi's ability to keep Italy firmly bound to the Atlantic Treaty and at the same time build up a dialogue with Russia, giving Italy a central position on the international map, and managing to lay the foundations for initiatives such as that of the South Stream pipeline that connected Russia to Italy. But what I remember above all was Italy's unwillingness to sign Europe treaties that were to its disadvantage, such as the European Fiscal Compact and the European Stability Mechanism.

If we assemble all the pieces of our recent history, the puzzle is clear to see for those who know how to look at it.

In Libya, we were forced to participate in the attack against Gaddafi, who was ousted from power. And I use the word "forced" fully aware of its meaning, because I, too, was at the Teatro dell'Opera in Rome on March 17, 2011, to watch the performance of *Tosca* for the celebration of the 150th anniversary of the Unification of Italy. I remember the echoes of a meeting that was held during the intermission between two acts when the President of the Republic Giorgio Napolitano had suggested that the government should participate in the intervention begun by the French against Colonel Gaddafi. The operation was clearly anti-Italian, aimed to weaken our interests. Berlusconi, who had already lost a great deal of his power because of a series of personal scandals, tried to oppose it, but in vain.

The advent of the Mario Monti government is another fundamental piece in this design. Because Mario Monti did not become Italian Prime Minister by chance, as an impromptu solution to Berlusconi's unexpected resignation. No, that operation was planned down to the smallest detail. By the European cliques, by some financial powers, and by the domestic supporters, some of whom held the highest offices in the state, Giorgio Napolitano first and foremost. They say that Berlusconi resigned because his own lack of credibility and that of his government had caused a panic in the markets, taking the spread to more than six hundred points. But the truth is actually much more complicated than that.

Why Mario Monti? Because he was a prominent figure within European circles, someone who could ensure certain unpopular decisions in Italy but popular ones abroad—especially if he came to power not by choice of the citizens but through underhanded power dealings.

Mario Monti was hailed as the savior of the nation, but here too, something doesn't quite add up. When I think of a "brave captain," according to my worldview, I imagine someone who defies fate to fulfill their duty—fearless, determined, and ready to take a personal risk to save others. "Captain" Monti, however, before taking the helm of a ship in the storm, had secured himself a very comfortable lifeline by being appointed a lifetime senator by the head of state. His government was, of course, met with unanimous praise and enthusiasm, but it didn't take long for the mask to slip. From signing the Fiscal Compact to the European Stability Mechanism (ESM), and introducing the so-called "Save Italy" decree (if there's one thing I've learned, it's that the more reassuring a law's name sounds, the more you should be concerned), Monti's government was marked by the fierce austerity policies. This, according to the European orthodoxy of the time, was supposed to put our public finances in order, but instead, it ended up causing nothing but social mayhem—worsening, moreover, our macroeconomic indicators.

* * *

When Berlusconi resigned, I was in a cabinet meeting. Within a few hours, thousands of people had gathered under the windows of Palazzo Chigi. At first, we heard a muffled noise, but then the threatening shouts became clear, and over them came the wailing sirens of armored police vehicles.

Between Piazza Colonna, the Quirinale, and Palazzo Grazioli (Berlusconi's headquarters), a dangerous and electrifying atmosphere took hold. The crowd of left-wing activists and members of the Five Star Movement celebrated the fall of the last Prime Minister who had been unequivocally chosen by the citizens through an election. They jeered with mocking whistles, raised clenched fists in the air, and chanted abusive slogans—"Buffoon! Buffoon!" "Caiman!"

Within minutes, all hell broke loose. The security agents told all the ministers to leave through the rear exit of Palazzo Chigi.

Each one got into their chauffeur-driven car.

With the flashing lights off, they fled into the darkness of the evening.

But I did not. "I've done everything I could. I have nothing to be ashamed of," I told myself. So, I decided to go out through the main door with my press officer, even as the DIGOS agents shouted at us, "Where are you going? Don't do that! What are you doing?"

The PDL meeting was to be held at Palazzo Grazioli, which meant crossing Via del Corso. I walked straight through the middle of the crowd of protesters moving in the opposite direction. When they recognized me, they began to shout insults in my direction. Many of them were incredulous: "Is that really Meloni?" But I kept moving, head held high and steps steady. No one dared touch me. I had learned as a young girl how cowards operate: if you run, they chase you; but if you confront them, nine times out of ten, they're intimidated and let you go.

* * *

At Palazzo Grazioli we had to discuss whether to support the Monti government. My memory of those tense hours is rather blurred. However, I clearly recall the gloomy atmosphere, the resigned expressions, and the weariness visible on Berlusconi's face and noticeable in his voice. I remember about fifty people taking turns to speak, offering arguments that were more or less convincing to support the statement in which the leader essentially said we should back the fledgling Monti government. I recall raising my hand to voice my opinion and the awkward silence that fell during my dissenting intervention. I told Berlusconi, in plain words, that the PDL should in no way support the Monti government. It was intolerable to hand Italy over to emissaries of those European cliques that had plotted and schemed against our democracy; it was like admitting our adversaries were right when they were not. Several times in my life, I've been looked at the way many looked at me that evening—as the naive, quixotic young woman who doesn't understand politics, who still has to grow up, who will one day understand the rules of grown-ups' games. And several times, years later, I've looked back to ask myself if I was right—and often, the answer has been "yes." As it was in that case.

Very few others followed my reasoning that evening. And at some point, I understood: they had given up—Berlusconi first among them. Perhaps, looking back, the first spark of the flame that would lead me to found Brothers of Italy a year later was lit that night, as I looked at the faces of a political class that no longer had the strength to fight. That was not the case for me.

The rest of the story is quite well known. It was a year of extremely difficult trials—both for many Italians, who bore the brunt of the government's decisions, and for me, constantly torn between my convictions and the responsibility of adhering to the party mandate under which I was elected. In my view, representation is a serious matter: one is elected within a party, and it is a duty to honor its line as a responsibility toward voters. My mandate was in the PDL, and I always respected it—though at times, I simply could not bring myself to vote for certain measures.

This was the case with the Fiscal Compact and the European Stability Mechanism (ESM), the so-called "State Rescue Fund." It has recently been claimed that Berlusconi signed the ESM, but, again, the truth differs. Berlusconi participated in negotiations for the creation of a support mechanism for national states, insisting that it be funded through common debt. The condition for activating such a fund, for us, was the issuance of Eurobonds. In practice, the "State Rescue Fund" envisioned by the Center-Right resembled the recent Recovery Fund more than the current European Stability Mechanism. However, that proposal didn't go through, Berlusconi resigned, and Monti signed the ESM as we know it today. I chose not to vote for the ratification of that treaty.

* * *

I did, however, vote for the "Save Italy" decree, albeit with great difficulty. And on that point, I want to clarify something. For years, no matter what I do, hordes of fake Five Star Movement profiles accuse me of the same thing: "Shame on you! You voted for the Fornero Law!" I think it's time to point out that an actual "Fornero Law" never came to Parliament. The pension reforms devised by Minister Fornero were entirely part of the "Save Italy" decree—a comprehensive measure that, at the time, everyone (no one excluded) deemed necessary to avoid default. Even Beppe Grillo spoke in favor of those measures, going so far as to praise Monti and his ministers in his blog.

The Five Star Movement can claim they didn't vote for the Save Italy decree, and therefore the pension reform, only because they weren't in Parliament. If they had been, they would have followed their mentor and voted in favor of it, too. Especially considering what we know now—they seem to have no problem supporting shameful measures if it means holding on to their seats.

The Five Star supporters either don't know, or pretend not to know, that it was thanks to me that the rule initially proposed by Minister Fornero, which would have frozen pension indexation for amounts over 900 euros, was changed to be applied only to pensions over 1,400 euros. It was our hard-fought battle in the Labor Commission that raised that threshold, though not as much as we wanted.

It was also thanks to me, and the fact that as an outgoing minister I had greater leverage to be heard, that the Save Italy decree included the full aggregation of contribution periods (allowing pension calculations to include contributions paid into a specific fund for less than three years, which previously would have been lost). Furthermore, it established that those receiving so-called "golden pensions" had to contribute to the nation's difficult moment with a solidarity levy.

This fight against "golden pensions" has been one of my long-standing battles, unfortunately later embraced (and subsequently trivialized and then buried) by the Five Star Movement. Nevertheless, I still firmly believe that it is a righteous cause. I have nothing against earned wealth, nor do I oppose high pensions resulting from properly paid contributions. What I oppose are injustices and abuses, such as pensions of 30,000 euros a month obtained thanks to laws specifically crafted to benefit a select few at the expense of everyone else.

This is why I have always advocated that beyond a certain threshold—still high, at 5,000 euros a month—there should be an evaluation to determine whether the pension received corresponds to the contributions paid. If not, it should be proportionally reduced. Sounds like common sense, doesn't it? Unfortunately, those who make decisions, like the members of the Constitutional Court, are often the same people who benefit from these generous mechanisms.

The disparity in pension payments between older generations, who receive pensions calculated based on their last salaries rather than actual contributions, and younger generations, who must comply with the strict contributions method requiring them to earn and pay for every cent of their pension, is the clearest sign of a country that has lost its sense of national solidarity. It's a truly unfair situation, and undeserved "golden pensions" are its most scandalous representation.

I refuse to accept this state of affairs, and perhaps it's for this reason that many would never want to see me as the leader of this country. It's true that I haven't made many friends with my fight against golden pensions. But as Charles Mackay wrote in his poem *No Enemies*, which Margaret Thatcher would read in difficult times: "You have no enemies, you say? . . . If you have none, small is the work that you have done." A sentiment, expressed differently, that has been understood in our part of the world for several decades.

* * *

But let's go back to those months that went by slowly, making me feel evermore distant from the PDL and the Monti government. Early on in December 2012, Berlusconi suddenly canceled the primary elections to choose the new party secretary. A primary in which I had declared my candidacy, challenging Angelino Alfano, who at the time was considered to be Berlusconi's protégé.

Faced with Alfano's candidacy, that part of the party hailing from National Alliance was split. Most believed it was necessary to strengthen the leadership of the former Minister of Justice with their support. However, there was also a minority convinced that it was important for us to have a symbolic candidate in the race. Otherwise, it would have been like saying our ideas didn't deserve representation at the highest levels of the movement.

I ran almost as an act of defiance, and perhaps for this reason—because I embodied a sentiment shared by many within the PDL—the support for my candidacy turned out to be significant, far exceeding expectations. In just a few days, we collected and submitted 20,000 signatures in support of my candidacy, complete with a photo opportunity showcasing boxes full of forms in front of the party headquarters. The newspapers began covering the start of the race with great interest, and someone must have thought things could spiral out of control.

And so, one morning, completely out of the blue, Berlusconi announced that the primaries would not take place. The decision was communicated through the press, without having been discussed anywhere.

That was it—over and done with, settled, nothing more would come of it. That was the last straw.

On December 16, the day the primaries were supposed to take place, we organized a rally at the Auditorium della Conciliazione. The title was The Primaries of Ideas. We were just a stone's throw away from St. Peter's, and people were thronging the street. "Are they here for us, or are they pilgrims?" I wondered as I arrived that morning, faced with that sea of people. I recognized faces of individuals who had stopped being active in politics years before. At a certain point, I realized that in that room there was an entire community praying to the Lord Almighty for something new to be born—something they could feel at home with.

That wonderful mid-December day convinced me once and for all. I wanted to be proud of my work again. I wanted those people to feel proud of their party once more, to love politics, and to engage in it. There was a right-wing community, lost at sea after years of scandals and economic crisis, that needed a voice—an uncompromising one. I didn't want to betray the ideals of a history spanning seventy years. With every applause ringing out from the audience, my belief grew stronger: to leave the PDL and create something new was the right way forward.

* * *

The problem was, however, that I had always seen myself as a foot soldier of politics, while that crowd was looking for a real leader. I didn't want to lead that journey alone; what was needed were sharp minds and broad shoulders, experience and passion, and someone to look straight in the eye when you need the strength to move forward.

Guido Crosetto, the gentle giant, was by my side that day. In truth, he had been there before, but perhaps until then, neither of us had realized how our destinies were becoming inextricably interwoven. We had bonded when I was a minister, and he was undersecretary of Defense. During the Monti government, he had often been a source of inspiration for me, such as when—standing alone in the entire party—he rose in the Chamber of Deputies to announce his vote against the Fiscal Compact. He had initially run in the primaries as well but later decided that we needed to join forces and withdrew to support me. That morning, on stage, he spoke just before I did and was right there beside me when, closing my speech, I said the words everyone had been waiting for: "We want a just place where we can fight. A place where we can turn our dreams into reality. If that place is the PDL, then that is where we will fight. But if that place is not meant to be the People of Freedom Party, then we are ready to create a new one, starting with the ideas we have shared this morning, with the people and the enthusiasm here today, and with anyone willing to lend a hand." Guido looked at me, and his eyes were shining bright. For once, I could actually see them because we were the same height—him seated, me standing.

A few days later, as we were about to announce our final decision to leave, he hesitated. I looked at him and said, "Don't abandon me now." He didn't, more out of friendship than belief, I think. Because that's who Guido is. His size reflects his spirit. He knows how to protect you, help you, and he won't betray you, no matter the cost. And that decision cost him.

In this, Guido and I became like siblings right away, in the madness of instinct, where saving your own essence is far, far more important than preserving your seat. I too nurtured doubts, of course, but not because I was jeopardizing the possibility of reelection. In this, I've always been a fatalist. I believe that politics, in the form of an elected office, should always be seen as something temporary in life. If you want to be a good politician, the first thing you must be is free, and to be free, you must be willing to take risks, always. It may go well, or it may go badly, or things may happen that, at the time, seem like terrible defeats but, years later, turn out to be great opportunities, and vice versa. In the end, I always trust in the Lord above.

* * *

After that rally, the path ahead was set. Many people began to approach us, and one of them was Ignazio La Russa. The former colonel of National Alliance, and a historic pillar of the Right, was none other than one of the national coordinators of the People of Freedom Party. At first, he had supported Alfano's candidacy in the primaries, I believe reluctantly so, but for him as well, the outcome of that situation marked a point of no return. Ignazio's presence gave the project a solidity that encouraged several parliamentarians from the People of Freedom, particularly those from National Alliance, to embark on this mad adventure. Of course, there were also those who snubbed us, voicing the usual rhetoric about new faces, but I want to make it clear that without Ignazio La Russa and his experience, we wouldn't have made it. And I believe that our entire movement should be truly grateful to him for how, generously, he left a certain and authoritative role to personally commit himself to a challenge with indefinite boundaries and uncertain outcomes. Now that I know him much better than I did then, I realize that for him, that choice was inevitable. Ignazio has essentially always remained true to himself. The heir to a lineage of strong faith, a young militant of Young Italy who, in the 1970s, broke the mold by hosting radio programs, the political leader who has never put his personal interests before those of the party. A man who is genuinely, wholeheartedly, and tirelessly right-wing, always ready to risk everything for what he believes in.

* * *

We sat around the table and began to seriously discuss the possibility of this new venture. There were many doubts, at least as many as the risks we would face. And before answering practical questions, it was the philosophical ones that had to be addressed. For example, is it better to have an egg today or (perhaps) the hen tomorrow? In other words, if the goal was to defend our ideas, did it make more sense to do so by holding on to positions we already had in a party that did not fully reflect those ideas, or by embodying that identity by rejecting any compromise, but risking being swept away? And if what is useful and what is right do not align, which one should we choose? We chose what was right. And so, on December 21, 2012, Fratelli d'Italia (Brothers of Italy) was born. A new party to continue an ancient tradition.

In hindsight, that choice was sheer madness. Every time I think back on it, Edmond Rostand's Cyrano de Bergerac comes to mind, with the simple and extraordinary words he uses after giving away all his money to repay the impresario for the performance that he had interrupted so he could launch into one of his tirades. "How are you going to live for the next month?" his friend Le Bret asks. "I have nothing left," Cyrano answers. When Le Bret remarks: "How foolish of you to throw it all away like that!" Cyrano replies: "But what a graceful gesture! Just think of it!"

Founding a new party just forty days before the elections, without resources, without friends in the media, without sponsors, was undoubtedly a risk, but it was even more of a risk if we look back at it now, knowing how much work goes into something like that. After all these years, and based on that experience, I am amused by those who think they can found a party from one day to the next. They do not realize, just as we did not, that it is incredibly complicated. And the number of arrows in our quiver were many: we had a history, a network across the territory, ten years' experience, and some of us were also somewhat popular. We weren't exactly starting from scratch, and yet a long, hard ascent awaited us.

The anxiety that came with having to do everything in as little time as possible kept us awake for days, holed up in a room in the building where the parliamentary groups met, just opposite Bar Giolitti. Surrounded by the smoke of a million cigarettes and rivers of coffee, we nominated three coordinators, we drew up a list of candidates, and we wrote the statute. But it was the choice of a name that took up most our time during those nights of endless discussions. In just a few days' time we had in fact decided what the party's name should be without the analysis of communication experts. "Figli d'Italia" (Sons of Italy), the name of the list with which I had run for the presidency of Azione Giovani (Youth Action), was our first choice, but someone timidly drew our attention to the fact that "Figli di . . ." in Italian, "sons of a . . ." in English, might sound like a double entendre.

I suggested "We Italians," but no one liked it. In the end it was Fabio Rampelli, who was also one of the founders of Brothers of Italy, who thought of the first line in the "Inno di Mameli," the Italian national anthem. Thus was born Fratelli d'Italia, or Brothers of Italy.

At a certain point in this process, I decided I would personally inform Berlusconi about our decision. When I spoke to him, at Palazzo Grazioli, he answered in the manner of a practical businessman who has learned that everything and almost everyone has a price. "Fine, I get it. . . . So, tell me: what is it you want, what do you want to do?"

"I want to be proud of what I do. I say that respectfully, but I truly no longer feel at home." He wasn't used to getting that kind of an answer, even though he had asked the question more out of the need to verify my determination rather than because he was truly convinced. He had dissuaded numerous people from leaving, but he knew that this time he would not be able to. I had wanted to have that conversation because of my esteem and affection for him, but I was saying farewell to all effects. I had decided to leave and that is in fact what I did. I believe that when a person is serious that is what they must do.

We said goodbye with a great deal of kindness, and I still remember the way he looked at me with the compassion of someone who is convinced that you're about to commit suicide. Rightfully so, because, as he often claimed over the years, none of those who left his party ever survived politically. No one, except us, but at the time this was something we could not take for granted.

* * *

On December 21, we launched the new party and immediately threw ourselves into the electoral campaign for the political elections, which were scheduled for two months later, with the Christmas season in between. Those weeks were experienced breathlessly because we knew we would have to make a huge effort to earn every single vote.

In the end, I totted up what I alone had done during those incredibly long forty days between mid-January and the end of February: over 20,000 miles, almost three hundred towns, and a small suitcase always packed. I had slept at home at most five nights. And those around me were no less committed. It was a superhuman effort, marked by great effort and enormous enthusiasm.

The rallies were packed, but outside those halls and squares, no one talked about us. Brothers of Italy's voice only existed when Guido, Ignazio, or I managed to appear in a televised debate. The major media outlets were polarized, inevitably reinforcing voters' belief that a vote for small parties was wasted. Posters were mostly put up by volunteers, and despite all the sacrifices, there were always too few campaign stands. We realized we were going to do poorly. And indeed, that fateful February 25 arrived, with its disappointing result: Brothers of Italy had gotten just 1.96 percent of the vote.

On the evening of the results, at the electoral committee where we had gathered to await the outcome, the atmosphere was far from euphoric. It was a resounding defeat, accompanied by the disappointment of seeing people like Francesco Lollobrigida and, even more so, Guido Crosetto not get elected. We had agreed to nominate Crosetto for the Senate so that there could be a strong, authoritative voice in the upper house of Parliament. The electoral law required reaching 3 percent in at least one region to elect senators, and we were confident we could manage that, at least in Lazio, and also in Campania, where thanks to one of Brothers of Italy's pillars, General Edmondo Cirielli, we had one of our most established and efficient operations.

Instead, we narrowly missed the target in both regions. In short, it seemed to us that things had gone very badly.

Then, however, I looked at the result not in terms of percentage but in absolute votes. The number of Italians who had put a cross on the Brothers of Italy's symbol was six hundred and sixty-six thousand, seven hundred sixty-five. In my mind, I tried to picture them lined up—faces, stories, and the hopes of so many people who, despite our marginality, had put their trust in us.

Their support had allowed us to elect nine deputies, a small but determined group. Other parties far more recognizable than ours, like Francesco Storace's right-wing party, which had existed for several years and could count on its leader being nominated once again by the Center-Right to lead the Lazio Region, hadn't made it.

We had to make do, and we did. We formed our parliamentary group in Montecitorio, but not without difficulty, because with fewer than twenty elected members, you have to request and obtain an exemption from other parties. Somehow, we managed to be present on every legislative issue. At the beginning, I was also the group leader in Montecitorio. Every role in the play was mine. I remember the loneliness and frustration of those years. We carried out meticulous work, as we do now—drafting proposals, conducting in-depth analyses, making precise policy suggestions—but all too often we felt like ghosts surrounded by people who couldn't hear us. My speeches, the ones that sometimes go viral today, were practically unheard for five years. I almost always spoke to an empty chamber. During voting declarations, we were among the first to speak, and the hall only filled up near the end, just before the vote. The few MPs in attendance paid me the kind of attention reserved for someone deemed unimportant. My colleagues from Brothers of Italy, overwhelmed by an enormous workload, were often busy elsewhere, and I often found myself speaking while surrounded by entirely empty benches.

In the Senate, we earned a minimal right to speak only toward the end of the legislature. Bartolomeo Amidei, formerly from Forza Italia (FI), and Stefano Bertacco, also elected with FI, decided to join the

Mixed Group, a component of Brothers of Italy. Both were from Veneto. Stefano, from Verona, was reelected with Brothers of Italy in 2018, but he's no longer with us. Cancer took his life in June 2020. I adored him. I remember when, with his calm voice and reassuring gaze, he told me he had been diagnosed with a tumor. And I remember the look on his face the day that I, having heard his condition had worsened, took a train to Verona as soon as the lockdown ended to visit him in the hospital. He didn't expect to see me, and when I walked in, his expression was both happy and conscious. I think he understood that my being there meant the news wasn't good. We hugged tightly and cried. "I'm not giving up an inch of the way," he told me that day, as he always did, as if it were his job to reassure me, not the other way around. He was so confident he convinced me too. But that was the last time I saw him. Yet the disease never broke him. Because that's who Stefano was. Like a character from a novel, he had been among the last and the first. As a young man, he had struggled with drug addiction and homelessness and was eventually rescued by the San Patrignano Community, to which he remained deeply attached. He made such good use of that experience that he dedicated the rest of his life to social services. And later, he stood with me at the Quirinale, during consultations with the head of state for the formation of the government.

He had seen it all, and because of that, he knew how to face anything. When I think of him, I'm convinced that true strength has his face. True strength smiles, looks you straight in the eye, takes your hand, and gives you courage. That was Stefano. Pure, aware, a quiet strength in a world of selfish and cowardly people. Stefano was one of the best, and I still can't accept that he's gone. But while we can't stop the people we love from leaving, we can choose to live up to their example. We will learn from you, brother, how to be relentless. And when victory comes, we will dedicate it to you.

* * *

I've asked myself a thousand times, "Gio, what made you do it?" Only those who've tried know what it means to create a party from nothing and establish it on the political scene when your resources are so limited that it feels like firing at tanks with a peashooter.

We went through some tragic moments, but thank God we had the courage to try. I never doubted that I had done the right thing, not even during the hardest times. Because the pride of always being able to walk with my head held high is worth any sacrifice. I never had to be ashamed of anything. I was always free to speak my mind without answering to anyone, no matter the journalist or the camera in front of me. I answered—and still answer—only for myself and my choices.

I think it's the same feeling an employee gets when they tell their boss to go to hell, leaving a safe job at a company where they no longer feel comfortable, to start their own business. It's a freedom that life rarely grants, and politics even less so. And that's why I'm especially proud of having founded Brothers of Italy.

The beginning was tough, I won't deny it. We mostly suffered defeats, always stuck just one step away from our goal. The 2014 European elections were another disappointment. We nearly doubled our votes, reaching 3.67 percent—but unfortunately, the threshold for electing representatives to the European Parliament was set at 4 percent. Once again, fate had played a cruel trick on us. Four years later, in the 2018 general elections, we ran again in coalition with the Center-Right and secured a still unsatisfactory 4.35 percent. However, that was enough to bring thirty-two deputies and eighteen senators into Parliament. Despite our small numbers, we finally had the minimum strength needed to push our proposals forward. Step by step, brick by brick, we built our political home. As the old saying goes, "Slow and steady wins the race."

It certainly wasn't easy to keep up our enthusiasm when others around us were racing ahead—even flying—thanks to a few sloppy slogans and a handful of promises worthy of the satirical movie character Cetto La Qualunque (Cetto the Anyman). Take the Five Star Movement led by comedian Beppe Grillo, which secured 32 percent of the vote by spreading the elaborate political theory known as "Vaffa" (Fuck You). It was a mix of lies, false promises, and demagoguery that had entranced the Italians.

I'm convinced that only those who were very naive believed in the Five Star Movement's propaganda. The vast majority of those who voted for them likely did so as the ultimate insult to a discredited political class. The slice of mortadella placed in the ballot with the words "Eat this too," obscene drawings in the voting booth, or the more restrained abstentions and blank ballots all turned into votes for the most grotesque political force in the history of Western democracies. The Five Star vote was one big middle finger aimed at the system by millions of (rightfully) angry Italians. The problem is that when you think you're making fun of history, you risk history making fun of yourself—and that is exactly what happened. The Five Star Movement was nothing but a huge bluff. A group of fake revolutionaries who, once elected, turned out to be the greatest defenders of the status quo, both in Italy and in Europe. They were also profoundly incompetent, suddenly finding themselves leading the nation at the most challenging time in fifty years. I'm sure many Italians regretted that rebellious vote and wished they could go back in time, hoping for a different political class to decide the fate of businesses, workers, and families battered by the pandemic and economic crisis.

* * *

Meanwhile, in 2018, five years after our inception, we were still struggling to muster between 3 and 4 percent. At some point, I began to suspect that, given the spirit of the times, I might have been the wrong person to lead a political party.

Things were not going well, and when I was asked what the problem was, I could only start from myself. Maybe I was the problem. Maybe my way of conceiving political life did not answer to popular sentiment, maybe my way of doing politics was too old, too traditional, too reflexive for an age that burns everything and does so instantly.

"Giorgia, the problem is that you think too much," a pollster said to me without mincing words. "You need simple catchphrases, slogans, and instant images, not complicated ideas that require too many minutes to be explained." But how can the problem for a politician be overthinking? For years even some of those in our group urged me to trivialize, "the way others do." A winning model, no doubt, or at least it appeared to be so, but it wasn't mine. "Guys," I would repeat, "I'm fighting against that kind of model. If you think it's the right thing to do, then you need another leader." In other words, when things aren't working as they should, you need to be ready to admit it and, if necessary, step aside. In a world where, when something doesn't meet one's targets, you tend to try to blame it on others, on adversity, on fate, I have always asked myself what was wrong with what *I* was doing.

The most difficult moment probably took place right after the 2018 elections. The terrible electoral law that, unsurprisingly, Brothers of Italy had spoken against, the only right-wing party to have done so, had produced a tripolar Parliament, none of which had a majority. The Center-Right had received the largest number of votes, but the numbers were still not enough to allow it to govern by itself. The President of the Republic preferred not to try to appoint one of our leaders, specifically Matteo Salvini, a leader in the party that had received the most votes in the coalition, and therefore the designated prime minister according to the rules that we have always adhered to. Salvini, on his part, hadn't insisted, officially because he thought it was dangerous to go to Parliament to search for the numbers he might not find, but unofficially, I believe today, because he was intrigued by the hypothesis of an alliance with the Five Star Movement. After all, while campaigning he had famously put forward the idea for "an anti-political wheeling-and-dealing pact," requesting that my allies exclude, in any case, after voting had taken place, alliances outside the perimeter of the Center-Right coalition. However, the morning of the declaration when this solemn commitment was supposed to have been underwritten, I had found myself to be on my own again.

So, after months of negotiations, the alliance between the League and the members of the Five Star Movement, had taken place. A young government, a new, breakaway majority, which intrigued many of our people as well. But not me. I have always believed that the Five Star Movement was a left-wing force, not at all disapproved of by the system, and that the margins to do something good and new with them did not exist. Now everyone knows I was not wrong about that, but at the time even within our own party the discussions were exasperating.

In any case, in the end, we did not join this bizarre majority. At the formation of the first Conte government, the political space seemed minimal: on one side, the "populist and sovereigntist" Five-Star and League government, and on the other, the moderate and pro-European forces. With us in the middle, trying to make our voices heard. We had to explain that the Five Star Movement had nothing to do with those who defend the sovereignty and the independence of the Italian people. Yes, they were populists, more accurately demagogues, but certainly not sovereigntists, and they had (and still have) nothing to do with the political Right. I knew that such a decision could be very risky for the future of Brothers of Italy. But I also knew, then as now, that respect for one's word, in politics, is the very foundation of democracy, of the relationship between the representative and the person represented. They call it consistency, but I believe it should above all be called seriousness. Responsibility. If you say something while campaigning just to get votes and then you don't follow through, it means you didn't believe in what you said, and fooled those who believed in you. Before making a pledge I think it over a million times, but when I do make that pledge I will uphold it, at whatever cost. We always promised that we would not govern with either the Democratic Party or the Five Star Movement, and we kept that promise both in 2018, when the first Conte government was formed, and in 2021, when the Draghi government came into office.

When it comes to choices such as these, Matteo Salvini has always been less strict than me, and I have often envied him for this. He always knows how to interpret what people want, it is his strength. When he, together with the Five Star Movement, brought the government to life, maybe because, at the time, he needed to find a way to wriggle free of Berlusconi's grasp, which was still rather strong, the numbers proved that he was right, given the remarkable growth of the League during that phase, to the detriment of Forza Italia above all. For us, instead, things seemed to be increasingly difficult, and in that time of a peak in the "Captain's" and the League's strength, along came the challenge of the 2019 European elections.

* * *

"If we don't get 4 percent this time, I am seriously going to consider doing something else in life. Enough. We look like hamsters running on a wheel." During those months, I had often used these words to vent my frustration with the people closest to me, and even though I think that no one actually believed what I said, I was absolutely serious. It was a huge opportunity to get rid of us. Lots of people, discovering it, must be kicking themselves now.

In early 2019, there were a few polls that gave Brothers of Italy just over 2 percent, the belief being that the growth of the League had to have taken some of our consensus away. There were some who began abandoning us to take shelter with Alberto da Giussano's more reassuring banner. It looked like it was going to be hard to get to 4 percent, even though in the meantime we too had received some rewards. In February, for instance, our party's first President of the Region had been elected in Abruzzo, Marco Marsilio. I was so determined to gamble everything that I put a huge amount of energy and focus into my work during those months. Competitive lists, relentless campaigns, never-ending effort. We left nothing to chance. If I were forced to quit, I would be able to do so without remorse or regret.

In the end, running counter to all predictions, at the European elections held in May 2019, we got an unexpected 6.44 percent of the vote, electing six members of the European Parliament. It was the start of something completely new for Brothers of Italy. No longer fighting in the backwaters to overcome the minimum threshold, but at last contesting the leadership in 2020 with the big parties. As I write these words, the polls say that Brothers of Italy is the third Italian political party, and there are some who say it is second, ahead of the Democratic Party and the Five Star Movement, a few percentage points behind the League. Amazing results that no one, I confess me included, would have bet a penny on in 2018.

However, I always knew that for us it would be harder to get to 5 percent than to go from 5 to 15 percent. In this, the democratic system is unappeasable; it's the syndrome of the practical vote. When the parties risk not surpassing the thresholds, the voters fear they will waste their vote. For years, I heard people from all walks of life say that they even though they supported our battles, they couldn't vote for us because our party was too small. Each time I tried to explain that we were a small party because they weren't brave enough to vote for us. That 6 percent and more from the European elections, which secured us above any electoral threshold, allowed all those who shared our struggles to vote for us without fearing that their choice would be pointless.

What I want to say to the Italian voters today is that they should trust their instinct more than the polls. Who will or will not count after an election is decided the day votes are cast, and they will be the ones to decide. A voter must not yield to influence, rather, they should choose based on what they truly believe. It's the only way to really make a difference.

* * *

The dramatic phase of being afraid to not elect our representatives in the institutions having been overcome, now comes the equally concerning one of electing people who are not worthy of the institutions. Being on the Right also means having a profound sense of the state. For us, the state apparatus, at every level, is sacrosanct, something to be respected and honored with one's work, especially if one holds an elected position.

This is why I am very demanding when it comes to choosing the candidates. I demand that they be people with values who have had the right kind of experience. People of quality, who have what it takes to claim to be part of the leadership, even if this means losing a few votes. I will not back down on this, I accept only people who are honest. Of course, over the years things haven't always gone exactly as I had hoped. In some cases, I was wrong, and in others—especially at a local level—people who seemed squeaky clean later turned out to be dishonest and inadequate instead.

Even after you've done the most thorough of background checks and lots of thinking, choosing someone always involves taking some risks: disappointment and betrayal come from where you least expect them. And you can't know every single thing about the thousands of people who represent you across the entire country. No one could, and mishaps can occur in every party. What makes the difference is how you react when it happens or what tools you implement to prevent it from happening. I try to defend myself from dishonest candidates by applying very strict criteria, making sure they haven't committed crimes, but also ruling out anyone who has no qualms about switching to the other side.

And yet, sometimes even that is not enough. When in just a few months' time as many as three members of Brothers of Italy were involved in investigations concerning the criminal gangs based in Calabria, besides taking measures immediately, I went straight to the anti-mafia chief magistrate Cafiero de Raho. Without mincing words, I asked him if he thought it was possible there might be a plan to infiltrate the party, and if that were the case, how could I defend myself from it. Because if there's something I am absolutely not willing to let my greatest enemies, the bosses behind organized crime, think, is that I am going to let them exploit the sacrifices I am making so that they can do their evil deeds.

I got into politics in order to fight dishonest people, and I will continue in this fight with every bone in my body, cost what it may. A real patriot cannot help but be an honest person, because they could never even imagine harming their national community with subterfuge and thievery. For this reason as well, there is no room for dishonest people in Brothers of Italy.

* * *

The day—with that 6.44 percent—we knocked down the wall that separated us from the big guys, was I happy? No, I wasn't. I went home and I was, simply, at peace. I remember wondering to myself why I couldn't just let myself go, celebrate the way any other person who had succeeded in such an important undertaking would have done. "You did your duty," were the words echoing in my mind. The same words that my mother would utter disdainfully after reading my report card, which was always filled with high grades, except for math, my bête noire.

Maybe it was that lesson that made me so unable to feel as happy as I should have felt about what I do. When things work out, I am simply at peace, and when they don't, I feel like it's the end of the world. It's not easy to live this way, but it's also what has made me so determined. The idea that happiness is just out of your reach, that there is still work to be done, another fight to wage in pursuit of a threshold that might actually not even exist.

Saving the Future

In the end, we made it. With Brothers of Italy safe from becoming extinct—notwithstanding the possible electoral law— we succeeded in our difficult task of protecting the history of the Italian Right.

Over the past few years, many of the people who grew up in the local branches of the Italian Social Movement and National Alliance have stopped me, shaken my hand, their eyes filled with tears, to say: "Thank you, Giorgia." And every time that has happened, I have been surprised, not because of their happiness to know they still had a party they could identify with, but because of the emotion, affection, and near devotion they showed toward me. As if, more than considering me a simple soldier who was just doing her job—this is how I see myself—they saw something epic in me.

One day, at the end of a political event, a husband and a wife, both of them rather elderly, came over and embraced me. "You're our hero, Giorgia, our Joan of Arc. This army that had lost its way needed a woman like you to lead it," the husband said. To which his wife added: "Did you know that you were born the same day as Joan of Arc?" No, I didn't know.

Of course, I'm not going to fall into the trap of comparing myself to the Maid of Orléans, but that day I realized that well beyond my true merits—above all, I'm attributed with having done something that has been done by many—a sort of minor mythology had been created around me.

It was the result of the power of communication produced by the contrast between the image of a young woman, a small one at that, and the enormity of the challenge that she led. The small, fragile person who faces a much more powerful adversary, and who, through her example, lays bare the cowardice of the person who backs away from that confrontation. Clearly, I see things completely differently, and I consider myself as just a person who has an average amount of courage in an environment where courage is lacking, or a woman who believes that honor is the most important thing that needs safeguarding in a society that prefers to protect values that are much more material. So there's nothing heroic to see here. Maybe my thinking is just old-fashioned, in spite of my forty-four years of age.

Yes, we made it, but I don't want there to be misinterpretations as to the reasons why we so stubbornly pursued the goal of saving the Right. Doing that, for us, was not simply a matter of affection, or loyalty to the country. It was not to guarantee a testimony, which would also have been a dignified thing to do. No. We saved the Right to save Italy. We saved the Right because today, here, more than in any other era, more than in any other place, we need the Right. We did all this looking forward, not backward, with our children more than our grandparents in mind, imagining the future more than recalling the past.

Our country and our people need a strong right-wing political movement. This is why I never considered all the hard work we did over the years to bring Brothers of Italy to life and to make it grow to be an ideological battle. Quite the opposite. As a patriot, I am convinced that what is good for Italy always comes before partisan interests. A concept that the Left, which does not acknowledge the value of a national identity, will never be able to fully understand, in spite of the fact that it so often appeals (foolishly so) to "the good of the country."

And it should come as no surprise that you, the reader, may feel free to use the word "country," but are always hesitant to say "nation" or "homeland." For many, the difference might seem insignificant, but it definitely is not. The meaning of the word "country" is "human settlement," a "nation" is a "group of individuals who are conscious of their own uniqueness and historical and cultural autonomy," and one's "homeland" is the "territory inhabited by a population and to which each of its members feels it belongs by birth, language, culture, history, and tradition."

A country is simply a physical place, where people live together; it is indistinct and material. A nation is also a place of the mind that one belongs to in which culture, history, and traditions are shared. Lastly, and more importantly, the homeland is a place that involves the heart, that willingness to share one's roots and participate in the fate of a community that is the very essence of the principle of belonging.

* * *

It goes without saying that the Left does not like the Right. I don't like the Left either, and I don't hide it from anyone. What's bizarre, instead, is that the Left has the chutzpah to explain to us, and not only to us, what the Right should be like. Journalists, opinion writers, commentators, politicians, intellectuals who are more or less respectable ones on the Left spend much of their time pontificating about how wonderful it would be to have a "modern Right open to dialogue" in Italy, "willing to abandon its unpresentable positions." Once again, that Left betrays its presumed and never proven superiority for which it believes it can even go so far as to decide how its adversary should be. Those on the Left would like a different Right, one that is to their liking. That is, a Right that no longer got any votes, was marginal, and that could easily be gotten rid of. Because, obviously, the day the Right is to the liking of the Left, it will no longer be to the liking of those who tend toward the Right.

As I wrote before, we went through this a few years ago, and we have learned our lesson. When the Left strokes your fur and flatters you for your "presentable" positions, it means you're doing something wrong. That is the reason why I prefer not to be liked by those people. I see their hostility as a North Star telling me I'm on the right path.

I am a person on the Right. I say that, I repeat it in my public and private encounters. I claim it with the pride and dignity with which one claims an identity, a belonging I have experienced. Even though I know that defining oneself as such means instantly being excluded from the circles of the elites, from the radical chic salons that Italy is filled with. It means attracting the hostility and the scorn of much of the media, the world of intellectuals, the academcs, the abstract custodians of forced truths. It means being pointed to as obscurantists, reactionaries at best. And at worst as the carriers of a virus of intolerance or racism.

In politics and in culture, Right and Left are often seen as having been surpassed by the offspring of the past century and its schemes. In the present era many see the Right and the Left as the archaeological relics of a time buried under the sands of history. I don't believe that. Of course, if we look at the stereotypes that defined the Right and the Left throughout the twentieth century and we compare them with the ones that define them today, a superficial observer might think that everything has changed, that some of those clichés have even been reversed. But a more careful analysis would easily show how its basic values, the framework it is based on, are still the same ones, adapted to a reality that has profoundly changed. I'm not talking about the stereotypes that Giorgio Gaber, a singer-songwriter, comedy writer, director, but above all poet, someone who was free, clear-sighted, revolutionary—and one of the few people I regret never having met—denounced in tongue-in-cheek style in one of his masterpieces titled "Destra-Sinistra" (Right-Left) "A nice noodle soup is to the Right / while vegetable soup is always to the Left / All the movies they make today are to the Right / but if they're boring then they're to the Left / . . . Gym or tennis shoes / still have something of the Right about them / but if they're soiled and unlaced / you're more a fool than someone on the Left." No, I'm talking about something that goes much deeper, that does not change with the seasons and is too complex to adapt to outdated labels.

Allow me to add that, usually, those who say that the Right and the Left as categories have been surpassed, at least in politics, do so to justify the ease with which they move from one side to the other of the aisle, often in exchange for an elegant seat. And this is the point: if you take away from politics the ideas, the distinct visions, and the opposing ones, all that remain are the interests to be defended, the personal objectives which too many people are willing to bow down to. As I see it, for as long as there are democracies, Right and Left will be of essential value because that topographical place (sitting to the right or the left in a parliament) will differentiate a system of values to be embodied and a plan to be implemented.

However, there does exist a coherent continuity between the Left that we are dealing with today, and that once sang the praises of the communist model. The fracture, after all, is always the same: the conflict between ideological delirium, on the one hand, and the reality principle, on the other. I already explained this concept in my contribution to the book *I comunisti lo fanno meglio (oppure no?)* (Communists Do It Better, or Maybe Not?) edited by Luciano Tirinnanzi. Communism was (and is) an ideology focused on the need to deny any form of identity in order to pursue the plan for a Marxist society, made up of people who are totally equal. Hence, the attempt to cancel national belonging via mass deportations in order to "mix" the ethnic groups within the USSR and impose state atheism, forbidding and repressing religion of any kind.

This same vision, which denies the role and the value of identity, can be found in liberal and globalist thinking today. Obviously, different tools are used now, but the final goal is still the same. The mass deportations of the Soviet era have been replaced by policies supporting immigration. The violent repression of religions has been replaced by the social and cultural demonization of every sacred concept. The fight against the "bourgeois model" has become that against the "superstructure" represented by the natural family. It's incredible how the communist vision has been reinforced in the world since real socialism was defeated by history in the early twentieth century. That's it: the clash between visions from the Right and the Left of society and the world has, after all, remained the same. On the one hand, let us rediscover the Left as it has always been, which theorized, and now attempts to impose, the best of possible worlds rationally and purposefully: a society of "equals" with no classes. In truth, without freedom, without faith, without history. But then there's the Right that wants to preserve the same profound identities that the Left would like to get rid of.

* * *

I have often wondered why, since I come from a family that is not ideological, I decided to go into right-wing politics, that cramped space that was considered at the time to be a place for losers or for exiles in their own country.

It might seem paradoxical to many, but the truth is that I felt there was a freedom to the Right that I could not feel to the Left. Freedom from conformity, freedom from having to bend to the "spirit of the time," freedom from radical criticism that the Left, because it was closed off in its ideological vision, did not allow.

I was struck by the fact that many of the young people who were involved in politics along with me did not come from right-wing families, while most of my friends on the Left came from left-wing families that were often orthodox. For them it was almost an obligation to follow in their parents' way of thinking, as though it were a form of unconscious imitation, as if they did not know how to be free enough to transgress from the way of thinking of the environment they came from.

But it wasn't just that. There was another important side to this. In those party branches that so often resembled catacombs I would find unexpected light. The kids there had an intellectual curiosity that was almost impossible to find on the Left. You might come across them seriously and somewhat temperamentally reading from the works of Antonio Gramsci, and right afterwards reciting by heart some line by Ezra Pound, or reflecting on Jung's rebel archetype. Because what reigned in that environment was the principle that "all men of value are brothers," regardless of where history had placed them, just as all valid, intelligent, or simply interesting ideas deserve to be analyzed regardless of who had them. This is what it means to be open-minded, because there are no "sacred texts" that must be followed. This is what gave us the freedom to read any book of our choosing, listen to any singer-songwriter, learn more about any historical figure, without exclusion and a critical support, in order to extrapolate the best that humanity had produced in our eyes, from every point of view.

It is the reason for which the Italian Right, in order to define itself, easily finds cultural and political references in a vast national and international heritage. And today Brothers of Italy aspires to serving as a synthesis of all the ideas that have matured at the core of conservative and liberal tradition, without, however, forgoing trying out new policies and new formats. So I'm not going to sit here listing the numerous intellectuals or texts from which to draw values and ideas. It would necessarily be incomplete, even unjust, a political trap that I prefer to leave to others. The sources we have drawn from are manifold. And each era, each generation, at times even in every battle, has added names, writings, thoughts to the list. If, for instance, I had to quote one of the thinkers who, in recent years, directed my vision, it would be that of the British champion of conservative thinking, Sir Roger Scruton, whom I mentioned a few chapters back.

I became acquainted with him late, too late, thanks to the European Conservative and Reformist Party, for which I have recently taken up the leadership. And yet, he still helped me to define the traits of what I do more than many of the authors I read when I was young.

Notwithstanding his characteristic British aplomb, Scruton, like many other right-wing intellectuals, had a multiform artistic life, an incredibly intense and courageously interventionist one. A life that was equally divided between the barricades in the streets, especially in the 1980s, and an armchair in front of the lit fireplace in his country home.

In love with Italy, a diehard supporter of beauty as the solution to the most complex problems of every era, albeit with all the possible differences, there is no right-wing party in the West that can say it is not indebted to Scruton. I often refer to a quote from *How to Be a Conservative*: "Conservatives endorse Burke's view of society, as a partnership between the living, the unborn, and the dead; they believe in civil association between neighbors rather than intervention by the state; and they accept that the most important thing the living can do is to settle down, to make a home for themselves, and to pass that home to their children. *Oikophilia*, the love of home, lends itself to the environmental cause, and it is astonishing that the many conservative parties in the English-speaking world have not seized hold of that cause as their own." So true. This is one of my favorite passages, which explains why Italy does not have a more coherently environmental political movement than the Right.

* * *

The freedom that has allowed the Right to draw without prejudice from all the national culture and beyond has never existed on the Left. They had Little Red Books, authors who you could read and those who were censored, music that could be listened to and that which was condemned. A cage. Because if you let someone else tell you what you can and can't believe in, then you'll stop using the greatest freedom that the Lord has given us: free will. I have always believed that books, like music, or philosophy, don't actually teach you anything, that they simply help you to better explain what you feel inside. If you give up searching for it everywhere, in the end you risk not knowing who you are. It was hard to convince a friend of mine on the Left to read a book by Céline, one of the greatest writers of the twentieth century, but also someone who was condemned for his mad sympathies for National Socialism; or get them to understand the heroic and narrative immensity of Yukio Mishima, the great Japanese scholar and patriot, as well as being a reactionary and a nationalist, whom even the twentieth-century Italian novelist Alberto Moravia was enthralled by.

During my declaration at the time of the vote of confidence in the Draghi government, I quoted Bertolt Brecht—an anti-Nazi German playwright beloved by the Left—to explain the Brothers of Italy's decision to remain the only opposition party: "We sat on the wrong side, because all the others seats were taken." Good heavens! It drove the Left wild. "How dare you quote Bertolt Brecht, he's ours!" As if culture belonged to one person and not to everybody. As if one were only allowed to quote certain authors, and not whatever they share with them, or find to be suited to their own context. My slightly perfidious reply to them was this: "Don't get mad. I know you yourselves would have liked to quote Brecht, but maybe you weren't able to find the quote when he praises support for a government led by a banker who never earned the popular vote."

Leaving aside the banter, I have wondered a lot about that agitation. Because if I had listened to a colleague on the Left and used a quote by, let's see, Gabriele D'Annunzio to argue in favor of one of his undertakings, I would have been proud to. But they would not, because their mindsets are simply too rigid.

* * *

I learned this when I was a kid. What struck me about my staunch left-wing friends was their confidence, the unbreakable sense of certainty that characterized their way of seeing things. An absolutism of ideas and visions that often made any sort of debate or discussion sterile: their conviction was always, and in any case, on the right side of history, even when that history was clearly wrong, and their ideas had produced unspeakable horrors.

I am reminded of a book I read about twenty years ago titled *In attesa di un pullman* (Waiting for a Bus). The author was a textile industrialist from Carpi named Renato Crotti—who has since passed away— the founder of Silan, one of the most important textile industries in Italy, which represented the economic miracle of that small- and medium-sized business that is the true wealth of our country and of our productive fabric. Crotti, during the postwar years and in the Emilia region of Red trade unionism and the most extremist communism, found himself doing business between the rock of competition from state-owned business and the hard place of the workers' protests. In short, the book tells the story of how Crotti succeeded in governing the explosive phenomenon of the communist-driven unionism of the barricades simply by paying his workers—the trade unionists first and foremost—to take bus trips to the Utopian Workers' Paradise: the USSR. On those trips he took along left-wing reporters who could see with their own eyes what the communism that the Italian Communist Party wanted to import to Italy was exactly. Many of them came back shocked, describing the hellishness of that fake paradise. And yet in Italy, they did not want to surrender their beliefs to what was being reported by trustworthy witnesses. In other words, if reality is different from my ideas, then it's reality that's wrong. Let's just say that the ideological vision of the Left is perfectly expressed in Georg Friedrich Wilhelm Hegel's famous words: "If the facts do not agree with the theory, so much the worse for the facts."

What I want to say is that the first thing about being to the Right is the "realism." Facing the world and its challenges without wearing ideological blinkers. What is known as the "reality principle": the rejection of any utopian embellishment, any ideological construct. For the Right, politics starts from reality, not from the idea we have of ourselves. We fight for the real man who lives in a real world. The reality is the present life, but also the past one: tradition, memory. Those "deep roots [that] are not reached by the frost," to quote Tolkien again. Roots that are the foundation of birth and growth.

I'm not talking about a materialist Right, however. Quite the contrary. I'm taking about a divine Right and, like others before me, to paint its shapes I will trust the most alternative Italian intellectual of the postwar period: Pier Paolo Pasolini. It might seem paradoxical, but the last composition written by the Friuli-born poet just before being murdered is truly a conservative, political manifesto of great beauty and consistency. In "Goodbye and Best Wishes" Pasolini delivers into the hands of a callow young fascist of the 1970s his ideal testament: "Take this burden onto your shoulders. / . . . You defend the fields between village / and countryside, with their corncobs / and vats of manure. You defend the meadow / between the last house in the village and the canal. / . . . Defend, preserve, pray!" In the lines that follow, Pasolini repeats, three times, his impassioned invitation to defend, preserve, pray. "And in our world, say / you are not bourgeois but a saint / or a soldier—a soldier without ignorance, / a soldier without violence. / Carry in a saint's or soldier's hands / your closeness with the King, the divine right / that lies within us, in sleep."

We would be hard put to find words more lyrical to define deep and widespread political thinking such as that which preserves the Italian right. Vertical thinking, that ranges from the Holy Scriptures to Roman law, from medieval chivalric codes to the great beauty of the Renaissance, from the young warrior poets of the Risorgimento to the Christian Europe of John Paul II and Benedict XVI. But horizontal thinking as well, of the kind that holds together the thousands upon thousands of church bell towers that Italy is made up of, from north to south and from east to west.

I have always identified myself in this part of the field more out of instinct, because of my character, than cultural awareness. Marcello Veneziani, using different words with respect to Pasolini, but ones that are equally effective, writes as follows: "The Right exists in people's heads, heart, and belly, even when they say they are not of this mind. It is a common feeling that struggles to become a common way of thinking. It is its strong point and its limit." Hence, the task of anyone who takes over its leadership at a specific time in history is to turn the Right into a lever to lift a common destiny, above any individual angst, with neither fear nor awe. However difficult that may be.

I am reminded of what Jean Guitton had Socrates say in a dialogue that he imagines to take place after his own death in the hereafter: "Thousands of ideas are not worth a single person. We have to love people; it is for them that we must live and die." That is indeed the Right I believe in. Filled with the humility, the humanity, and the compassion that only those who do not lose contact with the real world can safeguard. Values that cannot belong to anyone who is convinced they are in the right. The Left, on the other hand, pursues utopias, it arranges reality in a box, it peers inside a clean and transparent glass case that adheres perfectly to its own beliefs. For the Left, everything is linear, straight, all-embracing.

The thinking on the Left, past and present, is a totalizing ideology in the name of which one is willing to justify any form of abuse and violence.

From this point of view, ideological fury has many things in common with religious integralism. This is true in the abstract for every ideology and for every religion, but in this period of history it is typical of the Left and of Islamic fanaticism. If I believe I am the bearer of a "high and noble" mission aimed at building a better world or carrying out the wishes of Allah, then it is proper and dutiful to eliminate, by any means necessary, anyone who gets in my way. That is what terrorists do when they shoot at innocent people, or what the single-idea thinking does when it denies its adversaries the fundamental rights to freedom and free speech. I refer to them, quite deliberately, as progressive fanatics, for whom whatever method is needed to crush one's enemy is justifiable. And, like in Islamism, their globalist fury inevitably results in conflict. In fact, what is the only way for them to realize their utopia in a world without borders and differences? By forcing this vision of the world and of things on everyone. Even with violence if necessary.

For the sake of example, in American geopolitics, the Democrats—the left-wing liberals—are the champions of an interventionist vision in support of the destabilizing exportation of democracy in the world. Against all stereotypes, the Right is instead on the side of peace and balance between peoples throughout this debate. It is no accident that Donald Trump was the only US president over the past four decades to not start a war during his four years in office. The same cannot be said for Barack Obama, winner of the Nobel Peace Prize. The same is true of internal politics. What is it that encourages left-wing capitalists and *maîtres à penser* to invoke and practice censoring freedom of expression if not a Taliban instinct, claiming that theirs is a practice for the purpose of purification against "sinners"? What, if not fanaticism, is the iconoclastic fight of Black Lives Matter—coddled from the Left from every latitude—against the greatest figures from the past in the name of a Puritan rewriting of history and society? Before all this, I see being to the Right these days, and even more so now, as an act of resistance in the name of freedom. Of trust in the person and of peace among peoples. Freedom and peace that must be defended, yesterday like today, from the violence of such "democratic" fanatics.

We live in times of madness when a new, intangible dictatorship is on the rise. Intolerance imposed via the massive power of technology and the control of the imaginary. "Political correctness" has spread everywhere and dictates its absurd laws: from the ridiculous impositions of progressive bureaucrats who want to cancel what parenthood has always been by attacking the words "father" and "mother," through rich kids disguised as urban revolutionaries who destroy statues built in memory of war heroes, in memory of countries; even going so far as to censure fairy tales, children's stories, cartoons, movies that come up against the censorship of the language police.

One of the sensitive areas, perhaps the most important one, where this attack is taking place against what is "real" is, unsurprisingly, in the digital world, and social media in particular. Originally meant to be a formidable tool for sharing, communicating, and accessing information freely, in recent years social media has become a place where, on the one hand, there is a concentration of the repression of freedom of expression, and, on the other, the liberal propaganda—with whom the magnates who own these platforms flirt—secretly expects to dictate the narrative of the single and standardized idea, to build upon this sort of supranational "constitution." Obviously without opposition. And without even paying the taxes they owe to the various countries. Anyone and anything can be the victim and the hostage of this freedom-killing trend: from artworks removed from social media because they are too "offensive," to the sensitivity of the minorities, to the obscuring of nonconformist newspapers; from political movements banned for no reason, to the incredible decision to block the Twitter profile of the most important person elected on the planet, which is what happened to the President of the United States, Donald Trump.

If what occurs in the digital universe is somehow "obvious"—because every decision of this kind in any case triggers an intense debate in the newspapers—elsewhere intolerance spreads like a virus. Almost as if to instill in Western man a silent yet inexorable feeling of guilt for what his civilization built in the West, and not only there.

What I want to say is that the idea of political correctness is like a blast wave, a cancel culture that tries to overwhelm and remove all that our civilization developed that is beautiful, honorable, and human. Through pain, division, conflicts, and, obviously, the inevitable contradictions as well. It is a nihilistic wind of unheard-of ugliness that seeks to homologate everything in the name of One World. In short, that which is politically correct, the gospel of a stateless, uprooted elite, is the greatest threat to the founding value of identity.

* * *

What exactly are identities? That's a hard question I have always tried to answer, starting with myself. I am a woman, I am Giorgia, I am a mother, I am a Christian, I am Italian, I am European. I am many things at once that tell you where I come from. They define what I have decided to be, they indicate where I am headed. They are my multiple identities that, like concentric circles, frame my life on this earth and will leave a memory for those who loved me. I did not choose some of these identities, they were given to me. Others are the fruit of my freedom.

The first identity is my name, chosen by my parents. The first act of love I received. One's name is the first word that a child will hear. It is the sound with which they recognize their mother's and father's voices. Ernst Jünger wrote that names "have the power to invoke," they inhabit our soul, turning it into an immortal identity.

The second identity is my gender. Chosen by Nature or by God, you decide. It puts me in a specific area of humankind. I am a member of the female sex. Today this identity is threatened by the shadow of a "rainbow," which has come to symbolize the cultural decline that behind the rhetoric of inclusion crosses over into the denial of a simple reality, bringing with it incredible short-circuits, like the Arcigay association requesting that the Arcilesbica association be thrown out, "guilty" of claiming female specificity.

The third identity is my faith, handed down by my parents in my case, by the land where I was born and raised. It is an identity that can be chosen, changed, refuted . . . or perhaps even found when one comes to discover God in their life. However, Christian identity can also be secular more than religious because, for our culture, it is not just an individual identity, it is a collective one. "Why We Cannot Help Calling Ourselves Christians" is the title of an essay that the great Italian philosopher Benedetto Croce, layman and nonbeliever, wrote in 1942, recognizing that all of modern history is indebted to the Christian revelation. Because "no other revolutions will bear comparison with this; even the great discoveries which mark epochs in human history beside it seem incidental and limited." This identity underlies Western civilization. The very roots of the West can only be traditional and Christian.

My fourth identity, my being Italian, is the patriotism I feel. It is my belonging to a people, it is my love of this land, the language I share with others, the landscape that shapes an idea of the world, the traditions and customs I have inherited and love because they are so deeply connected to our ancestors, their legacy, that which is called Tradition. It is the "Us" that builds the national loyalty underlying democracy itself. For conservative thinking, democracy and the rule of law cannot be separated from loyalty to one's country, and the construction of a political Europe can only be carried out if we take nationhood into account.

* * *

What emerges from the awareness of this identity—based on the faith, origins, culture, and traits we are born and grow up with, or, more simply put, God, Country, and Family, in the words of Giuseppe Mazzini, not with a fascist slogan, like some ignorant people believe at times—is a clear and inevitable vision of the world. A vision that we give ourselves the job of bringing back to the public debate, because it represents the center of gravity not only for us but for all of Western culture. Yes, it's true that the Right puts the person at the center. And yet, I do not believe that this principle must belong exclusively to a political party. But on this point, unfortunately, the Italian Left has recorded a chronic imbalance toward illusory dehumanized anthropologies. For it is from the integrity of a person that harmonious belonging develops and extends by concentric circles: family, country, and Europe, which make up, all together, the thousands of years of civilization that have shaped the West. Putting a person at the center means recognizing all that is sacred about life, the uniqueness of each individual: that is why, for me and for us, the defense of life from the moment of conception is more than an epic battle. It is a nonnegotiable principle.

Furthermore, for a culture that puts the person at the center, the concept of freedom cannot be anything but essential. An absolute principle for the Right, clearly accompanied by the constraint of responsibility. Freedom either does or does not exist, and it concerns speech, choice, and expression. Freedom means self-determination when it comes to economics: because it is a question of promoting general interest. And freedom is privacy, too, because I am the master of my life—which I answer to conscientiously or in good faith. But I cannot answer for it either to the state, which must necessarily stop at my doorstep, nor to the Big Tech bosses.

The last stage of identity is that of the family and its role that has never been fully recognized. The family is the fundamental core of sociality from which everyone develops their own formation, shares their destiny, and ties to itself a continuum that represents the most important tonic of society, ever since the dawn of time. The person and the family are the inescapable elements required for the creation of a community of citizens. And Italy is the humanistic homeland par excellence when it comes to the identity of its cities. Those thousands of bell towers became one single thing thanks to the Unification of Italy, cemented in turn to the sacrifice of every Italian with every one of their dialects in the trenches of the Great War, whose victory allowed this country to become a part of the foremost powers in the world. That is why for the Right there is neither contradiction nor conflict between city and state. Between local identity and national belonging.

As people, as citizens, and as Italians we identify ourselves intimately—and have always done so—as Europeans and Westerners.

Because the acknowledgment that we are part of a common myth rooted in tradition and Christianity embraces the people of Europe, but its sphere of influence extends well beyond the Old Continent. For me, saying the words "I am" means belonging to all this at the same time. And recognizing all these "circles" does not mean subordinating one to the other, but rather discovering an intrinsic symphony. And a crescendo. Which resembles an inexorable cavalcade. To the rhythm of music.

I AM A CHRISTIAN

I Believe in Us

My grandmother Maria was deeply devout. Hers was a kind of folk devotion made up of small, everyday rituals. After losing her father to tuberculosis as a young girl, she was sent to a boarding school run by nuns, where she absorbed all the lessons they taught her. And when her husband nearly died of his first heart attack, her devotion to God became unwavering. She prayed and prayed, promising the Lord that if he saved the love of her life, the only man she had ever known, she would go to Mass every single Sunday for the rest of her life. Every time I listen to one of my favorite songs by one of my favorite singers, "Mon Dieu" by Édith Piaf, I think of my grandmother praying: "*Mon Dieu! Mon Dieu! Mon Dieu! / Laissez-le-moi encore un peu / mon amoreux. / Six mois, trois mois, deux mois. / Laissez-le-moi pour seulement / un mois.*" *(My God! My God! My God! Leave my true love here with me for a bit longer. Six months, three months, two months. Leave him here with me for just one month.)* My grandmother kept her promise to the very end, even long after my grandfather had passed. She preferred to go to Mass on Saturday afternoons, forcing us to go with her.

So, for much of my childhood, we all went to Mass every week in a tiny church in the San Paolo neighborhood. To be honest, looking back now, I can't help but wonder whether God saw my grandmother's promise as truly fulfilled, given that she always dozed off in church. Nevertheless, over time my sister and I came to know the words of the Mass by heart. We even copied them, word for word, into a notebook, turning it into a game to see who could memorize them better. In church, we read from the Scriptures and even served as altar girls. The parish was a vital part of our lives.

But our true parish wasn't the one we attended on Saturdays. It was San Filippo Neri, located in Garbatella, and at its heart was Father Guido Chiaravalli—though to everyone in the neighborhood, he was simply Father Guido. In fact, I didn't even know his last name until he passed away. For me and countless others, Father Guido was the closest person to holiness I have ever known.

He was a father in every sense of the word: guiding, educating, and supporting the kids of Garbatella for decades. You'd often see him walking briskly around the neighborhood, always in the same jacket, no matter the season. Born in the Bergamo region, he was tough when he needed to be, striking as hard as a blacksmith. But when you stood before him, his piercing blue eyes, protective gaze, and powerful words had a way of opening your heart to him. He cared for each individual soul, and saved many kids from drugs and bad influences. When he died at the age of eighty-six in 2014, thousands attended his funeral. His former "kids," spanning generations, came together by word of mouth to bid farewell to him one last time. Arianna and I were there too, of course.

It was Father Guido who convinced my grandmother and mother that we should be baptized—by then, we were already six and eight years old. When we were born, my father, a staunch atheist, had opposed our receiving the first of the sacraments. But it was Father Guido who prepared us for our First Communion. For that special day, my sister and I were dressed to the nines in white dresses and a confection of lace on our heads—complete with huge bows that we were immensely proud of at the time. I recently came across photos of that day and I must admit that the kids who bullied us weren't entirely unjustified. But please don't tell my mother—she remains incredibly proud of our outfits, and she made a million sacrifices to afford them.

When we were little, Father Guido would take us to the seaside on a bus. We'd spend the day on a public beach at the Cancelli di Tor Vaianica. Even as we grew older, he never stopped looking out for us. He wrote a letter to my grandmother expressing his disapproval when Arianna had children without being married. Not a single sheep could escape his flock. It was thanks to him that I grew closer to God. This closeness wasn't born of simply memorizing the words of the Mass, but it was the deep meaning of the liturgy, which can only be understood as an adult. Perhaps I fully grasped it only years later, when I took a Confirmation course so I could be my niece's godmother.

* * *

Beyond the sacraments, Scriptures, and liturgies, my conversation with God has never been interrupted. Still, I've always thought that the Lord probably has more pressing concerns than my relatively fortunate life. So instead, I prefer to bug Harael, my guardian angel. That's the name I use for him because I once read that Harael is the guardian angel of all those born on January 15.

It's not easy for me to discuss this topic in a rational way. Some things are processed with your heart rather than your mind, and there's always the risk of veering into New Age territory. However, I firmly believe that angels manifest themselves in each and every one of our lives. All you need is to know how to listen. Over time, I've become convinced that the voice of our guardian angel is none other than what we commonly call our conscience. That voice speaks inside us, often playing counterpoint to our thoughts, offering guidance we don't always want to follow. How many times have we ignored our inner warning, only to later say, "Damn, I knew this would happen." I think that voice is your guardian angel. I talk to mine constantly—asking for advice, listening, and eventually (almost always) discerning the angel's answer. To me, a guardian angel is a guide, a mentor, a best friend. Someone you can't deceive because they know everything about you, yet remain devoted to helping you discover and nurture the light within yourself.

At one point in my life, I became completely captivated by angelology—the study of doctrines concerning angels. Around the age of eighteen, I began collecting angel statues. Today, I've lost count of how many I own. My angels are strewn about every room, office, and house I've ever had, and they come from all over the world, crafted from the most disparate materials, in every shape and size imaginable. Yet, my favorites will always be the hand-painted wooden ones. Collecting them is a way of honoring my own guardian angel and, through her, thanking God for sending her to watch over me. Every night, when Ginevra falls asleep, I lean close to her and whisper the words of the *Angel of God* prayer into her ear. She isn't able to say it on her own yet, but I hope that one day she will form a genuine, daily bond with her own guardian angel, just as I have with mine.

* * *

There was another great man who brought me closer to God, thanks to his powerful example—the saint Pope John Paul II, born Karol Wojtyła. To me, he was the greatest pope of the modern age and the greatest statesman of the twentieth century. But he was more than that. They say we often don't understand the value of something until it's gone. Pope John Paul II was elected in 1978, just a year after I was born. When he died in 2005, I was twenty-eight. In those nearly thirty years, he had always been there. When he died, it felt as though I had lost my grandfather because he had always been there for me.

A saint and a human being, Pope John Paul II became a part of my life as though he were a member of my own family. When his earthly journey came to an end, it felt natural for me to go to Saint Peter's Square to pay tribute to him. I wept more than I ever had for someone with whom I didn't share a personal, day-to-day relationship. Of course, I'd had the privilege of meeting him—four times, in fact. Back then, it was customary for the pope to meet elected government officials at the start of each year, regardless of their level—city, provincial, and regional administrators. I was elected to the Province at just twenty-one, and I never missed a single one of those events. I remember the first year of the ceremony, he mistook me for the daughter of one of the councilors. I was barred at the entrance, as family members weren't allowed in. My colleagues quickly reassured him that I was, in fact, one of the councilors. When it was my turn, he smiled at me with his trademark expression—strong and compassionate—and said, "The youngest in the council." It was both simple and electrifying.

In those five years, I had the privilege and the pain of witnessing his suffering up close. Year after year, he became more physically bent over, yet his dignity shone ever brighter. He chose to transform his suffering into a lesson, demonstrating the heroism of accepting his fate to the very end. Though he couldn't predict it, his courage in the face of pain brought him closer, in our eyes, to the figure of Christ. His message was as powerful as that of Pope Benedict XVI, yet more accessible. His humanity was as incisive as that of Pope Francis, yet felt more rooted in the universal sentiment of Christians. I have followed every pope, though not with the same profound connection. Maybe it's my age or the awareness that comes with it, but although I am Catholic and have never criticized a pope, I must admit that I haven't always fully understood Pope Francis. At times, I have felt like a lost sheep. I hope that one day I will have the privilege of speaking with him because I am certain that his big eyes and direct words will help me make sense of what I don't understand. I see too many atheists praising him while many believers remain confused. I'm certain there's an explanation that has eluded me so far.

* * *

I have never stopped believing in God. Yet, the dimension of faith is so intimate that it must not and cannot serve as a model for a collective political movement, nor for a nation. My faith in God, imperfect, uncertain, and sometimes painful, is mine alone. I think that's true for everyone on this earth.

Like many, I have questioned God's design when faced with certain events. Like many, I have sought His help during difficult times and offered thanks when I recognized His blessings. It is through Him that I strive to be a good person, convinced that He sees and values—here on this earth, not just in the afterlife—those who remain aligned with His will. Through Him, I've come to understand that each of us has a mission in life. I never feared death until I became a mother—the truth is, when you bring a child into the world, you realize that you are no longer free—not even to die. Thanks to Him, I believe that life should be navigated with your eyes upward, not forward. The true purpose is not how far you advance, but how much you ascend, striving toward perfection. Paradoxically, to ascend, you need to dig deep into the foundations of your existence. This is why I've always been intrigued by great cathedrals, with their foundations dug deep into the ground, and their towering naves symbolizing those who have ascended in their attempt to reach God through prayer. I remember the emotions I felt the first time I set foot in Notre Dame. I thought the French must be crazy to choose the Eiffel Tower as their national symbol—a mass of iron—when they had a site like this. When I watched my favorite cathedral burn in 2019, my pain was profound. It moved me to organize a crowdfunding campaign to help rebuild it, and I wasn't alone. The images of the cathedral enveloped in flames stirred something deep in many people. It triggered an emotional and intellectual response that stood in stark contrast to the prevailing mindset in the West. At the time, we were struck by how keenly ordinary people felt the loss—spiritually and as part of their identity—far more than the political and cultural elite of the French state. In Italy, Ernesto Galli della Loggia best captured the meaning and tragedy of it all: "No doubt the flames of Paris were caused by an accident, but all it took was to see one of the icons of Christianity on this continent reduced to ashes, for a vast part of the European public opinion to have a reaction that was beyond any traditional political or confessional division. An effusion of identity self-awareness: 'We are this thing here, this place, and this church as well, and we are not willing to renege on what we are.' Without any arrogance, but also without hesitation. Showing, however, the extent to which the man on the European street had formed a common sentiment, a sentimental and psychological mindset, light-years away from the current ideas and the biases of the political and media-cultural elite."

To this day, the cause of the fire remains unknown, but those haunting images resonated deeply. When certain symbols go up in smoke, it feels as though a part of our identity burns with them.

I'm not talking about Italian symbols alone, but of European ones. I wept in Paris, surrounded by the soaring walls and rose windows of that Gothic masterpiece, Notre Dame. I stood in awe at Stonehenge, waiting for dawn, marveling at those massive stones—seemingly impossible for humans to transport—which still today predict the sun's path. I was moved in Andria, standing before Castel del Monte, the fortress commissioned in the thirteenth century by Frederick II of Swabia, Emperor of the Holy Roman Empire and King of Sicily. His court was a remarkable meeting point where Greek, Latin, Germanic, Arabic, and Hebrew culture converged. And in Westminster, I felt a mix of admiration and sadness before its monumental grandeur. It struck me that, yes, perhaps more than others, the English had truly mastered the art of inheriting the legacy of Ancient Rome.

These are pieces of my identity—not just Italian, but also European.

For me, Europe has always been a big source of hope. It makes me laugh when people describe me as the leader of an "anti-European" party. My mind immediately returns to the years of my youthful activism: the protests, the slogans, and the many songs that have long defined the cultural heritage of the Italian Right. Back then, our vision of Europe was one our elders had dreamed of—strong and independent, unbound by the two Cold War blocs. It was a Europe that would unite its people, not through arbitrary parameters, or a common currency, but through the shared strength of thousands of years of its civilization. Then, when the Berlin Wall fell, everything changed. Once more, we embraced our peers from the East—those who had lived through decades of Social Realism firsthand. Europe could finally, as Pope John Paul II so beautifully put it, "breathe with both lungs." That moment should have been the launch of the European dream. Yet, sadly, the opposite happened.

I learned to love Europe through travel, reading, and above all through the heroic figures whose actions shaped my imagination—men and women who defended our borders and ensured the survival of our civilization. I think of the brave King Leonidas I of Sparta and his three hundred soldiers who, obeying his command, sacrificed their lives in the Battle of Thermopylae to hold back the Persian Empire. I think of the Frankish warriors led by Charles Martel, victorious at the Battle of Poitiers in 732 AD, halting the Islamic tidal wave that had already swept through Spain. For this, they were the first to be called "Europeans." Like Constantine XI, the last Emperor of Constantinople, a legendary warrior who died in 1453 alongside a handful of heroes—Italians and others from across Europe—during the desperate defense of what was then the capital of Orthodox Christianity, now Istanbul. I think of the thousands of Venetian sailors from the Serenissima who perished in the Battle of Lepanto in 1571, fighting to stop the advancing Turks. Or the epic charge in 1683 led by King John III Sobieski of Poland, who, with the Winged Hussars and the Ukrainian Cossacks, saved Vienna from the siege of the Ottoman Empire. More recently, there was Jan Palach, the Czech student who, in January 1969, self-immolated in Wenceslas Square to urge his fellow citizens to resist Soviet Occupation. And a few years before him, the "youth of Budapest," who challenged the tanks arriving from Moscow. I have reflected often on Europe—on its glorious past and its uncertain future.

To me, a united Europe is an ideal that reaches back through histories, rooted in three magnificent cities: Athens, Rome, and Jerusalem—where it all began. Christianity undoubtedly gave these foundations cultural unity. During a remarkable event organized by Youth Action in Rome, we posed the question: Why hasn't Brussels officially recognized the irreplaceable value of Christian roots? This should have been included during the attempt—an ultimately failed one—to provide Europe with a constitution.

Not because I personally favor confessional visions, but because no political project can endure without a shared sense of belonging. Moreover, I'm convinced that only by valuing and fostering our shared identity can we strengthen the understanding among Europeans that we are bound by a common destiny. Some, like me, believe that our identity must be defended and safeguarded with the same commitment we apply to protect the natural heritage left by our forebears. Yet others consider Christian identity "unmentionable for the public discourse of official Europe," to the point of criminalizing the conservative governments of Hungary and Poland, which remain steadfast in defending their national and Christian identity. They have gone so far as to use, in a cowardly manner, accusations of violating the rule of law as a weapon—striking at the hearts of the Hungarian and Polish people during the worst pandemic since the postwar period.

* * *

What is Europe, really? Can we even speak of Europe without acknowledging its classical and Christian identity? How far do the boundaries of its civilization truly extend? I believe the then-Cardinal Ratzinger expressed it best when he repeatedly stated that "ours is not a continent that can be comprehended neatly in geographical terms; rather it is a cultural and historical concept."

No one can deny that the history of Europe and the very essence of its civilization are indissolubly linked to its Christian roots. Today, the borders of Europe largely reflect the perimeter within which the distinct identity first asserted itself, and later defended itself.

Consider the pivotal role played by the powerful evangelization movement in the complex process of unifying the Romans and the Germans—a fundamental milestone in Europe's formation. Nor can we overlook Christianity giving rise to the development of the concept of the "person," a notion infinitely more profound than the simple idea of the "individual." It introduced unprecedented values, such as solidarity with the marginalized, the poor, the sick, and the needy. Christian religious ethics also laid the foundation for the gradual abolition of slavery.

This historical narrative is supported not only by the works of scholars such as Franco Cardini and Giovanni Reale but also by the tangible legacy scattered around Europe: great roads leading to sacred places like the sanctuary of Santiago de Compostela, the shrine of Częstochowa, the Cathedral of Our Lady of Chartres, the Abbey of Mont-Saint-Michel, the Hermitage of Camaldoli, and the Monastery of San Benedetto in Subiaco. These and countless other sites make it impossible to overlook the inescapable significance of Christianity in shaping European culture. As we journey through Europe, we encounter evidence of what we learned in school: monasteries were vibrant centers of cultural production, and it was thanks to the work of diligent monks who doubled as scribes that much of our classical literature survived. In these same spaces, women like Catherine of Siena and Hildegard of Bingen emerged as influential intellectuals—figures now "rediscovered" and celebrated by feminist scholars. And let us not forget the great women of the Middle Ages, such as Eleonora of Arborea, the Judgess (Laura Boldrini should be proud of herself for being called by the same name), the ruler of Southern Sardinia. A trailblazer, she promulgated the Carta de Logu, a legal code considered by many to be a precursor to modern penal codes.

Grand cathedrals, often built at the very heart of cities, were the vibrant centers of life. They played a pivotal role in the significant culture advancements that arose from episcopal schools, which, notably, were open to laypeople as well.

The need to defend Europe's Christian roots goes far beyond secular and rational acknowledgment of their relevance in shaping the historical trajectory of Europe. If it were merely a matter of history, this defense would amount to a noble but ultimately symbolic gesture of loyalty to values at risk of fading. However, I am convinced that defending these roots is not just about history—it is a current and urgent necessity. Again, Benedict XVI articulated this urgency in his 2006 lecture at the University of Regensburg—a speech of extraordinary intellectual value. Though it has often been misquoted and unfairly criticized by those who failed to grasp its prophetic nature, it remains a clear-sighted vision for Christians and Europeans alike. His key message reminds us of the indissoluble bond between faith and reason: "Not acting reasonably is contrary to God's nature."

It is precisely in this encounter between Biblical faith and Greek thought—along with the invaluable contributions of Roman civilization—that Benedict XVI identifies the foundations of what we can reasonably call Europe.

When Joseph Ratzinger speaks of Greek thought as essential to European identity, I am reminded of the timeless warning carved on the pediment of the Temple of Apollo: "Know thyself." What would our modern idea of man be without these words? I also think of the Roman notions of law and citizenship—ideas that shaped the Empire's remarkable capacity to integrate diverse cultures without ever losing its own identity. As I was saying, this is not merely a matter of history.

To engage in meaningful dialogue with someone different from ourselves, we must first recognize who we are—human beings endowed with two sources of understanding and love: reason and faith. This is why I have never subscribed to the culture of tolerance, though I wholeheartedly profess the culture of respect. Tolerance, after all, implies enduring something that, deep down, you would rather not have in your midst. "Respect," on the other hand, comes from the Latin *respicere*, meaning "to look deeply." From this, it follows that you cannot love the Other without truly knowing them, just as you cannot expect someone to love you if you do not know yourself. This brings me to what I consider a surreal paradox in today's Europe: while promoting the culture of inclusion, we are also asked to erase the symbols of our identity to make that inclusion possible. If you want to be good, we are told we must hide the symbols of our faith. And so begins the removal of Christian imagery—starting with the crucifixes that once adorned the walls of our schools. This is a grave mistake. That symbol belongs in places of education, no matter what someone may or may not believe. Whether or not you believe in

God, the crucifix contains the values on which our civilization is built. It is not about imposing a religious creed, but of teaching who we are. Solidarity, reason, and equality among men—these are lessons transmitted by that symbol. A crucifix on the wall does not impose religion; it is a testament to the roots of our civilization. It is not a tool of exclusion, but a reminder of who we are and what unites us. While history has added countless layers to our thinking, our foundations are undeniably rooted in Christianity. Cutting those roots risks leaving us unstable, on the brink of collapse. And this, I fear, is exactly what is happening—in Italy and across Europe. You can be an atheist, a Buddhist, or a Muslim, but if you were born and raised in Europe, those Christian values are part of your heritage, whether you like it or not.

The other great message from Pope Benedict XVI's Regensburg *lectio magistralis* is encapsulated in this enlightening sentence: "Without reason, faith threatens that it will become fanatical, and without faith, reason is entrapped and deprived of its dignity."

I'm not inclined to wade into theological debates, but personally I believe this distinction highlights a fundamental difference between the Christian and Muslim visions of the world. At the core of Christianity is man and his free will. Made in the image and likeness of God, we are entrusted with the ability to discern right from wrong. To be a good Christian is to "simply" love your neighbor. Islam, on the other hand, presents a sacred text that is itself divine and prescriptive, instructing believers in precise detail on what they must do. For this reason, while Christianity allows for the separation of religion and state ("Render unto Caesar the things which are Caesar's"), this separation is inconceivable for Islam, which inherently ties itself to politics through sharia—a legal and social model rooted in the Qur'an.

These are not merely religious differences; they are two very different philosophical frameworks. Personally, I choose the Greek, Roman, and Christian framework. It is the foundation that I want to see prevail in Italy and Europe. Does this make me an ignorant xenophobe or a bigot?

* * *

I have always believed that without classical and Christian roots, Europe would be nothing more than a geographical expression. I have long thought that Europe needs a shared celebration—a day of remembrance that can unite its people beyond the scars of the "European civil wars" that tore it apart in the twentieth century. That is why we chose November 9th, a date that marks the evening in 1989 when an officer of the German Democratic Republic announced that citizens could now travel freely between East and West without a permit. Just hours later, the Berlin Wall was torn down piece by piece by a jubilant crowd. Since the ten-year anniversary, our community has commemorated the event annually, organizing many events. Thanks to the efforts of young people from Youth Action, November 9 is now officially recognized as World Freedom Day. It is a day of such importance that it deserves to be a topic of discussion in schools. Yet, the so-called pro-Europeans of today—many of whom were the communists of the past—continue to struggle with a guilty conscience and prefer to emphasize other, more divisive moments. Or perhaps it's because they wish to suppress the uncomfortable truth about our collective Western conscience: that after World War II, we bartered away our freedom and peace in exchange for the people of Eastern Europe by delivering them into the hands of a communist dictatorship. No, democracy in Europe did not truly return in 1945 when Nazi Germany and Fascist Italy were defeated, despite what we like to tell ourselves. It returned in 1989, with the collapse of the Soviet bloc. We owe a debt to our Eastern European brothers and sisters—one that remains unpaid, even as some viciously attack the Visegrád Group or other former Socialist countries. It makes my blood boil to hear politicians and commentators on the Left declare that "those who do not respect our vision must be thrown out of Europe," as though Europe were a private club where unwanted members can be shown the door. As though the EU is synonymous with Europe itself, rather than just one specific organization among many possible ones.

In truth, my relationship with Europe is akin to that of a disappointed lover. I believed in it deeply, and maybe that's why I feel so embittered now. Maybe even angry. Angry with those who took a grand dream and turned it into an amusement park of technocrats and bankers, feasting at the expense of ordinary people. They endlessly invoke the teachings of the "founding fathers," yet they have betrayed them in their very name.

Sir Roger Scruton (I can't help quoting him again—it's his fault for writing so many clever things) once explained that conservativism stems from the belief that while it's easy to destroy good things, it's far more difficult to create them. This is especially true for those intangible yet vital aspects of our collective heritage, such as peace, freedom, safety, and civilization. Scruton also warned us about the dangers of a "false Europe." This "false Europe," represented today by the institutions of the EU, is utopian in nature and potentially tyrannical. By contrast, the "real Europe" is a community of nations now under threat from this stifling false vision and the supposedly "pro-European" rationale that is presented as the only viable path forward.

All the flaws in the EU's current design continue to provoke growing hostility among its citizens, yet the so-called "pro-Europeans" pretend not to notice. For them, any problems are always someone else's fault—blamed on those who "no longer want Europe" or on the alleged ignorance of voters. As we've sadly seen in situations like the vaccine rollout, their solution to every crisis is always the same: to further cede sovereignty to Brussels. I am certain that if we want to preserve what is good about the European Union, we must rebuild it from the ground up, basing it on values and ideas free from the confines of "pro-European single-thought."

That's right—contrary to what we are often told, there's not just one way to be "pro-European." Handing over ever-greater sovereignty to the EU—based on the federal model of the "United States of Europe" and the mantra of "Ever Closer Union"—is not the only path forward. This model has been experimented with for years, and it has failed disastrously, alienating citizens from European institutions and worsening the democratic deficit of our time. Democratic sovereignty, first and foremost, resides in nation-states, where governments and parliaments are directly elected by the people. By devolving legislative powers to unelected European bureaucrats, we undermine the very foundation of democracy.

Yes, I know, it's like this almost everywhere, except in Italy, where we continue unperturbed to have heads of government that no Italian has ever voted for—not even in a condominium meeting. Normally, though, that's not how it's supposed to work. Let's say that, in Italy, the concept of the "external restriction"—a sort of autopilot from Brussels telling us what we should and shouldn't do in our own backyard—has been replaced by what I call "internal restriction." We go a step further by appointing prime ministers who are already preapproved by Brussels, sparing the EU the trouble of being seen as the bad guys. In the end, Indro Montanelli's wry prediction has proven true: "When the European Union is constituted, the French will enter as the French, the Germans as Germans, and the Italians as Europeans."

We, however, believe it's entirely possible to be part of a great union of European nations while still safeguarding the national interests of each member state. That's why we, as European conservatives, advocate for a confederate model, not a federal one. Those three little extra letters represent a radical difference that deserves explanation. In our political vocabulary, federalism refers to the devolution of powers from the center to the periphery—what was once described as "from Rome to the territories." When applied to Europe, however, federalism means the exact opposite: the centralization of power in Brussels. Those of us who want to keep power closer to the citizens—at the level of the nation-state or local autonomies—advocate for a confederate model instead.

The Europe I envision is one that deals with the major issues: foreign policies and defense, protecting external borders, bolstering the internal market, and responding to cross-border challenges like pandemics. After witnessing the disastrous management of COVID-19 and the chaotic vaccine procurement efforts of the European Union, this is a clear priority. But beyond these major issues, most decisions should remain in the hands of national governments and local authorities. This principle is called subsidiarity, and while it's enshrined in the EU treaties, it's also the principle most frequently violated by Brussels. For us, our concern is simple: Brussels must not take responsibility for issues best dealt with in Rome, Warsaw, Budapest, or Madrid.

* * *

My Europe is the "Europe of Nations, but also a nation itself," as dreamed of by General De Gaulle, and the "Europe that moves to the Right, or isn't made at all," as Giorgio Almirante often said. We have our languages, our traditions, our borders. This unity in diversity has always felt natural to me, and I am determined to defend it. Now that I have the honor of serving as president of the European Conservatives, I feel the full weight of this responsibility.

Europe is a part of who we are, and European policies have become an integral part of national policies. The days when they were merely an extension of foreign policy feel like a distant memory. That's right, foreign policy. It's always been a passion of mine. As I described earlier, when we were young, we would be at each other's throats in our endless meetings. . . . We didn't deal in shades of gray, white, or black—we had clear ideas. But to participate in those debates, you had to be prepared. For my generation, those debates were an extraordinary political training ground, as were the student assemblies. You couldn't risk embarrassing yourself, so you had to study. When I compare the ruling class of today to the improvisors who have jumped into Parliament on the back of the Rousseau bandwagon, I am so very proud. We learned so much in those smoke-filled, dusty rooms where we debated everything—from the Yanks and the Native Americans to the Israelis and Palestinians, the English and the Irish (like Bobby Sands), and all the way to Tibet with its peaceful yet unyielding monks. We followed the movements of Commander Massoud as he led the Afghan Mujahidin against the Soviets, and we were inspired by the legendary Almerigo Grilz, whose daring reports brought us into the world's most remote and forgotten wars. Now that I'm no longer a young woman, I carry the lessons of those days with me, and I've come to understand that for a patriot, the best approach to foreign policy is always rooted in the defense of the national interest.

That's what I told Mario Draghi when, during his swearing-in speech, he proudly declared that his government would be "pro-European and pro-Atlantic" (*europeista e atlantista*). But that's not the point. Italy is already a part of Europe and NATO.

The real question—one that those who have governed us in recent years have failed to answer—is how Italy fits into these supranational bodies. Will it assert itself with pride and strength befitting one of the world's major powers? Or will it continue to act as a colony, slavishly following the policy directives of its partners and competitors? Will Draghi's authority be used to address pressing issues like Europe's tax havens, which siphon billions of euros from the Italian treasury each year? Will he take on the low wages of Eastern European countries that undercut our labor market? What about the banking regulations that have penalized Italian banks by turning a blind eye to the derivatives bubble? And will he challenge France's predatory behavior towards Italian companies? Or will the former president of the European Central Bank become yet another Trojan horse for the Franco-German domination of Italy?

In other words, what does Draghi's authority matter if he does not intend to use it to do what no Italian prime minister has done in the past decade: unequivocally defend Italy's national interest? No ifs, buts, or maybes, and no subservience to foreign masters.

Too often, we Italians are afflicted by a kind of provincial mindset—a habit of assuming that what happens abroad or what comes from outside our borders must be better than what we can achieve ourselves. Yes, we have our flaws, but I believe our greatest failing is that we do not love or take enough pride in what Italy has represented—and still represents—to the world. This is not about chauvinism or disdain for others; it's about respect. We love ourselves and respect others, based on the awareness that being Italian is a gift we must strive to honor every single day.

This is what we, Brothers of Italy, are working to achieve, guided by the teachings of one of the most Italian of Italians: Nazario Sauro, an irredentist. A citizen of the Hapsburg Empire, he enlisted in the Italian Navy to fight Austria. Captured and sentenced to death, Sauro wrote a letter to his eldest son the day before his execution. He could not have known that his words would become a testament for us. His letter concluded with this: "Swear on this Nation, Nino, and have your brothers swear that when they have come of age and can fully understand, that you will always be, wherever you are, Italians first and foremost."

The Racism of Progress

I can't stand those TV shows that invite you on, pretending to be interested in your point of view even when they don't share it. Instead, they build a kind of circus around you, where you inevitably end up playing the role of a monster to be condemned—a ferocious beast to be tamed. I've experienced this dozens of times, and at a certain point, I decided I wasn't going to play their game anymore. If they truly believed I was so unpresentable, so dangerous, so chilling, and if they were consistent with their own convictions, they wouldn't use me—or the ideas I represent—to boost their audience ratings.

One evening I found myself on La7's *Piazzapulita*. Corrado Formigli, the show's longtime host, started out gently: "When I see you holding your daughter in your arms, I think about how all of us, as parents, have dreams for our children. We only want what's best for them, and we work our tails off to give them opportunities in life. Then I think of this little girl—her name is Alima. I believe she's about your daughter's age. She was saved by an NGO while her father was fleeing war and her mother was coming from Niger. If she hadn't been saved, she would still be in a Libyan refugee camp. So, my question is this: why shouldn't this little girl, who is fortunate enough to be in Europe right now, be given the same chance as your daughter? Because if we applied the rules you advocate, such as the naval blockade, this little girl would never have reached Europe."

Of course, the question is flawed. Under my proposals—which include a naval blockade and focus on distinguishing refugees from illegal migrants—a family fleeing war, like Alima's, would have arrived in Europe anyway. When I pointed this out and added, "I'm very sorry because, even though we've known each other for years, you still haven't had the patience to read my proposals," Formigli was visibly annoyed. It was a heated exchange, but once again, I showed how the immigration policies of Brothers of Italy are light-years away from the superficial, self-serving narrative some members of the Left-intelligentsia try to impose.

What truly drives me crazy, though, isn't the TV shows themselves, but something deeper—the reason I've shared this episode in my life in the first place. Does anyone really believe, in their heart of hearts, that someone like me has no compassion, no inkling of solidarity for children like Alima, or the countless others who have died in the Mediterranean after being loaded onto makeshift boats by heartless, cynical traffickers—traffickers the Left never mentions? Yet, this is exactly the message they've managed to convey. In 2019, during the same period, I came across a story about a Nigerian woman who had been mocked in a hospital for screaming in anguish after losing her young daughter. Witnesses described her cries as "inhuman." I posted about it, saying those comments made me sick. The hospital quickly denied the incident, but it was my reaction—banal, inevitable, and obvious—that became the focus of attention. It was as if people found it shocking that I could express empathy for a grieving mother from another country. Only a fool could believe that.

I will never forget the wailing of little Joseph's mother from the boat at sea, crying out in desperation after losing her tiny son off the coast of Libya. Nor will I forget the stories of many—too many—shipwrecks that for years have tragically turned these so-called "journeys of hope" into journeys of despair. When faced with a heartbreaking scene like this, you don't need to be a mother to feel empathy, to be utterly horrified and devastated. Anyone who remains indifferent to such tragedies is, in a sense, no longer fully human. Like everyone, my instinctive reaction to such suffering is to open my heart, my arms, my borders, and the doors of my home—to offer refuge and shelter to those in need.

As a girl, I read *The Man Who Laughs* by Victor Hugo. One scene remains etched on my mind: the story of the young protagonist, Gwynplaine, discovering a baby in the snow, cradled in its mother's lifeless arms. The mother had managed to protect her child through a fierce storm, making it to a village. Just as you breathe a sigh of relief, thinking they've made it to safety, the real tragedy unfolds—no one will take them in. Hugo writes that, seeing those closed doors, "the child felt the coldness of men more terribly than the coldness of night." The indifference of people in the face of suffering has always frightened me. When confronted with such stories, it is natural to want to emulate the teachings of Saint Francis of Assisi: to strip ourselves of everything if it means saving the poor and the needy, freeing all of humanity from suffering. But instinct alone isn't enough. To give it substance, we also need reason. And so, without diminishing the principle of humanity, we must ask ourselves a difficult question: would opening our doors unconditionally and giving everything up truly be the right path to ease the pain of the most fragile among us? If this is a question that every human being must grapple with, it is even more pressing for a legislator.

The great philosopher Niccolò Machiavelli offered an essential lesson for anyone dealing with the res publica. While I have always hated the notion that politics can be divorced from morality—and have been skeptical of the oversimplified interpretations of Machiavelli's teachings as "the end justifies the means"—I believe his true lesson was something far less cynical. His real message, I think, is that the role of politics is to act for the greater good, even when decisions can seem dangerous.

To answer whether it is right to welcome everyone who knocks on the door of our country, we must first ask ourselves another question: if we allow anyone who wishes to enter Italy, will we truly mitigate the suffering in the world? The intellectually honest answer is no.

There are hundreds of thousands of people in the world living in conditions far worse than ours, who legitimately aspire to come to Italy or Europe in search of a better life. Africa alone has over a billion people who would see an objective improvement in their circumstances if they became part of the Western world. But can Italy, Europe, and the rest of the West realistically welcome these hundreds of millions and offer them the standard of living we enjoy? No. Let us be sincere and responsible: not because we don't want to, but because it is objectively impossible—a utopian idea. We've seen this happen with far smaller numbers. Large waves of immigrants, far beyond what our system can integrate with dignity with its limited resources, have often been left on the margins of society, vulnerable to exploitation by organized crime, or even forced into prostitution on our streets. One of the tragic truths that the do-gooders consistently ignore is where these people—whom the magnanimous West "saves"—actually end up. The greater the number of migrants, the worse their living conditions become. And with them, the conditions of those communities that receive them also deteriorate. Instead of alleviating suffering, we risk multiplying it.

Over the years of debate on immigration, I have yet to get clear answers from any proponent of immigration to what are, in fact, quite simple questions: Should everyone who asks to enter be allowed to do so without distinction or limitation? If not everyone, then how many? A million? Two? Ten? And if the number were to rise to twenty million or more, what happens once that threshold is exceeded? Do we stop migrant number 2,000,001? And how? Do we turn them away? Do we implement a naval blockade? And if we draw that line, why should our humanity extend only to those we see arriving while ignoring the plight of those who cannot reach our shores—perhaps because they lack the money to pay traffickers and are enduring even worse conditions than those who do manage to come?

The Left often accuses the Right of being demagogic when it comes to immigration. But in reality, the opposite is true—it is the Left that has consistently approached the issue with vague, simplistic platitudes like "volemose bene" (let's love one another) or resorted to the laughable tactic of labeling anyone who discusses possible solutions as a racist. They rarely, if ever, provide concrete proposals or rules of engagement. Instead, they refuse to confront the numbers and the realities of the situation, hiding behind a nebulous rhetoric of open doors. This makes it clear that it is the Left that has been demagogic—and has often profited—at the expense of migrants.

Of course, there are those on the Right who are also guilty of demagoguery, even stooping to using disdainful or racist rhetoric. But that's not true of me, nor of Brothers of Italy. We have always maintained that immigration is a complex matter that requires serious governance and clear, common-sense rules.

The first rule is that no one should enter Italy illegally. A responsible nation cannot reward those who break the law to enter while penalizing those who abide by the rules, who wait their turn, and apply for entry through legal channels. Yet, this is exactly what has happened in recent years with the resetting of the decree on immigration numbers—the system the Italian government uses to set the quotas for legal immigration based on nationality. The quotas for regular immigrants authorized to enter have often been zeroed out due to the overwhelming influx of illegal mass immigration, which has saturated our ability—and willingness—to accommodate foreign nationals. The result? Thousands of Filipinos, Peruvians, Moldovans, and Ukrainians who had applied to enter legally have been unable to do so. Is that fair? I don't think so. The message sent by this policy is scandalous and criminal: *Dear foreigner, if you want to come to Italy, the only way is to pay a people smuggler and enter illegally.* It implies that the state does not decide who enters based on its laws and assessments, but that the traffickers of the twenty-first century are in control.

To act responsibly—and out of respect for those who legitimately aspire to come here—any serious state must do everything in its power to stop illegal mass immigration. This includes measures such as building walls or implementing a naval blockade if these prove effective.

The latter proposal has been a cornerstone of Brothers of Italy's position in recent years, to the extent that we were often labeled "the naval blockade party." We stood firm in supporting this approach despite relentless attacks and lies from the mainstream media, which tried to paint the measure as inhumane, impossible to carry out, or—their favorite mantra—"the naval blockade is an act of war." The exact opposite is true: our proposal is the only real solution that respects international law, halts illegal immigration, and ends the tragedy of deaths at sea.

First, the claim that a naval blockade constitutes an act of war is entirely false. Our plan involves coordinating with North African authorities to prevent boats from departing in the first place. Second, our proposal is much more humane than the status quo, which effectively prioritizes those who can afford to pay smugglers to reach Italy—typically economic migrants—while abandoning those truly fleeing war and persecution. As part of our plan, we advocate for the establishment of international, community-controlled processing centers in North Africa. These centers would allow genuine refugees to apply for entry to Europe under international law, while illegal migrants will be sent back home. Finally, our approach is unquestionably more serious than the current situation, in which a sovereign state—via NGOs—openly negotiates with smugglers. These arrangements often involve coordinating with traffickers to pick up illegal migrants at sea, ultimately enriching some of the most ruthless and most shameful criminal organizations of our time.

Once it is established that no one enters the country illegally, we can begin to have a serious discussion about the immigration "quotas" Italy needs. The demographic data, as I've written before, is alarming: our population is gradually decreasing, with a significant reduction in the number of residents in Italy. There are more deaths than births. Put simply, as a people, we are on the path to extinction. The first answer to this crisis should be a comprehensive plan to incentivize births. It's no coincidence that the first point in the Brothers of Italy's manifesto has always been "the most ambitious plan to support families and increase the birth rate in the history of the Italian people." The deliberately bold words reflect the magnitude of the challenge we face. Sadly, what needed to be done to address this issue has not been done, and the decline in the birth rate has continued unabated for years. While Brothers of Italy will strive to reverse this trend when it leads the government, alas, it will take decades—if not centuries—to see meaningful results.

In the meantime, Italy cannot avoid setting immigration quotas, and no one denies this fact. It is the State's specific responsibility to determine these quotas for legal migrants (distinct from the issue of refugees—I emphasize this point because confusion abounds on this topic). These quotas should address the needs of the national community while ensuring a dignified future for the migrants we choose to welcome. Once again, let's approach this without demagoguery. The facts are clear: the single most critical factor influencing demographic trends in any "gathering" of human beings is the number of fertile women within that group. If immigration is needed to combat demographic decline, the priority must be the number of women of childbearing age arriving in Italy. So why, if the Left insists that migrants are essential to reversing our demographic crisis, has it not prioritized families? Instead, roughly 90 percent of the 700,000 illegal migrants who have arrived on boats these past few years have been men. These are the mysteries of blind faith in immigration.

Then there's the other surreal sound-bite: "Immigrants do the jobs that Italians don't want to do." How many times have you heard someone say this? Plenty. Yet, unless the Left intends to use these words to mask its undeclared hope that thousands of immigrants will eventually vote for them, the statement is misleading. A more accurate version would be: "Immigrants are willing to do certain jobs under conditions and wages that Italians, rightly so, refuse to accept." Which, I'm sure you understand, is a very different statement. Mass migration floods the labor market with millions of desperate individuals, driving wages down and eroding workers' rights. And who profits from lower wages and fewer protections? The major economic powers, of course, as well as financial speculators who, not coincidentally, fund pro-immigration NGOs and push pro-immigration narratives with the help of the mainstream media circus.

I recall a controversy that arose between me and Alessandro Gassmann on social media. The actor had written, "Do you like tomatoes?

Vegetables? Strawberries? Wine? Without them [migrants] you can forget about all that." The irony is that Gassmann is also a UNHCR ambassador, and I truly believe he cares about immigrants, but he failed to see how his argument eerily echoed the rationale used to justify the exploitation of slaves on cotton plantations. His statement has little to do with principles like "welcoming" and "solidarity." True solidarity and bravery would involve acknowledging that Italy should accept immigration only when it aligns with the needs of the labor market and protects all workers without weakening their bargaining power. That is precisely what we, Brothers of Italy, demand.

Unregulated immigration disproportionately impacts the most vulnerable—those in the labor market, those relying on social services, and those living in the suburbs of our largest cities. This is why the Left, tucked away in its comfortable, velvet-chaired salons, can afford to pretend that these problems don't exist. It's no accident that in Western countries, the working classes—the poor, and those in more peripheral neighborhoods—are increasingly gravitating toward right-wing political movements and moving away from a Left that seems indifferent to their struggles.

Another important point to consider is that a state that seeks to protect its citizens' interests should unapologetically prioritize the entry of foreigners who are most likely to integrate successfully. Cardinal Biffi caused shock waves when he dared to suggest that Italy should favor Christian immigration. I see nothing scandalous about this—quite the opposite, in fact. It is entirely reasonable for a country to favor immigration that aligns as closely as possible with its national community. Such an approach increases the likelihood of successful assimilation and reduces the potential for social and cultural conflict.

And yet, the very idea of "compatible immigration" unsettles the Left. Why? I've explained in detail throughout these pages that immigration is often a tool wielded by globalists to erode national identity, to create a homogenous mixture of cultures, to ultimately create a world that is all the same, made up of weak people. Immigration that is culturally compatible undermines this agenda. It has nothing to do with addressing the suffering of migrants or fostering their development as a positive element within the national communities. That's the truth—and the evidence supports it.

Take Poland, for example. For some time now, the country has faced relentless criticism for resisting the redistribution of migrants who arrive illegally in Southern Europe. In response, Warsaw has pointed out that it hosts a million Ukrainians on its territory—people fleeing a war that has claimed 14,000 dead in just a few years. Nothing like the fake refugees who have landed on our coasts. And how does the mainstream respond to this defense? Ukrainians don't count because they are Europeans, Christians, and culturally very similar to the Poles. So, as we've said, they're no use to the globalist agenda, which seeks to undermine national identity. And never mind that these Ukrainians are also people, many of them with small children. As the journalist Corrado Formigli might put it: whether they're trying to save themselves or not, they're of no use. It's worth noting how for Eastern European countries, which have always fought fiercely to preserve their identity and sovereignty (also because they've *really* had to fight to defend it), there are no distinctions between Right and Left on this point. Take, for instance, the stance of the former Slovak Prime Minister Robert Fico (his name may be similar to the Five-Star Roberto Fico, but their affinities end there). Despite being a prominent member of the European Socialist Party, Fico has consistently argued that Slovakia, as a small Christian country, cannot accept mass Muslim immigration without sacrificing its identity.

This whole discussion becomes even more relevant to Italy for a rarely acknowledged reason: we have around sixty million people of Italian origin scattered around the globe—a "second Italy." Many of these Italians dream of returning to their motherland, yet we continue to overlook them. I believe it makes sense to argue that if we do need immigration, we should first prioritize the return of those of Italian origin, as their arrival would not pose integration problems.

And what about the Christians? Christianity remains the most persecuted religion in the world, facing widespread and aggressive hostility.

Why do we pretend not to see this reality? Why should we, as the cradle of Christianity, not offer refuge to those who share this heritage—especially since they cannot easily find asylum in Islamic countries, where they are often marginalized or outright persecuted?

* * *

I can already hear the cries of the opportunist champions of doing good—those who are lenient with the bad and ruthless with the good—reacting to my "thorny" opinions. They'll likely assign me the modern equivalent of a large scarlet letter sewn onto my chest, screaming, "Racist! Xenophobe! Shame on you!"

Really? Are we truly trivializing complex topics like these, which I present with logic and reason, by resorting to superficial, decontextualized accusations? If we want to talk about racism, then let's talk about it. I have nothing to fear from that conversation either.

Let's start from a simple observation: only someone ignorant can be a racist, and I don't consider myself ignorant. Far from it. I'll go further and say this: it's not in my nature to hate anyone. The idea that I could hate someone based on their physical traits—such as the color of their skin—is absurd. On the contrary, I know what it feels like to be hated. From a young age, I've been on the receiving end of hostility because of my ideas. My views—alternative to the mainstream and unwelcome to the "progressive" culture of my opponents—have made me more than just an *adversary*, an *enemy* in their eyes. For these self-proclaimed enlightened arbiters of truth, I should never have been allowed to speak freely. Expressing my opinions or organizing initiatives has always caused scandal and indignation among those who were raised to see me as something "nonhuman"—someone unworthy of civil discourse. Ironically, these are the same people who enjoy parading slogans like "let's keep it human" while implicitly labeling anyone who disagrees with them as animals and nonhumans. Paradoxically, this happens in good faith. After all, if you truly believe that the person standing before you embodies every form of hatred—responsible for exterminating millions of Jews in gas chambers, planting bombs in train stations, enslaving Black people, and abusing and raping women (as some radical feminists might claim), a woman on the Right is both an accomplice to and a victim of her male oppressors—then of course you'd feel justified in treating that person with disdain. I, too, would detest myself and fight with every means at my disposal if such a description were even remotely true.

And I would indeed feel deep disdain for myself if, as some shamelessly claimed, my ideas and battles were somehow linked to the murder of Willy Monteiro Duarte. On the evening of September 6, 2020, Willy, a twenty-one-year-old chef from Cape Verde, lost his life after being savagely beaten. His only "crime" was attempting to defend his friend who had become the target of a group of local thugs. They punched and kicked him to death, simply because he refused to look the other way. Willy was a young man who could not remain indifferent in the face of injustice. For this reason, in my eyes, he is a hero—especially at a time when indifference reigns supreme.

When I read the news of his death, I cried, thinking of him and, as always in such tragedies, of his mother. She had raised him with sound values, as a man of integrity, only to have the love of her life stolen away. I tell Willy's story because he deserves to be remembered, and because neither he nor his family deserved for his death to be exploited.

When the details of that dreadful incident came out in the news, and I saw the images of the stereotypical violent, macho, tattooed cokeheads, the usual superficial and irresponsible people tried to turn the story into a political agenda. Those animals were labeled as "young fascists," and indirectly—or directly—the narrative took shape that the murder of a young boy of color by those brutes was the result of the "culture of hate" supposedly championed by me and others. I felt deep shame—not for myself, but for a political class willing to exploit anything for its own purposes, to distort reality just so it could be used to their advantage. Willy did not die because he was a person of color. Willy died because he was a good kid. His killers didn't take his life because of his race, but because they were high on cocaine, in an Italy where cocaine has become a status symbol. And allow me to add: those four vile individuals who beat Willy to death have nothing to do with the culture of the Right—unlike what a few idiots have tried to claim. In fact, they don't share our ideas at all. They are the offspring of a whole other "culture" that promotes models like Gomorra to rake in millions, while turning a blind eye to the spread of drugs. (In fact, two of Willy's killers already had records for selling drugs. If our proposals had been accepted, they would not have been free that night to commit this atrocity.) These killers are also the product of the "role models" cherished by certain "progressive" artists—or "communists with a Rolex," as we might call them—who equate success with the horsepower of a car, the price of a handbag, the number of partners you have, and how many drugs you consume. Without fear of being contradicted, the Right has always fought against these false myths of success. So maybe someone else should bear the responsibility for what happened to poor Willy and his family.

When the spotlight on Willy's story began to fade—as it always does, when people's lives and tragedies are treated like disposable tissues—I called Willy's mother to offer my personal condolences. I will never forget her frail tone that expressed her desperation. I will never forget the composed dignity with which she answered me. She greeted me with the words, "It is an honor to hear from you," proof that at least she, Lucia, had not fallen for the hateful accusations that had been leveled against me.

* * *

No, I cannot hate foreigners, those who are different, or those who are unlike me because I am naturally curious, drawn to the world, to other cultures, and to the richness of diversity. In fact, it is precisely my desire to safeguard the value of "diversity" that underpins one of my greatest aversions to the Left. They are obsessed with underscoring the value of "equality," a word that, in practice, often masks their intent to make everyone and everything the same.

The Racism of Progress

I've been accused of racism since day one. It is screamed at you to silence you, to shut down the conversation before it even begins. Along with the word "fascist"—whose intimidating and defamatory power it has now replaced and absorbed—"racist" is the epithet used to discredit you. It is designed to render you unworthy of respect or even the most basic acknowledgment. Obviously, if you're a racist, then your arguments are deemed irrelevant, unworthy of consideration, time, or evaluation. The only thing that matters is to condemn them. Even better, they think they can prevent you from expressing those arguments in the first place—using preemptive censorship to silence not only you but all those of your "race."

The champion of this strategy is Rula Jebreal, the Palestinian journalist with Israeli and Italian citizenship who we often see pontificating on Italian TV shows. In every debate we've had, without fail, she eventually comes out with the line, "I realize it's hard to look at a woman of color like me." Once, I turned to the audience and blurted out, "I'm starting to think this nutcase has got it in for me." It wasn't a tactic on my part—I was sincerely thrown for a loop by that accusation. Not only because, as I've said hundreds of times, I don't have a racist bone in my body, but also because the image Jebreal accuses me of harboring is, ironically, the one she projects to avoid engaging me on equal footing.

I'll admit, I've found myself struggling with Jebreal—not because of the color of her skin, but because it's difficult to have a meaningful discussion with someone that shallow. What I see in Rula Jebreal is far removed from the victim she portrays herself to be. She is a beautiful woman, comfortably ensconced in the financial elite—qualities that likely contribute to her media credibility—but she's incapable of holding her own in a debate of any depth.

From my days in student assemblies to the Parliament and TV talk shows, I feel as though I've spent my entire life defending myself, countering accusations, explaining, and demonstrating that racism has nothing to do with me.

It has been this way for us forever. But, on reflection, it's been a good thing. Constantly confronting accusations of racism—and dealing with the real racists who approach us, convinced they'll find like-minded people in our midst—has pushed our group to dig deeper. It has forced us to understand and to craft ever more rational and convincing arguments. Especially because, on this issue, the Right always finds itself at a disadvantage, burdened by the terrible weight of history—the legacy of anti-Semite and Nazi-Fascist persecutions cast a long shadow.

Practically speaking, this means starting from the premise that you must prove you're not a racist *in spite of* being on the Right. For the past seventy-five years, the collective imagination has tied racism almost exclusively to one political and cultural side. If you're on the Right, you're automatically assumed to be racist, intolerant, and xenophobic. At the same time, the narrative assumes that other political cultures are somehow entirely immune from this infection of the spirit. In the simplistic storytelling that has dominated since the postwar years, racism was supposedly born with Mussolini's Blackshirts, later imitated and followed by Hitler's Brownshirts, and then both were vanquished by the *good guys* in the world who fought against the *bad guys* in the battle against racism and totalitarianism. Before this and elsewhere, it's as if racism had never existed. But is that how things really played out?

This one-sided narrative is the product of the cultural hegemony that progressive ideology has imposed since the end of the war. Over several decades, this has shaped a European and Western discourse on racism centered around the theme of "repression." Traumatized by the horrors of the Holocaust, Western culture, *wanting to be racist no longer*, has attempted to absolve itself so it can claim *never having been so*, offloading the full weight of this terrible legacy solely to the Nazis. However, it's an incontrovertible fact that racism was deeply embedded in our civilization for at least two or three centuries (with some exceptions). Today, this historical reality is resurfacing in ways that are sometimes grotesque—such as the defacing of statues of Winston Churchill or Christopher Columbus).

When you analyze and really dig deep, not only do you find that racism is present in all "developed" nations—those which, not coincidentally, once classified others as "underdeveloped," before politically correct language sweetened the term. Moreover, racism is not exclusive to any political and religious culture. It even exists in places where it is most vehemently denied—within the enlightened and progressivist philosophy that forms the backbone of modern left-wing culture. The Right is nothing by comparison. In fact, conservative thought, which is closely tied to Christianity and the unitary conception of the human race, provides a bulwark against discriminatory and xenophobic tendencies. Christianity's core teaching—that all people are equally children of the same God and equally loved by him—offers an inescapable and categorical equalitarianism that is inherently opposed to racism.

Marco Marsilio, the current chairman of Brothers of Italy for the Abruzzo Region and a philosophy graduate, explains this well in his book *Razzismo: Un'origine illuminista*. Consider some examples: Social Democratic Sweden sterilized women deemed "socially useless" until 1975. In the United States, the *Dictionary of Races* was used to control immigration until the 1950s, with devastating consequences. (There's even a well-known anecdote about Albert Einstein filling out an immigration questionnaire and writing "human" under the category of race.) This policy denied visas to thousands of Polish, Ukrainian, Russian, and Baltic Jews, leaving them trapped in Europe on the eve of war. And until the 1960s, Black Americans in the United States were forced to sit at the back of the bus, were barred from many colleges, and were often denied service in restaurants. The British Empire fired on unarmed Indian protesters led by Mahatma Gandhi in their struggle for independence. During World War I, Anglo-French colonial troops were notoriously sent as "cannon fodder" to face enemy fire first. The European colonial powers only granted independence to their colonies after years of bloody revolts. Until the 1930s in Europe and North America, human zoos drew crowds to see families of "savages" placed in cages alongside monkeys and orangutans to demonstrate the "missing link." Say what you want, but it's clear that these countries didn't wage war against Germany to combat racism. It was, in some ways, a fortunate accident of history that, in the aftermath of war, humanity emerged more aware of the tragic consequences of racism.

Society began to reflect on the issue, driven by the shock of racist atrocities. Slowly but surely, the walls and barriers that divided men, cultures, and religions were torn down.

The world would indeed be much simpler if "absolute evil" actually existed and was confined to the historical period of Nazi-Fascist ideology. If that were the case, all we'd need to do is condemn and combat that ideology, and the problem of racism would be solved. Unfortunately, racism is a much broader phenomenon, and denying its pervasive dimensions does nothing to counter this societal disease. The road ahead is long, but we must continue on it—steadily, without shortcuts, without hesitation, but also without the distortion and excessive guilt that often turn "racism" into something it is not.

* * *

Take, for example, the time when Brothers of Italy was accused of racism because it was the first political party in Italy to raise the alarm about the Nigerian mafia—a brutal criminal organization involved in drug dealing, prostitution, human trafficking, and macabre practices like juju rituals and, allegedly, ritual cannibalism.

The Nigerian mafia is, in fact, Italy's "fifth mafia," ignored for too long by the media and underestimated by institutions—precisely out of fear of being accused of racism. The reluctance of the media to confront this issue is striking, as though discussing a criminal organization made up of migrants, which has expanded operations and planted itself in certain parts of Italy, might embarrass the advocates crying *"Refugees welcome here."* These are the same people who spend their days writing articles to convince Italians that mass illegal immigration is a choice that can only bring benefits. The writer Roberto Saviano, who built his career on exposing the Italian mafia and the Camorra, once found evidence of organized crime everywhere but has been quiet. (Although, given the court sentences, it seems he has limited himself to cobbling together work carried out by other people.) Saviano was silent for many years on the

Nigerian mafia, and it was not until 2019 that the anti-mafia champion timidly mentioned this phenomenon. However, he still hasn't dedicated a single one of his precious literary or journalistic contributions to the subject. It seems unlikely we'll ever see a TV series focused on this scourge. Maybe Saviano is waiting for someone else to write an article or book on the subject from which to draw inspiration. For the time being, there's not much around, except for a book I cowrote with Alessandro Meluzzi and Valentina Mercurio. Perhaps he could start there. Or better yet, he could start in Castel Volturno—a city in Campania, the very region Saviano hails from.

I have been to Castel Volturno many times, once a jewel of a town, now ruined. Its mayor, Luigi Petrella, is a member of Brothers of Italy. Known as a "città nastro" (ribbon city) because it stretches along the coast on both sides of Via Domiziana, Castel Volturno was once a favored holiday destination for the wealthy of Caserta and Naples. Over the decades, however, it has become a territory where half the population lives as part of an invisible mass. Those fifteen miles of coastline have become the headquarters of one of the most ruthless criminal organizations in the world: the Nigerian mafia. Walking through the streets lined with buildings overlooking the sea—once vacation homes but now crumbling and abandoned—you encounter a forgotten humanity. The decay is overwhelming and impossible to ignore. Castel Volturno is an absolute no-man's-land: men working in the fields for mere euros, drug dealing, and criminal activity at all hours of the day, and places like the Connection House, where women—often minors—live as slaves, forced into prostitution.

During a meeting in the Prefecture, I had the chance to speak with one of those women—one of the few who had the courage to report her pimp and to escape from that hell. Even now, she lives in constant fear that her former captors will make her pay for her freedom. The story she told me, with a mix of pride and terror on her face, could be made into a movie. She hadn't come to Italy by choice, but by force, driven by her love for her child. Her tormentors had cast a voodoo spell (the juju I mentioned before) on her son, and to save his life, she was told she had to pay them

25,000 euros. There was only one way to earn that kind of money: travel to Italy and sell her body. For years, she endured inhumane conditions: battered, raped, forgotten. Her body and heart were devastated, but her mind remained steadfastly focused on saving her son. Eventually, she met an Italian man who helped her rescue her son and escape her captors. Now, she is slowly piecing her life back together, and she says she feels content, hoping to help the many—too many—other women trapped in the same situation. Don't the do-gooders here in Italy know about this? Have they ever spoken to these victims? Where are the feminists? Are they too preoccupied with trivial battles—like insisting people say "capa treno" (female train conductor) instead of "capo treno" (male train conductor, the traditional term)—instead of joining the fight against these horrible injustices? Why do they pretend not to see what's happening? Perhaps it's because confronting this reality would force them to reevaluate how frivolous their priorities are?

Regardless, we've been fighting this fight for years—even without their help. We've even formalized a proposal to ensure that when these slavers are caught, their crimes against these women are charged as "enslavement" rather than "exploitation of prostitution," the latter carrying lighter penalties.

As I listened to this woman's story, her suffering brought to mind a poem by Charles Baudelaire—something I had read many years ago. I've always had a passion for the Decadent movement, and although my favorite Decadent poet has always been Arthur Rimbaud, I find that Baudelaire wrote some of the most extraordinary poems in the history of literature. One of these, "To a Woman of Malabar" (Malabar being a region in India), ends with these haunting lines:

> Happy child, why do you long to see France
> our suffering, and over-crowded land,
> and trusting your life to the sailors, your friends,
> say a fond goodbye to your dear tamarinds??
> ... shivering under the snow and hail,

how you'd pine for your leisure, sweet and free,
... if you'd to glean supper amongst our vile harms,
selling the scent of exotic charms,
sad pensive eyes searching our fog-bound sleaze,
for the lost ghosts of your coconut-trees!

How can these lines, written almost two centuries ago, still be so relevant today? What is human about any of this?

* * *

The fight to protect migrant women forced into sexual slavery is just one of the many battles I and Brothers of Italy have waged in defense of Africans in these past few years. Among these issues, however, there is one I consider the most significant of all.

Whenever the topic of immigration arises, the mainstream narrative is always the same: we have a "Christian" duty to welcome African refugees fleeing war. But if we attempt to probe deeper, we are immediately silenced with the effective, yet hollow, cry of "Racist!" But I'm not buying that. For years, I've sought to understand the dynamics at play. I've asked myself: What wars are we talking about? What are these young people really escaping from? What drives them to leave their countries? Why is the continent of Africa so poor?

I discovered something that confirmed my convictions. Africa is not a poor continent. Quite the opposite—on paper, it is potentially the richest continent in the world, with vast reserves of raw materials: oil, diamonds, gold, precious metals and rare elements ... the list goes on. So why, if the land is so rich, are its people so poor? Because the land is exploited by foreign powers, who extract everything, leaving only devastation behind. This exploitation thrives amid global indifference and the complicity of corrupt local governments. And who exactly are these foreign exploiters? There are several, but chief among them are certain European nations—most notably France. Get it? We pretend to be benevolent because we welcome those fleeing to escape the consequences of our own exploitation, only to abandon them at the margins of our societies. But rather than fill Europe with Africans, wouldn't it make more sense to free Africa from the grip of certain Europeans?

Curiously, this story remains untold—its paradox and shame ignored by almost everyone. Everyone, that is, except Brothers of Italy.

Over the course of the past two years, we organized a highly attended meeting at the Chamber of Deputies to shed light on the CFA franc, a colonial-era currency through which France continues to exert control over many African countries. The event featured young African patriots—individuals who have long fought for the freedom of their land. Through their firsthand accounts, we revealed how the very European nation whose president, Emmanuel Macron, once described Italy as *"dégueulasse"* (essentially disgusting) for refusing to allow yet another migrant ship to land on its coastline, continues to mint currency outside its borders to control the economies of various African countries—fourteen to be exact. The raw materials buried in Africa's soil are coveted by the whole world, and France's control of their exportation is the same as exercising a true seigniorage over wealth.

Let's take the example of Niger, a former French colony in the Sahara region, and a key crossroads for migratory routes from Central Africa toward Libya. Niger is one of the world's richest countries for uranium, a raw material essential for nuclear power plants. Since 1957, French state-owned companies have been extracting uranium from Niger. Today, thanks to Niger's uranium, France is able to meet a third of its national energy needs. Yet, in 2021, over 80 percent of Nigeriens still had no access to electricity. The situation in the villages near the uranium mines is even more dire. Residents are forced to drink radioactive water and farm land contaminated by acids used in the extraction process. Niger also has the highest illiteracy rate in the world, and just 5 percent of its population has access to the internet. Their life expectancy is among the lowest in the world.

* * *

I could share countless stories like these, ones you won't find in the major newspapers or on TV because the situation in Niger is just a small glimpse of a much larger and unprecedented exploitation. But there's more to this story: while Europe, the United States, and the developed world debate "energy transition" and the push for a green economy, few people know what's happening behind the scenes of this new paradigm. There are few who realize that without Africa, there could be no energy transition, no green economy. How many people have heard of indium, gallium, cerium, lanthanum, or promethium? These metals and rare elements are indispensable to the production of modern technologies and are essential for the development of the green economy.

We never wonder how electric car batteries, solar panels, or wind turbines are manufactured. The same goes for all the other tech we use: cell phones, tablets, TVs, computers. Everything is made thanks to the metals and rare minerals that Africa is so rich in. And yet, the paradox remains: these precious natural elements, which are the "new oil" in our global energy economy, represent its ruin.

The world leader in extracting and transforming these metals into technology is China. For decades, Beijing has had its sights firmly set on the Dark Continent. The Chinese dictatorship has offered enormous loans to African nations to build infrastructure—projects that primarily serve China's global trade routes. Many African countries have fallen into the Chinese debt trap, ceding control of their land and the underground resources to Beijing.

And so, Africa has become a gold mine fueling the Chinese empire, making the West more and more dependent on Chinese technology in pursuit of its energy transition.

The plundering of African resources not only deprives its people of their wealth but also exacerbates desertification, fuels tribal conflicts into which Islamic fundamentalism often creeps, and drives migratory flows that benefit neither Africa nor Europe. No one willingly leaves their homeland, their family, and their roots. If young Africans had a future in their own countries, they would never abandon them. As African Cardinal

Robert Sarah wrote in a recent book: "We need to do everything that is necessary for men to be able to remain in the countries where they were born." The connection to one's roots, traditions, and identity is intrinsic to human nature. The fight by young Africans for sovereignty and independence is fundamentally a fight to protect their identity. This reality leaves the Left floundering, as they resort to their usual do-gooder rhetoric to "solve" Africa's problems. In truth, their platitudes only perpetuate the exploitative systems that are strangling the continent.

In 2019, I attended an event on safety in Ferrara. Just days earlier, several Nigerian gangs had caused a massive riot that had transformed the GAD district—an area of three different districts plagued by rising crime—into a tinderbox. Carrying a large Italian flag, we marched through the district to symbolize the need for the state to reclaim control of these territories. At one point, we saw a group of Africans in the distance, waiting for us and calmly holding the flag of Cameroon. A reporter approached me and said: "Doesn't it bother you that these people feel threatened by you?" I didn't respond, uncertain of what would happen next. We continued walking until we passed the group. A young man came up to me dressed in bright, traditional clothing that is worn in many of these countries, and said to me: "Onorevole Meloni, may we speak?" To which I replied: "Of course, please go on." But instead of protests, there was silence all around me. He looked at me and said, "We are Cameroonian patriots. We want to thank you because you and your party are the only ones condemning the exploitation of our country. Please help us explain to the Italian people that we don't want to come to Europe. We don't want to be forced to flee our country. We want to stay in our homes. Please help us free our nation." They handed me a megaphone, and I found myself haranguing the crowd, telling the story of our battle against colonial France, surrounded by reporters who were shocked and angry because they now had to rewrite all the articles they'd already prepared, to instead describe Italian and Cameroonian patriots embracing.

Europe must completely rethink its relationship with Africa. It needs to take a step back, abandon its neocolonialist ambitions, and embrace a path of genuine cooperation—one that fosters mutual prosperity. Only through this approach can Chinese dominance be curtailed. A free and prosperous Africa is crucial to redressing the global balance.

We can play a pivotal role in this by drawing on the fruitful and pragmatic teachings of Enrico Mattei, who made ENI (the National Fuel Trust) and Italy great by striking deals with major oil producers—a choice that likely cost him his life. His model for Italy is far removed from the predatory ones of other Western nations, and should now be implemented in this crucial phase in history. Africa is the world's greatest reserve of "new oil." Ensuring that Africans can benefit from their own riches is essential to inaugurating a new era of global prosperity and freedom. An Italian model for Africa—it's not just an idea. It could become the greatest challenge in the coming decades if our nation could only forge a clear foreign policy, and if the ruling classes could finally find the courage to seek the truth rather than hiding behind convenient labels.

I AM AN ITALIAN

It Didn't All Go Well

I had never been to the Festival di Sanremo, a song contest held annually in the town of Sanremo in Liguria since 1951, but I've always watched it on TV. Some years I didn't miss a single minute of it, while other years I watched it without paying much attention. I think it's safe for me to say that the appeal of Italy's most important national popular event has always been there, drawing me in, even though my favorite singers have seldom taken part in it.

My life, like every one of our lives, has its own soundtrack. And in my case the collection of songs is a packed one. That's because I love all kinds of music: from opera to heavy metal, from the most sentimental pop to the so-called introspective music, like that of Marcello De Angelis or of the Aurora, which accompanied me throughout my teenage years. And it might come as a surprise, but of all the singer-songwriters it's the music and lyrics composed by Francesco Guccini that I know best. In fact, I used the lyrics from "Cirano" to end my speech in which I announced I was running for leader of Youth Action. For some of the press it was a surprise, for the audience listening to me it was not.

How could I, like others in my political community, ever remain indifferent to the words of the music of Fabrizio De André, or of other great names in Italian music, however integral it may be to the Left in the twentieth century.

You can easily imagine how sad and bitter I felt when I heard the revised version of "Bella ciao" sung by Guccini in which he used the names Giorgia Meloni, Salvini, and Berlusconi, accompanied by the invitation that we be "taken away" by the partisans in 2020.

It reminded me of how I felt the time when I discovered that the Santa Claus who had just rung the doorbell was none other than my tipsy fool of an uncle. I pretended I hadn't really recognized him, although it made me truly sad to think of the gifts he had brought for me.

And so, for as long as I am allowed to, I will continue to sing "Cirano" and "Cristoforo Colombo," because I am convinced they are among the most wonderful and profound lyrics in Italian music.

* * *

But let's go back to the Sanremo Music Festival. It was February 17, 2011, and I remember that the evening was devoted to the 150th anniversary of the Unification of Italy. Roberto Begnini entered the stage at the Teatro Ariston riding a white horse and waving an Italian flag. He had come to present a critical interpretation of the lyrics of the Italian anthem, "Fratelli d'Italia," which means Brothers of Italy. Soon it would become the name of our party, so it was a sort of premonition.

I will never forget the following fifty minutes with Benigni on the stage. I, like every Italian who was lucky enough to watch the performance, was overwhelmed with a wave of emotions.

There were many phrases about Prime Minister Berlusconi, some of them more unpleasant than others, but the history of the Risorgimento told in the most popular theater in Italy triggered an extraordinary feeling of belonging.

"An unparalleled greatness, steeped in youth. . . . You will never know how many young people died for us. . . . They died for their country so we could live for our country." Benigni was right to underscore this fact several times, because no world congress, no enlightened monarch, no great statistician, none of them were responsible for the creation of a unified and free Italy. The people were the ones who had taken on this important task, particularly its young warrior poets. Willing to die if it meant transforming an ancient dream into a new nation.

"Italy is the only country in the world where first culture was born and then the nation." That was another one of the most beautiful and truest statements that Begnini made that night. To the extent that I believe we can safely say that Italian's own flag is not the offspring of some foreign concession, but rather of the prophetic lines written one of the world's greatest poets. "olive-crowned above a veil of white /appeared to me a lady / beneath a green mantle, / dressed in the color of living flame." These are the words Dante Alighieri pronounces upon seeing Beatrice, the love of his life.

Being a part of this beauty is a privilege, but it is also a serious task for those in Italy who are involved in politics. Unfortunately, over the years the sentiment of love of country has either been mocked or denied, especially in the aftermath of World War II. I believe this was unjust not only for all the young men who died for Italy, but also counterproductive for a coherent and shared development of the Italian state.

* * *

"We have made Italy, now we must make Italians." These famous words attributed to Massimo d'Azeglio represent the critique we receive the most: the fact that we are not united as a people, and as a result are a country where everyone thinks for themselves. But the reality is much more complex than that. There is a great contradiction in the Italian people: they have been conscious of themselves since much before the birth of the Italian state, and yet they often appear detached with respect to their country. At times there have been doubts about the Italians' sense and feeling of national belonging. This has occurred historically: for instance, before the Risorgimento, when Klemens Von Metternich wrote that Italy was just "a geographical expression." And Italians themselves, every now and again, believe in this definition, which substantially says that

Italy does not exist as a nation, and that its sole homogeneity is local and communal. Except for when they change their minds: when faced with History, with a capital "H," and its great challenges, they prove in the first person that they have a strong sense of national community.

Proof of this can be found, besides in the Risorgimento, in the trenches of World War I, where the blood of all Italians flowed together and became one indissoluble thing. This was also proven by the heroes of the battles of El-Alamein, and we are often reminded of this by Italians who find themselves in the most unthinkable places at the most unthinkable times. A case in point was the young Fabrizio Quattrocchi, who was born in Sicily and had grown up in Genoa. Taken hostage in Iraq where he was working as a security contractor, he was murdered by his cowardly kidnappers, but not before trying to pull off his hood and shouting "I'll show you how an Italian dies."

* * *

It's not true that Italians are incapable of being altruists when times are hard. So much so that those who read this book will recognize themselves as the protagonists of stories of courage and solidarity. How can we forget those who rushed to the earthquake zones of Amatrice in 2016, Modena in 2012, l'Aquila in 2009, Colfiorito, Umbria in 1997, and, farther back in time, Irpinia, Friuli, Belice in Sicily, not to mention the many other places hit hard by Nature's force? And how can we forget the many Italians who came forward in Vermicino, in 1981, to try to rescue Alfredino Rampi, a six-year-old boy who had fallen into an artesian well and was stuck there until his tragic death? During the tragedies that have affected our country in different ways, organized emergency services have often been lacking, but those who were ready to lend a hand have always been there. The ones who, having found out that other Italians are in trouble, have taken action, bringing water, food, blankets, and hands to remove the rubble. Some, many, have raced to the scene holding the Italian flag, as if to say: "Thanks to this symbol we are all brothers, and so here I am, this is where I belong."

The most recent dramatic events are told in photographs, in videos, in the reports of those who were there and remember what it was like to dig through the rubble of those destroyed homes to find someone who hadn't been able to get out, or the symbols of an everyday life lost: a toy, a book, a photograph.

Stories of remarkable solidarity, with a list that is wonderfully and dramatically long.

We were a nation just forty years of age when on December 28, 1908, over eight thousand people died in an earthquake in which Messina, Reggio Calabria, and the other towns on either side of the Strait were razed. It was an apocalypse.

And what about the rest of Italy? Spontaneous committees to collect funding and "passeggiate di beneficenza" (charity walks). It was an incredible solidarity effort.

Just seven years later, on January 13, 1915, the earth shook again. In Avezzano, in the Abruzzo region.

Thirty thousand dead. And again more solidarity and lots of volunteers rushing to dig through the rubble. One of them was Nazario Sauro. Yes, the very same Istrian hero I quoted before. What did an Istrian sailor and an Abruzzese shepherd have in common? Perhaps very little, certainly not their dialect, but there was something they shared and it sufficed: being Italians. That is why the Istrians went there. And they were not the only ones.

In the same letter I mentioned before, which Sauro sent to his son before dying, he wrote: "The country will come to your aid." It is there, in Abruzzo, and then at the front during World War I, that we become a nation, that we are united.

Those moments of solidarity don't end here. In addition to the more recent ones, which I have already mentioned, I cannot help but think of the "mud angels" who in Florence (the same epithet would be used for Genoa and Parma in 2014) helped to rebuild the city immersed in the mud that the 1966 flood had left behind. Works of art were saved, books, invaluable cultural records. Because that is who we are. Perhaps distracted, perhaps lost in our particular interests, but ready to come to people's aid without thinking twice.

* * *

In other words, Italians have always demonstrated with their actions just how strong their sense of community is: from north to south. This is not the anomaly. So what is it then? It is what is witnessed, with respect to the normality of other great countries, with a disaffection vis-à-vis the country and its institutions. That's right. Because, unfortunately, Italians have little faith in the state. This is due to a series of manifest historical issues that have made it so that their trust has occasionally been betrayed. Perhaps it's the legacy of being the nation of a thousand bell towers. Or perhaps it's because we are the children of a great empire that crumbled, as if the most important part of our path as a people were behind and not ahead of us. We Italians feel this syndrome of a "great past" more than many others due to the greatness of the history of Rome for all of humanity. Then came the Unification of Italy: a crucial turning point in our history, but also a difficult passage because it came about more as an annexation of the southern territories to the Kingdom of the Savoy than as a harmonious composition of a single country. And this in part contributed to fueling people's mistrust before the authority of the state and its ruling elites. Thia idea was crystallized by Giuseppe Tomasi di Lampedusa, one of Italy's greatest writers, in the 1958 novel *The Leopard*, where he writes: "if we want things to stay as they are, things will have to change."

And in the early twentieth century many things did change. The rapid changes in the liberal state that was very distant from universal suffrage, in which only a limited portion of the aristocratic and bourgeois population was represented; the advent of fascism and then the birth of a Republic rising from the ashes of the regime; and all in just twenty years' time. It would be like experiencing these ongoing changes from 2000 to the present time: a state that changed completely as many as three times, disavowing almost everything that came before. Including the move from the monarchy to the Republic. Then, of course, we had a bright phase in the postwar period—the one known as the "Italian economic miracle"—followed, however, by a long stormy period determined by the worst of the First Republic. It was precisely that moment in history that marked a rift between the people and the government.

The result of this is a country that has a strong sense of national community, but that deeply distrusts its own rulers, the perception—alas, often justified—being that those who govern are not doing so in the name of the community, its good, and its future. A vicious circle is generated according to which, if the commander is inadequate, poor, and totally indifferent, then the infantry feel they are free to do whatever they want. That is Italy's challenge: to try to solve its great contradiction, having a ruling class and a state that are good enough for the Italian people and for the strong feeling of unity that the Italians have shown so often.

* * *

It won't be easy to restore the faith of the Italians in the institutions. All too often, their solidarity has ended up in tatters. For years. Not just in a figurative sense. Why then, are we forced today, as Brothers of Italy, to fight in Parliament to destine the resources of the Recovery Fund to the areas hit by earthquakes in 2009 and 2016 as well? Why do we see, like on too many other occasions, makeshift housing, some of it covered in snow, and the inhabitants desperate for help that could restore stability and a future, but that never arrives?

Maybe we don't feel like a people because, sometimes, the state has no respect for its people. And we aren't a people because there are some who don't want that.

When the earthquake of 1915 flattened Avezzano, the greatest intellectual and poet at the time, Gabriele D'Annunzio, said that the Italians rushing to help symbolized an Italy that could be better. He added that the books kids were reading in elementary school said the same thing. The children's novel on social issues and patriotic themes *Cuore* by Edmondo De Amicis is a perfect example of this.

That Italy was united because culture, history, and education encouraged us all to be so.

What about today? How many movies tell the story of the volunteers working for the Civil Protection Department? Wouldn't the story of two such volunteers falling in love as they save lives be great? Wouldn't it be moving to watch a university student as they discover their place in the world while rushing to help strangers that are, just like them, Italians?

But they don't make movies like that.

This is because for too many years culture has been in the hands of a nationless Left, the party that sold our identity to make us weaker and less capable of being a people.

Nonetheless, in spite of decades of anti-Italian propaganda, there are still some who believe in our country. Because, after all, the only lesson that counts is that of a song we are all familiar with, our national anthem, which reminds us each and every day that: "United, in God's name, who can defeat us?"

* * *

We are the sons and daughters of our history. Of all of our history. Like every country, the path we took was complex, more articulated and complicated than we would care to mention. I know I'm stepping into a mine field, but I am not afraid to emphasize yet again that I don't worship fascism. On the other hand, I know the name and the history of each of the young people who lost their lives in the 1970s on the altar of anti-fascism. Sometimes they had written an essay at school, and for this reason were condemned to death. This violence, both cultural and physical, has certainly generated in me a firm rebellion against political anti-fascism. I cannot deny that. But that is where my relationship with fascism ends. Truly, I would not know what else to add. That is better done by a historian who wants to analyze the features and impact on society of fascism a century ago.

And if they asked for my opinion on the infamy of the racial laws, I could only reply by describing my own personal feelings inside the Yad Vashem Memorial in Jerusalem. Better still, after I left.

I visited it during an official trip to Israel, where I participated as a minister of the Italian government. I was welcomed with curiosity and respect by the Israeli authorities, even though I had wanted to visit a Palestinian refugee camp. The cold modernity of the museum building itself dedicated to the victims of the Holocaust would later seem to be at odds with the stifling atmosphere inside it. A horrendous tale made up of images, objects, sounds. The Hall of Names ends the museum tour and it is the very essence of this journey through memory. It consists of two cones, one suspended in the air, the other situated at the base, filled with water. Collected in that unique space are the faces and the names of those who lost their lives in that madness. There are thousands of pictures, stories, and it is as if they were all there looking at you, asking you what you are willing to do to prevent such a thing from ever happening again. This way, those victims live on eternally. Because the remarkable law of retaliation that is on display at the Yad Vashem means restoring life to the dead, restoring humanity to those who brutally lost it. Taking a backward path to do so: from number to name.

I believe that no one can leave that place the same person as when they entered.

I have continued to think about it for a long time, wondering how that horror was even possible. Genocide that is consumed in tiny steps, a little at a time. One act of cowardice after another. Eventually achieving the complete dehumanization of the victims through apparently innocent vignettes, offensive songs sung without thinking, gossip disseminated more and more insistently.

This was a low point for humanity, I have no doubt about that. And we cannot take for granted the idea that it will not happen again in the future, somewhere on the planet, in spite of the greater knowledge that the world can more easily draw from today. The persecution of the Jews was not carried out in ignorance: it was supported by intellectuals, philosophers, writers. Especially in Germany, which at the time represented a high point in economy, thinking, science, and music in the world. But this was true of Italy as well, during fascism, even though many of the protagonists of Mussolini's rise were Jews, as were many of the Italian heroes in World War I. This is something I have never been able to understand, and I believe it was the same for many Italians at the time.

In the pathway behind the Children's Memorial of the Yad Vashem, there's a tree dedicated to Giorgio Perlasca. Farther ahead there's a whole forest where ten thousand trees were planted, symbolizing the lives of the Jews he saved in Hungary. Perlasca was not just a fervent supporter of fascism, a Blackshirt, he was also a protagonist of the war on Ethiopia and a volunteer in the Spanish Civil War at General Francisco Franco's side. That is where he learned Spanish, which allowed him to pretend he was an Iberian general consul, saving millions of lives, putting his own life at risk. The paradox surrounding the shrewd, courageous miracle that Perlasca carried out is that it would have slipped away, lost in the oblivion of human events, if it had depended on his reluctance or on the national anti-fascist chronicles. Today, if we (a small number) are aware of his story it is because the people saved in the ghetto of Budapest have never been able to forget him. Especially the women, the ones who would become mothers and grandmothers, with their thousands of children who would otherwise never have been born. Who in turn became parents themselves, and so on and so forth. It is impressive how an act of courage or of altruism can have such important consequences, even immortal ones. Just like the opposite, unfortunately.

And this is something within everyone's reach, at every turn in history. It is something that concerns us all.

* * *

During my trip to Israel, as well as to the United States, the United Kingdom, Ireland, Spain, Japan, South Africa, and Kenya, and to all the places that I was able to visit to meet so many people and enrich my life, I have had the great advantage to be able to speak directly with many of them, without needing an interpreter. It might seem odd that a person like me who is so closely tied to what she feels she belongs to is at the same time a foreign language enthusiast. Because the truth is that my life's dream was to work as an interpreter. When I graduated from high school, I tried to enroll in the school for interpreters and translators, but I had to give up on that idea because I couldn't afford it. The school was in Trieste, it was very expensive, and attendance was mandatory. I was already working to support myself and to help out my mother, so there was no way I could study there.

But the truth of the matter is that my love of languages isn't at all out of sync with respect to how important my Italian identity is to me. Rather, it is precisely because I believe in the indissoluble value of my identity that I am so curious about others. I love everything about foreign languages. The grammar, the etymology of the words, and, above all, the idiomatic phrases that tell you more about a population than its history will ever do.

I was lucky. I grew up substantially bilingual, speaking both Italian and Spanish fluently thanks to those weeks in the summer I spent with my father in the Canary Islands. I am convinced that a person who learns a second language when they are still a child will find it natural in the future to be good with idioms in a language that is not their own. I don't know whether it's true, but that is how it was for me. To think of it, I don't know all the grammar rules that allow me to speak English and Spanish pretty well, and to manage with French. I think that a person's foreign language skills are very similar to their musical ones. It's a question of sounds. Sometimes I don't know how to explain why a sentence in English sounds so right, but it just does. For me languages are mainly a question of having an ear for them, and, in consequence, training the ear in that sound. I convinced myself that there is no greater gift to a child than that of teaching them to speak a foreign language when they're still little. I'm not talking about the scientific knowledge of a foreign language, I'm talking from my own personal experience, so please take what I say with the benefit of the doubt. When you learn another language as a child, you automatically do the most valuable thing you can do to be able to speak in a foreign language: you can think in the language. This is why I have insisted that Gigì start learning English from a very young age.

Of course, I have always loved this subject, and like in all the things I love, I put a lot into it: my devotion, my head, my concentration. I enrolled in high school by myself, desperately looking for a diploma in languages, at a time when the linguistic high school was private. The only choice I had was to enroll in what at the time was the Amerigo Vespucci School—later renamed for the former mayor of Rome Ernesto Nathan—a secondary school where you trained in tourism. It was also an experimental school where your diploma would be in languages. Over the years, there are those who have criticized my studies. But I am proud to have made that choice. If you really want something you have to go and get it, even if it means making sacrifices or giving something up. So, after the first year, I found myself in a separate branch of the school on the Nomentana Road, which for someone who was living in Garbatella meant a total of three hours a day on the bus. It wasn't that bad. In the end, those long trips were a way for me to study. I never stopped listening to music on my yellow Walkman, and I learned a lot of my English that way. So, I can't say I learned languages thanks to school alone. Quite the opposite. A lot of what I learned was self-taught. I learned English because I wanted to understand the meaning of the lyrics in Michael Jackson's music, and in those of many others. I perfected my French because I wanted to read the works of the Decadent poets in the original language, since something always gets lost in the translation. As I said before, I needed Spanish to survive those summers spent in the Canary Islands. That's the way it was when I was a young girl, and that's the way it still is today. Because the trick with foreign languages is that you must never stop using them. Music is still today my main training method, but there are others as well: for example, when I see a foreign movie for the second time, I watch it in the original language, with English subtitles. I read all the lyrics of the songs I love, when I don't fully understand the meaning. Andrea lived in France for a few years when he was a boy, and sometimes we practice speaking French. At home, we speak English with my daughter's nanny, Betty (Ginevra adores her, and so do we, and I will never be able to thank her enough). Every chance I get to practice is a good one.

In the end, this youthful (and not so youthful) passion has proven to be an important key to many of the things I have done in my life. Especially as concerns building an international network of alliances and friendships that has recently led to my election to the prestigious post of chairman of the European Party of Conservatives and Reformists, which includes forty-four European and Western Conservative parties. Being able to speak directly in English on the phone, or send text messages in English to my British Tory colleagues, the Poles in the Law and Order Party, the Likud Israelis, the American Republicans or the Australian Liberals, and at the same time in Spanish with Santiago Abascal, the leader of Vox, which is the Spanish party that is Brothers of Italy's twin, has made it much simpler and faster to manage my role.

From this point of view, I am seen as a rare breed, along with very few others on the Italian political scene. Not just at home but abroad as well, where I have often been told "For an Italian you speak English well." Each time it has upset me, and I have replied irritably. But, unfortunately, that's the truth. There are still too few Italians who speak English adequately, and whether we like it or not, in our globalized world this serious gap diminishes the opportunities, especially for our young people. And the paradox is that while we are not concerned about just how much our kids are behind in this subject matter, at the same time we try to show off by abusing English loanwords, terms that do not belong to us, even going so far as to give English names to laws produced by the Parliament of the Italian Republic. Yet another expression of a certain ridiculousness, of hollow provincialism. As I see it, it should be the opposite. English should be mandatory and taught properly from kindergarten, but at the same time we should defend the use of the Italian language—whose importance is not even acknowledged in the constitution, another one of the battles waged by Brothers of Italy—at the highest levels of our institutions, and in Europe, where it isn't even one of the languages used for daily work purposes.

Of course, for many months, this, like many others, has seemed like a surreal battle. From early 2020 time has been as if suspended, swallowed up by the COVID-19 pandemic that has swept across the entire world and turned our lives upside down. In the West, Italy was the first to be hit hard and, once again, the Italians stepped up with discipline, love, and generosity that amazed the world.

* * *

Whether or not we accept this fact, COVID-19 was like being hit by a hurricane. It took away hundreds of thousands of lives, thousands of companies, jobs, and more or less all of the certainties we had. And when I say certainties, I don't mean just those of the person who had built a future for themselves with blood, sweat, and tears, only to see it all disappear in a few months' time. I am talking about the basic achievements of our civilization as well. At a certain point we realized that the things we had always taken for granted were actually not so at all. Democracy, for instance, which, because of COVID-19 as an excuse, was put on hold. President Mattarella, in announcing that he would ask Mario Draghi to form the new government, exploited the risk of contagion as the reason why it would be impossible to vote. As if the rights of the people to choose who their leader should be, especially at times such as these, was a practice of secondary importance. As if democracy were less vital than working, buying clothes, going to the hairdresser's, all the activities that in those days, in Italy, continued to be carried out.

And even more importantly, we cannot take our freedom for granted. The most fundamental human right, the one on which all other rights depend, crashed into the wall of the decree laws, the administrative acts with which Giuseppe Conte first, and Mario Draghi later, decided if and when we could leave the house, and where we could go when we did. We took for granted that it was inevitable, that the citizens' health had to be safeguarded at whatever cost, even at the cost of our freedom. But are we sure that one of these rights can completely be sacrificed on the altar of the other? I'm not sure it can. It is a reflection I owe to Maria Fida Moro, Aldo Moro's daughter, who at a certain point underwrote the appeal made by Brothers of Italy, at the time, against the liberticide tendency of Conte's infamous decrees and those of the Five-Star-Democratic Party executive that even suspended the constitutional principles. "That the government do its job as best it can, something that it has not known how to do so far, instead of tyrannizing the Italians," her letter reads. In it she reiterates our battles when she exhorts the people not to accept the fact that in the name of the containment of the epidemic an entire country has waived its fundamental freedoms. Because, while it is very true that a person will have no use for freedom if their life is compromised, it is worth remembering that the exact opposite is also true: free men are not willing to trade their freedom for their health. Because otherwise we would be saying—as Maria Fida Moro did—that our heroes, who sacrificed their lives for freedom, hadn't understood a thing.

Of course, it was necessary and understandable to take drastic measures at the beginning of the pandemic when we had no idea what we were dealing with. But the "philosophical" question must now be raised. For how long should a curfew be imposed on a free people? And what about the shuttering of public places, or the ban on friend and family gatherings, or needing permission to work and study? This exceptional state of affairs cannot last indefinitely, nor can the concept be accepted that when faced with an emergency citizens' freedom can be limited and democratic principles waived. The time has come to put an end to this "exceptional" parenthesis and go back to the rules of democratic life on which Western societies are founded. The state must lay down prescriptions of use to containing the epidemic, rules to follow, anti-contagion protocols. Individual protection, distancing, etc. It is up to the state to do this, and it is of use for it to do so. But it is not in the power of the government, nor of the state itself, to limit the fundamental freedom of its citizens indefinitely.

The third apparently obvious thing we had to give up was our social life. Spending time together, embracing, even kissing, in short, that ensemble of habits without which our relationships cannot truly be described as human. And if deprivation such as that can have a huge impact on the lives of adults, it is devastating when it comes to young people. Even before the pandemic we were concerned about the new generation's difficulty experiencing their relationships with others without having to filter them through a computer screen or a smartphone. I have two nieces, Vittoria and Rachele, respectively aged twelve and ten, whom I adore. They are beautiful, intelligent, brilliant. They are exactly what you would want your own kids to be like. I haven't been able to devote as much time to them as I would have liked to, so when we do spend some time together, I try to make up for my failings as an aunt. And yet it's not easy to enter their world, to understand it fully. It's not easy to interact according to our models. The impression I have when I observe Vitto and Rachi, as I call them, like many other young kids, is that whatever they need to tell each other that's important they prefer to do via chat, social media, and text messages. From their shelter. As if they didn't have the courage to be able to deal with their emotions by looking at each other eye to eye. Even when they're in the same room they'll talk to each other via their phones, in silence. And if I thought that this kind of behavior was cause for alarm before the pandemic, after over a year of sheltering inside, online learning, with many schools closed, gyms too, and no chance to go out and spend some time in the company of others, the risk involved is leading the younger generation to a point of no return. And the paradox is that instead of wondering why we allowed young people to be the ones to sacrifice the most during COVID-19, when those who were most at risk were the elderly, we almost always made them responsible for anything happening. A ten p.m. curfew to prevent any sort of nightlife, talking heads on TV explaining how the second wave was the result of the discos being open in August—when the fault was clearly that of a government that hadn't prepared properly during summer months, for instance by enhancing public means of transportation—turned, in the minds of the people, those who on a social level, in the long term, will be the main victims of the pandemic, into the most credited disease spreaders.

COVID-19 heavily impacted my own life as well. I can clearly remember the fear of the first months, that feeling of anxiety that stemmed from not knowing what we were dealing with. I think I was among the first to call Roberto Speranza to ask him for information, during the first days of January 2020, when the problem was still limited to Wuhan, China, and everyone believed it was too far away to reach us. I was influenced by my memory of one of the most beautiful novels I have ever read: *The Stand* by Stephen King starts with a lethal strain of influenza escaping a lab and in just a few weeks' time exterminating almost the entire human population. I said to him: "Roberto, this Chinese stuff about the virus reminds me of a book I read when I was a young. Simply put, almost everyone died. What's going on here?" I asked. Speranza told me that it wasn't a virus like the one King described in his book, but the situation was delicate and still being monitored. I told him to keep me posted and that he could obviously count on our help if necessary. My anxiety was heightened by the fact that there was an incredible incongruency between the scenarios being described in China and what was being said in Italy. Do you remember? On TV, we could see images of Chinese soldiers surrounding the city, people dressed in hazmat suits that you normally only see in the movies, the population shut inside their homes, and the blanket sanitization of the cities. The situation was even more striking because China does not easily give in to panic, it does not have the same interest in health or in human life that we do in the West. And it isn't famous in the world for having high standards of hygiene. So, if the Chinese were adopting such drastic measures, did it mean that we were facing something really terrible, an apocalypse? That was what I was trying to ask our ministers. Faced with all this, instead, our government—the second Conte government at the time—was telling us that there was no need to be alarmed or to start panicking, because everything was under control. "We are more than ready," Conte reassured us. My party was suggesting quarantining all those who came from or were returning from

China. The reason, during that phase, was clear: if those were really the scenes taking place in China, then we weren't sure what to do. In short, we needed to be very cautious. And instead what happened? We were immediately accused of racism and demagogy, along with all the scenes we remember so well: drinks before dinner at the Navigli in Milan with Nicola Zingaretti, the "Hug a Chinese person" campaign with the protest group known as the "sardines" warning us with the slogan "Racism is a virus, too," the TV shows with spring rolls being eaten to show there was no discrimination, the "influencers" launching reckless reassurances *urbi et orbi*. And, lastly, the TV virologists talking about COVID-19 as being no more than like a "common cold." To complete the picture, the World Health Organization, emulated by our health authorities as well, told us that masks were useless, and that only those with the symptoms could transmit the virus. Obviously, they had gotten it all wrong. One month after my phone call with Health Minister Speranza the virus had spread everywhere in Italy. It was not going to be the apocalypse, but it would be the worst shock since the two world wars, with dramatic outcomes for national and international healthcare and the world economy.

I remember the Health Minister Roberto Speranza coming to report to Parliament on the situation, stating that there was no cause for alarm. For a long time, COVID-19 was managed as if the evidence everyone could see with their own eyes did not exist. Once again, reality was distorted to blind ideology or self-interest. However, in a short time, the situation got worse, and we witnessed a radical change of course, marked by total lockdowns and measures that tried to catch up with a situation that was already spiraling out of control. Suddenly, reality could no longer be ignored.

All this reminded me of Nassim Nicholas Taleb, a Lebanese American essayist and mathematical statistician, and the author of *The Black Swan*. Specifically, how humans fool themselves into believing that the reality they have known in recent years is destined to remain unchanged forever, instead of being aware that the unexpected is a fundamental part of history and life. The difference between those who survive unforeseen events and those who are overwhelmed by them lies in the ability to always be prepared for a sudden change in the state of things. It is clear to everyone that Italy was not ready to face up to this emergency. The West was not ready. When the "black swan" of COVID-19 burst onto the scene, we suddenly discovered that Europe did not produce masks or medical devices to handle the emergency—not even latex gloves. Worse still, we discovered that we were not in control of our medical production because a large portion of our medicines relies on active ingredients manufactured outside Europe, mainly in India. Italy lacked an updated pandemic plan, and the EU, despite its daily output of regulations on every conceivable human matter, had no strategy whatsoever for dealing with the unforeseen, even though analysts and virologists had been predicting such events for years. The European Union, once again, laid bare all its fragility and inadequacy in addressing the great challenges of our time. In the face of the pandemic, of course, but the same would happen in response to a major natural or historical event—anything that disrupts the routine of its bureaucracy.

I am referring to the insightful observations of Giulio Tremonti, who, reflecting on COVID-19, did not dwell on debates about the nature of the virus—"laboratory experiment or not?"—but instead started from the concrete reality: the pandemic is undeniably an experiment in the history of the last thirty years. Because a contagion that erupted in a live animal market in Wuhan, an area relegated to the darkest backwaters of civilization, with unchecked globalization, immediately involved the entire world. A globalized but unprepared world.

"This time the monster came in the form of a virus," Tremonti observed in the *CNEL Notebooks*. "In the form of a global virus that demonstrates and/or causes the intrinsic fragility of the global world. A virus that marks (or nearly marks) the end of the phantasmagorical, happy but artificial three decades of globalization. A virus that is already altering—and will greatly alter in the future—the blueprint of social engineering applied so far to the global world. This represents a radical change in the hitherto positive and progressive paradigm of globalization."

What will stay with me most from that year (2020) is the deep sense of frustration—frustration at not having been able to do enough, at not being heard, at not being able to provide sensible answers to those who called me asking for help. Even though I am in the opposition, for them—and rightly so—I represent decision-making power. There are those who call me to ask for interpretations of incomprehensible decrees, or the reasons behind completely nonsensical measures; others complain that we cannot get those measures corrected. Some have confided in me that they cry at night, in secret from their children, out of fear for the future. I've spent many sleepless nights myself, searching for workable solutions. I delved deep, studied hard, together with other leaders and parliamentarians of Brothers of Italy. We set ourselves a rule: never offer criticism without also offering a possible solution. It didn't help much because our proposals were almost always ignored by the government, particularly Conte's administration. They simply weren't interested in our ideas because they came from us. And no matter that Italy was sinking—what mattered more to them was maintaining the narrative that the opposition was irresponsible. Accepting our proposals—even implicitly acknowledging their seriousness—would have interfered with that narrative.

This attitude was symptomatic when we tried to understand the scale of the COVID-19 phenomenon at the start of the pandemic. I remember we were in a phase where, on the one hand, there were those who were saying, "We are dropping like flies," claiming that the emerging numbers were just the tip of the iceberg; and on the other, those who were saying the exact opposite: "They're trying to scare us; COVID-19 is just a sort of 'flu.'" Those were the dramatic days of coffins being taken away by the army in Bergamo: we couldn't just stand still and stay silent. We had to provide Italians with clear answers. That's why I told Giuseppe Conte, during a meeting at Palazzo Chigi between the government and opposition forces, that there was only one thing to do immediately in order to understand what was happening: compare the absolute number of deaths in Italy in the first months of 2020 with the deaths in the same period of previous years. Region by region, municipality by municipality.

Were we or were we not experiencing an increase in the mortality rate in Italy? If the answer was yes, by how much? How was the virus impacting people, and who was being impacted the most? We asked the government over and over again for this information. They didn't respond. So, we did the only thing we could do: we calculated it ourselves. Thanks to the Brothers of Italy Research Office, led by the excellent Francesco Filini—though we didn't have the resources and structures that were available to the government—we took the few publicly available data points, analyzed them, and produced a study accessible to all. The resulting picture was alarming: a spike in deaths in specific areas of Italy, particularly in Lombardy, and the realization that if the virus had spread in the same way across the entire country, it would have triggered a massacre.

At the same time, another important fact emerged: the vast majority of the rise in deaths involved the elderly population. COVID-19's mortality risk decreased with age, becoming almost negligible for younger people without severe underlying conditions. We were beginning to identify the weaknesses of this "unknown" enemy we were facing—a devious enemy that targeted the most vulnerable, particularly our elderly. This observation was later confirmed in much greater detail by ISTAT (Italian Statistical Office) and the Italian National Institute of Health, and it has since become a widely accepted fact, even by those who initially denied it.

Based on the study we conducted, as early as April 2020 we presented our proposals for combating the epidemic at a press conference. Even now, many—too many—months later the proposals remain largely the same.

The first is that every effort must be directed toward protecting the elderly and the most vulnerable. This could be achieved through widespread home assistance, reserving specific times for them in public offices, post offices, and supermarkets. We also suggested offering those who wanted it the option of safe accommodation in hotels or apartments, preferably in smaller towns less exposed to contagion. And, of course, in-home medical care and giving absolute priority to the vaccines.

We stated that it was essential to address the main factors in the virus' transmission, starting with public transportation. This could be strengthened by involving private transport: taxis, rental cars with drivers, and tourist buses, which were largely being unused at the time.

We called for strict controls on those entering the country and, of course, for stopping mass illegal immigration. We were not heeded. No specific measures were put in place for the elderly, and we were told that the virus didn't spread on public transportation or the boats carrying migrants. The response from the Conte government, and later the Draghi government, was the easiest one: lockdowns.

Overcrowded subways and open borders, but bars, restaurants, gyms, museums, cinemas, and shops were closed. At that point, COVID-19 had the last laugh, thanked the government for its cooperation, and continued to spread—and to kill. It killed our elderly, it killed the most vulnerable. And it killed off our economy, thousands of businesses, and millions of jobs. I will never forget the heartbreaking scenes of the young restaurant owner sitting on the ground with her head in her hands, or the shopkeepers and artisans unable to hold back their tears in front of journalists. A lifetime of hard work wiped away.

This is the unacceptable contradiction of a situation pictured for us as a "war" to justify lockdowns and restrictions, but that hardly seemed like a war when billions of euros were squandered on useless initiatives instead of securing our productive fabric and protecting jobs. If we were truly in the middle of a conflict, it would be unacceptable to waste resources on cashback schemes, shop receipt lotteries, e-scooter bonuses, vacation bonuses, job advisers, business-class trips to Dubai for ministerial delegations, wheeled school desks, and countless other pointless handouts. And above all, it is unacceptable that the coronavirus became a feeding trough for the "usual suspects," conveniently from the usual circles close to the Left. The judiciary will determine whether crimes were committed, but whether or not they were, I find the way the funds for managing the emergency were spent appalling and disgraceful: masks purchased at three times the market price, shady contracts awarded to shell companies, millions of Euros in orders and consultancies. While the Italian people gave it their all—volunteers, doctors, nurses, pharmacists staying open without proper personal protective equipment (PPE), cashiers risking their lives every day, and the dedication of our armed forces and law enforcers—the government revealed all the squalor of the worst kind of cronyism. This is also why I could never have joined a government with those who were complicit in all of this.

* * *

No one can convince me otherwise: Conte and his majority, especially the Five Star Movement, navigated the pandemic crisis with their eyes more focused on the polling curves than on the infection curves. They must have thought that COVID-19, in the end, was also an opportunity. The carefully timed press conferences on weekends, right before the evening news, became so routine that at a certain point, it wasn't clear whether Conte held the press conferences to explain the emergency decrees (DPCMs) or issued those decrees just to secure yet another public appearance. Then there were the calculated soundbites, sometimes directed at us, and the triumphant press releases about audience numbers. As if Italians were watching those press conferences out of admiration for Conte, and not because, in an Italy where even the constitution had been effectively prorogued, the Prime Minister had become the law himself, and listening to him was the only way to know their rights.

I was particularly struck by the opening words of a phone call I had with Giuseppe Conte at the beginning of the second wave of the disease:

"Hello Giorgia, how are you?"

"Worried, Giuseppe."

"Why?"

"Why? Because of the situation."

"Oh. . . . Well, we're better off than others."

"If you say so."

At times, I even envied the former Prime Minister's confidence—his belief in his abilities, which bordered on recklessness. If I had been faced with the decision of risking the deaths of 20,000 people or the economic collapse of 500,000, I doubt I could have maintained such composure. But he understood before anyone else that, in the face of an external threat, citizens rally around the flag and place their trust in institutions. That's why he was confident he could gain personal popularity from the storm. And, as much as I find this behavior cynical, he wasn't wrong. By leveraging that dramatic period, he managed to carve out a space for himself that today has elevated him to lead a non-party like the Five Star Movement.

Politically, this last year was tragic for me, as I fully experienced and still live with the nation's anguish. On a personal level, however, the COVID-19 emergency introduced me to an almost normal daily routine I had never known before. Staying in Rome for three consecutive months during the first lockdown, without taking a single flight to another city, was an absolute novelty for me. Having lunch at home on weekdays was another. Being able to play with my daughter several times a day was the most beautiful of these new experiences. Amid the tragedy of the lockdown, being able to spend every day, almost all day, with Ginevra was the only true gift. Even though I never stopped going to Montecitorio to work—it wasn't easy working at home with her—I vividly remember the deserted office, the ghostly building. I remember Rome during the day as I had never seen it before, and hope never to see it like that again.

What I take with me from those strange months is a deeper awareness of the value of time and the certainty that nothing can be taken for granted—because everything, absolutely everything, can change from one day to the next.

Attacking the Decline

I am really unlucky when it comes to vacations. My karma probably believes that my job is to work, always and whatever the situation, relentlessly, because the truth is that every time I try to take a break a tragedy occurs somewhere, or there's some mess I need to deal with. I've gotten to the point that if I even think about organizing a vacation my anxiety starts to grow. When I decided to take a few days off to visit London, the Italian army was struck by the terrible Nasiriyah bombing. I was so shocked I decided to come right back so I could go to the funeral and be close to the families of the nineteen Italian victims. When Andrea gifted me a weekend in Paris to fulfill my desire to see the big Christmas market that's set up on the Champs Élysées (I adore Christmas markets), there was an Islamist terrorist attack on the Bataclan, and I practically ended up working as a correspondent throughout those days of shock and horror. Last year (2019), having sacrificed my entire summer for the electoral campaign (Italians were going to be voting in seven regions on September 20), I took the liberty of organizing a week in Southern Sardinia with a small group of friends. But what happened that time was that the day before we were supposed to leave my mother was rushed to the hospital with the risk of dying. I could go on, but I won't because I wouldn't want you to say that maybe I'm the one who brings bad luck. What I can say, though, is that at one point a friend of mine who was working at the crisis unit of the Ministry of Foreign Affairs called me and asked: "Giò, where are you thinking of going on vacation this year, so I can organize any extra help that might be needed?" He was only half-joking.

The biggest of these episodes of bad luck occurred in the summer of 2019. Ginevra was almost three and after my pregnancy and summers spent taking care of a newborn I thought I might try to organize a vacation. I am a licensed scuba diver and when I travel I like to see the places I like from above and below the water's surface. But I have never been able to fulfill my dream of seeing whale sharks live. They belong to the shark family, but like whales they're huge, harmless, and feed on plankton. They're not easy to come across, because they migrate while following their food. In fact, I've always just missed them, sometimes by a hair's breadth. But in some places around the world you actually can free-dive with those huge, and very beautiful, giant sharks. One of those places is Isla Mujeres, in the Mexican Yucatán. So, in 2019 I decided I would go to Mexico, via the United States. My departure was scheduled for the eighth of the month, and I was so excited about that trip that I had spent the two previous months thinking, as I waited to fall asleep, about what I was going to pack in my suitcase. That date had become a sort of goal for me. Obviously, I hadn't taken into account my karma that was averse to vacations.

Around August 5, when I was feeling happy and counting the hours before my departure, the winds of a government crisis were just beginning to blow. The Five-Star-League coalition executive was in full swing, later known as the Conte I government. Matteo Salvini and the League had started to clearly show signs of dissatisfaction, and they were saying that the Captain had come to an end, that the experience was over. On August 7, the evening before my departure, the rumors had become so insistent I called Matteo to find out if there was any truth to them. He didn't answer, which was a bad sign. I tried asking for information from other members of the League, but they didn't answer either. Total panic. At ten p.m. I decided to go full steam ahead regardless, and started packing. The following morning I was so excited I woke up at five. I was feeling very optimistic, and no longer thinking about the tension inside the Conte government.

I flew from Rome to New York. As luck would have it, as soon as I got comfortable on the plane, Ginevra, who was seated next to me, looked at me and said: "Mamma, why do you always leave me by myself?" Children know exactly when to say that sentence that will linger inside your head forever. But at that moment I was feeling euphoric, so I answered her reassuringly, "Don't worry sweetheart, for the next few days we're going to be together all the time." She hugged me, and we started playing, coloring animals with a special felt-tip pen. After a few hours the food was served, and then we both fell asleep. I slept a few hours, and when I woke up I noticed that my phone was filled with messages. I had activated the Wi-Fi, available on intercontinental flights, and that stream of messages seemed very suspicious. My anxiety started rising again. When I finally got up the courage to read, my fears were confirmed. The Conte government had fallen. At that very moment. Not several months earlier which its nonconclusiveness would have deserved, not in two weeks when I would already be back, but on the very day I had taken off with my family. I must confess, I couldn't hold back the tears. It was a hysterical kind of weeping that expressed all the fatigue I had accumulated and my guilty feelings concerning my daughter, who was going to have to be without her mother once again. In short, I never made it to Mexico. The whale sharks are still a chimera, and I spent August between my house and the consultations at the presidential palace. Ironically, they were held on the very same day that I had booked my scuba diving session.

* * *

In the entire history of the Italian Republic, which is certainly not short of ups and downs and plot twists, this will always be the wildest legislature.

It seems like ancient history, but if you think about it, only three years ago we inaugurated this eighteenth legislature with a small trauma for Italy and Europe: the Five-Star-League government, a sovereigntist-populist executive that presented itself as a disruptive experiment. That shock was accompanied by exhausting negotiations and moments of extreme tension from the very first rumors that emerged concerning its composition. I remember when Sergio Mattarella opposed the appointment of Paolo Savona as Minister of Economy because he considered him too far from a certain European orthodoxy, insisting on appointing a "guarantor" figure to lead the Ministry of Economy and Finance. That decision made me really mad, even though I had no role in selecting Savona as minister. I simply did not and do not believe that it falls within the President of the Republic's powers to prevent the government from setting its political direction, including through ministerial appointments. Mattarella, evidently, believed that the first Conte government aimed to undermine the balance and status quo in Italy and Europe and took action to prevent it, overstepping, I believe, his constitutional role.

Things, however, did not go as Mattarella feared or as many Italians had hoped. We of Brothers of Italy were among the few who predicted this. We chose not to be part of that government experiment, despite its enormous initial support and momentum, and I admit it was not an easy decision to make. Unlike what happened later when the Draghi government was formed—when our internal meetings unanimously voted to remain in the opposition—during the birth of the Five-Star-League government, many within our ranks pushed for Brothers of Italy to join in. There were times when we were hesitant because the pressure to join, even from many of our voters, was pretty strong. Of all of us, I was probably the one who was the most against the idea, but I wasn't completely convinced. I knew that staying out of what presented itself as a disruptive government could be a fatal decision, especially since our results in the previous political elections hadn't been particularly impressive. I sought advice to ensure I was making the right decision. I spoke with Luigi Di Maio in my office one May afternoon. He candidly told me that if we wanted to be part of the majority with them and the League, he would agree only on the condition that the Prime Minister came from the Five Star Movement. He explained that our presence would shift the majority too far to the right, and given that they also had a strong left-wing base (today I would even go so far as to say *predominantly* left-wing), it was important to redress the balance. That condition was, of course, unacceptable to us, and I want to thank Di Maio for helping to make the decision easier and more justifiable within Brothers of Italy. I also discussed the matter several times with Salvini. At first, he asked me to join the government, probably to raise his bargaining chips vis-à-vis the Five Stars, but later he told me that even if we did decide to enter the government, our presence would not be accepted. In the end, I managed to do what I believed was the right thing to do, also thanks to them.

Why was I so firmly opposed to being part of a government experience that presented itself as youthful, disruptive of old patterns, and initially enjoyed enormous support? Simple. Because notwithstanding the excitement of the moment, which Italy is often prone to, I knew the Five Star Movement well and understood the difference between a populist entity like M5S and a sovereigntist reality—viewed as a patriotic force—which is what Brothers of Italy represents. The two concepts, populism and sovereigntism, have often been portrayed as one and the same. In actual fact, they are very different. To put it simply, sovereigntism is the belief that sovereignty should be returned to the people and national states in an era where decision-making power is increasingly delegated to ambiguous entities that transcend the States and are disconnected from the control and will of citizens. As such, sovereigntism is a clear worldview and philosophy. Populism, on the other hand, is the exact opposite. It is the anti-vision—the idea that the role of politics is to follow the public's mood, pursue momentary impulses, and respond to society rather than lead it. The Five Star Movement is the most successful form of populism. More than a political party, Grillo's creation is like a disposable container: something you can fill with whatever you need at any given time. For this reason, Di Maio and his colleagues can seamlessly shift from being staunch anti-Europeans to loyal defenders of the European balance so cherished by Brussels' bureaucracy. In just a few months, those who claimed they would open up the political establishment "like a tin of tuna" became its most ardent supporters. In fact, they became the establishment themselves.

The perfect Prime Minister for such a movement could only be Giuseppe Conte, also known as "Barbapapà," because, much like the cartoon character from my childhood, he can morph into whatever is required in that moment. The closing of the circle in this scenario comes with the rise of Mario Draghi. It might seem like a paradox, but if you think about it, it isn't: the very Parliament where the Five Star Movement is the largest party began with the promise of a disruptive government and ended up bringing Mario Draghi to Palazzo Chigi—the representative, even the guarantor, of the existing national and international balances. Precisely those balances the M5S had promised to overturn during its election campaign. This is why I never understood the decision of my Center-Right allies, particularly Matteo Salvini, to follow the Five Star Movement down that path. I do not consider the League to be a populist movement, and such varied alliances don't seem natural for them. But I don't want to judge the legitimate decisions of my allies. After all, it's not the first time that Center-Right forces have taken different paths during complex situations. It has never been an insurmountable problem. On the contrary, the diversity of parties within our coalition has always been a strength, not a disadvantage. I believe it will be the same this time.

* * *

Still, what happened in Parliament during this legislature—I've said it before and will say it again—is rather incredible. It cannot be taken for granted as normal or inevitable. So, I believe that to make sense of it all, we need to try to look at these events with enough distance from the daily political disputes. We must try to piece together the parts of this puzzle and see if, in the end, a clear picture emerges—even if that picture turns out to be disturbing.

As I wrote before, it all began with the Five Star Movement securing over 30 percent of the vote in the general elections by presenting itself as an antiestablishment force and promising not to form alliances with any other party. Then they changed their mind and entered into a forced alliance—a sort of political GMO—with the League. That government lasted just over a year before Salvini rightly pulled the plug, realizing that no real revolution was possible with the Five Star Movement. When the Five-Star Movement-League experiment collapsed, it took the former party only a few weeks to form a new government. With whom? With those they had previously labeled their worst enemies—the Democratic Party, whom they had called the "party of thieves and Bibbiano." This was likely a choice driven by desperation, as the Five Star Movement had lost all credibility and squandered more than half its electoral support within fifteen months. But it was also driven by the illusion that they could leverage their status as the largest parliamentary force against a confused PD led by Nicola Zingaretti. In other words, they believed they could dictate the political agenda to a Democratic Party playing second fiddle to Conte, Di Maio, and Azzolina.

This notion, which might have seemed plausible from a naive perspective, soon clashed with reality: the Five Star Movement failed to consider that the Democratic Party represents what Americans would call the "Deep State." It was, therefore, predictable that, at the first opportunity, power would shift from a Five-Star-led government—with Conte and Casalino in leading roles—to a government where the Five Star Movement would be insignificant. And what actually happened? Giuseppe Conte was shown the door with the approval of key sections of the Center-Left. Let me take this opportunity to say that I have nothing personal against Conte. In fact, I acknowledge that, despite never having governed anything before, he showed great tactical skill. The same goes for his Rasputin-like adviser, Rocco Casalino, who was so ruthless and skillful that he managed to turn a complete unknown into a true media phenomenon. But the fact that the Deep State would get rid of this "Mr. Nobody" and his overbearing spokesperson at the first opportunity—given their delusional belief that they held an entire nation in their hands—was very much in the cards. This became even more likely after a year of dealing with the sudden

COVID-19 crisis. Conte, skilled at turning the state of emergency into a political opportunity, eventually succumbed to a delusion of omnipotence. This led to a communication frenzy, reckless and manipulative use of emergency decrees (DPCMs), and reckless and irresponsible management of the vast resources put at his disposal by the Parliament.

The rise of Mario Draghi was meant to be a return to "normalcy." The same people who once supported the "populist" Conte now enthusiastically applauded the former president of the European Central Bank. In certain political circles, it took no time at all to shift from "Conte or death" to "Conte is (politically) dead." This is the magnitude of the situation. Perhaps in Italy, we've become so accustomed to political shape-shifting that even something this grotesque no longer surprises us.

Let's be clear on this. With Mario Draghi, we all—myself included—feel more reassured having someone with extensive experience and international prestige leading the country, rather than an enterprising amateur like Giuseppe Conte. But where is the democracy in all of this? Is a good résumé enough to lead a sovereign nation without asking its citizens what they think? They've labeled Draghi's administration the "government of the best," though clearly it isn't. I challenge anyone to argue that Di Maio is the best possible Foreign Minister for Italy, or that Speranza deserved to be reappointed as Health Minister. But even if it were the "best" government, the underlying problem still remains: who decides who the best are, and based on which criteria? Is it academic credentials, physical appearance, communication skills, empathy with the people, or social status—as was the case more than a century ago? What criteria can be considered objective? For two thousand years, Western civilization has wrestled with this question, and the answer it ultimately settled on is that the "best" people to govern are those chosen by the citizens in free elections. The argument is simple: those elected by the people are accountable to the people, at least in theory, while those imposed from above—through more or less legitimate means—answer to entirely different forces.

This question applies, of course, to Mario Draghi as well. Did the esteemed former Governor of the Bank of Italy take on the task of leading our country during a crisis to defend its interests—or to ensure something else? To my mind, the answer to this question remains unclear.

Other elements of this story are clear, though, and they are not reassuring. I'll try to explain it with a metaphor. Italy is a ship navigating through a storm, and that ship has a captain, Conte, who is clearly inadequate. It is then decided to replace him with a long-experienced captain with universally recognized qualities. But the crew remains the same, the storm grows ever stronger, and moreover, it's no longer clear under which flag this new captain intends to sail. Is Draghi the patriotic captain who hoists the Italian flag high and defends the Italian ship, its interests, and its strength, or is he rather the captain imposed by others so that this ship gets back on the course deemed right in some other European or non-European capital? This is no small difference. Not for us. A patriotic Draghi can always count on Brothers of Italy, even from the opposition. A Draghi who is a guarantor of interests other than Italy's will find Brothers of Italy standing in his way. I told him this when we met during the consultations that preceded the formation of his government. It seemed to me that, deep down, he appreciated our genuine frankness.

I think that the only "government of the best" Italy should hope for is a government of patriots. People who are so courageous and in love with this nation that they are not going to exchange it for anything or anyone. That is the real revolution our country needs. That is the mission of Brothers of Italy and, as I see it, of the entire Center-Right. Because, after all, the political and historical dynamics of what is happening in Italy are actually rather simple if, here too, you look at it with detachment, as an outside observer might. When a medium-power nation goes through a period of weakness—which, unfortunately, is the case for Italy from 2011 to the present—it is inevitably subject to the interference of neighboring States. This creates a political divide within the struggling nation between those who believe it is better to cooperate with the overbearing neighbor and take on a cautious position of subordination, and those who claim the full sovereignty and independence of the nation. In some contexts, this opposition degenerates into bloody clashes, while in others, fortunately, it remains within the realm of political debate. In Italy, this struggle manifests between those who demand "more Europe" and those who call themselves patriots. On one side, those who are convinced, perhaps even in good faith, that Italy's proper position is that of a subordinate state to an EU controlled by the Franco-German axis; on the other side, those who demand a role for Italy of equal dignity with the other founding states of the EU. Simplifying, on one side, the Democratic Party, the "collaborationist" party of foreign interference, and, on the other, Brothers of Italy, the movement of patriots. And I am convinced that this will be the growing bipolarity of the coming years in Italy. Indeed, because, after all, the Left—but not only the Left—believes that Italians are not capable of "keeping to the straight and narrow" on their own, and therefore need a kind of hidden shareholder with veto power over national decisions to teach us how to redeem ourselves from our age-old sins.

I disagree with this. I believe that our counterparts are too focused on their own national interests to offer true help that is not tainted by their selfishness to help with our fluctuating affairs. I believe that the only ones who can pull Italy out of its difficult situation are us Italians, with a bit of fresh courage and self-respect.

* * *

Healing the relationship between the people and the state is the historical task that belongs to us. A movement of patriots is needed to authentically interpret the spirit of the nation, to defend its cultural, strategic, and economic interests. And in a divided and fragmented nation, the task of patriots is primarily to heal the many wounds we have inherited. I remember the founding principles of National Alliance courageously asserting that a shared historical memory had to be rebuilt to overcome the great divides in recent Italian history. Yet today, this is no longer enough: a movement of patriots must, above all, have a long-term vision, to defend Italian identity as the safe home where we can raise our children and give them a future of serenity, security, justice, and prosperity. The individual is too alone in this vast world, and the world itself is too vast and wonderfully rich in diversity to make it one's dwelling. The "citizen of the world" is nothing more than someone who, in chasing the illusion of making the whole world their home, eventually discovers themselves to be a "homeless person." This is why we still need homelands. Especially in our day and age.

I want to devote all of my energy to this "we" that is Italy, without which words like "I am Giorgia" would ring hollow, banal, and meaningless. However, it is a burden we must carry on our shoulders, I have to admit. Sometimes I think how much easier it would be if I just disregarded all the big problems that cause my country to suffer. Don't ask me what the future is for this curious nation that we are, and think only to my own "garden." I remember a grand provocation uttered by Vittorio Feltri on TV once. The subject was immigration, and to his interlocutor, who kept asking him whether he had it in for migrants, Feltri replied, with a ruse that only he can afford to use, saying: "Why should I care whether these people are allowed to land here or not, I live in a beautiful home, I'm even well-off, the more of them arrive the better, they work for peanuts, and I'm fine with that. I'm saying it for those poor Italian wretches who live in the outskirts of the city, not for myself." Feltri had brilliantly, in just a few sarcastic words, made a complex and profound statement that anyone else might have tried to explain in a much less effective way, with words such as these: "I'd like to look at things while thinking only about what's in it for me, but unfortunately I cannot." Needless to say, the person interviewing the director of *Libero*, the usual left-wing opinion maker, didn't grasp the irony and said he was shocked by the words he had just heard.

The truth of the matter is that if you think you can wash your hands of the fate of your country, reality will soon be there to shatter that illusion. Here again, I will describe this based on a picture of my life. A few years ago, one summer's day, I was having lunch at the beach in Maccarese. There was still no COVID-19, so there were no restrictions. There were two young girls with us: Lucrezia, the daughter of an old friend of mine, and Ania, the daughter of a Polish couple I had met that day. The two small girls, who had just met each other, were the same age and had even been born on the same day. Lucrezia would grow up in Italy, Ania in Poland. Do you know what emerged as we talked about those two girls that day? That Ania, by the time she had grown up, would probably be living in a country that is richer than the one where Lucrezia would instead live. So Ania would have more job opportunities and live in a better social context. Get it? Projecting the data for economic growth, in a few decades Poland would have a higher per capita income than Italy's. Until not long ago, this was out of the question. Italy, one of the great world powers, now risks being overtaken by countries that used to be less rich.

I don't want that. I don't want to throw in the towel to our country's decline. And I won't, whatever it may cost. For the good of my daughter, so that she and other young Italians will not find themselves, one day, leaving their country in search of a better life, the way millions of Italians had to in the past. I won't do that because of the profound gratitude I feel for those who have made Italy great over the centuries, only to see us squander that wealth. I won't do that simply because I love my country even though, at times, it does everything it can to push us away. However, I will work to make this country think big once again, aware of its strengths. I will fight for my country to regain an awareness of the fact that the decline can be halted, that Italy can go back to growing, racing, flying, the way it did, unexpectedly, during the years of the "Italian miracle."

And I am convinced that you don't need brilliant and extraordinary ideas. All it takes is the proper dose of devotion, seriousness, and common sense. Along with the courage required to take apart a system that is convenient for a few, to the detriment of everyone else.

* * *

I don't intend to reassert Brothers of Italy's whole manifesto here. Anyone who has decided to read this book and has gotten this far, to the last chapter, didn't do so just to find what can easily be looked up on the party website (do look, though, if you're inspired to: you'll find the texts from

Brothers of Italy's most recent meeting, our ideas, and many documents that are both useful and interesting). Nevertheless, I want to quickly sketch, for those who are reading this, an idea of what Italy could be like. The country I believe in and for which I fight together with many others.

I've already said a lot about support for families, female employment, and the birth rate. I could bore you for another three hundred pages on the same subject. But I won't (this time). However, I do want to repeat that this should be our absolute priority. It isn't, and I don't get why it is not.

What already a century ago Gramsci referred to as the "southern question" is still today the country's biggest wound. The big differences that exist between the different parts of our country are shameful and unacceptable. I am concerned about what is commonly referred to as the Mezzogiorno (the South) not because I am bound to an old centralized, welfare state, and pro-southern idea. The exact opposite is true. I think of the growth of the South as an indispensable element if there is to be a great revival. I think with admiration, as well as with some envy, about how Germany managed its country's reunification phase starting from the 1990s, and how it devoted all of its energies to absorbing the eastern regions that had been freed from communism. It was a huge effort, also sustained by the generosity of Europe, worthy of a great people. And it is also what I would like to see for our South. The South's economic fragility is, paradoxically, a huge opportunity for the rest of Italy as well. Because it increases the potential for growth that the nation has overall. If we aimed seriously, and without charitable intentions, at the development of the areas that are struggling the most, not just in the South, we could achieve overall growth rates that are greater than those of our European neighbors. What we need are infrastructures, public investments, support for those who have the courage to invest and hire staff in difficult contexts. The Mezzogiorno needs the preconditions for it to be able to grow—not charity. This is why you have seen me get angry many times, over these recent years, when all that was offered as a prospect for growth in the South was just the worst of the welfare state's aid policies. Let's start from something that's very concrete: allocating 50 percent of the budget to infrastructures in the South, instead of the current 30 percent, more or less, when we're lucky.

The issue of infrastructural underdevelopment is no longer just the South's problem, it now affects the entire national territory. For too many years, we have stopped thinking about the future and stopped investing in public projects. Brothers of Italy was the first party to make a clear-cut distinction between "good spending" and "bad spending," a matter that has recently become fashionable. When, for years, the debate was polarized between the austerity enthusiasts loyal to the EU and the third-millennium pseudo-Keynesians with their naive theory that "debt doesn't exist, the more you spend, the better," we alone argued that not all deficits are equal. The issue is not "deficit, right or wrong," but rather "what is the deficit being used for." Just as it makes sense for a family to take on debt for a mortgage to buy a home to live in but not to take out loans to vacation in the Maldives, so too should a state incur deficit spending to build infrastructure, modernize the nation, build hospitals, and secure the territory. It is a mistake, however, to borrow to increase unproductive current expenditures, such as financing a "bonus for eighteen-year-olds."

Infrastructure must be built to serve Italians, not foreign interests or economic elites. Brothers of Italy is the only party in the Italian political landscape to place the issue of ownership of strategic infrastructure at the heart of its political agenda. This is a challenging topic to tackle, primarily because it is rarely discussed. Perhaps this is because the financial groups that derive enormous benefits from managing infrastructure also heavily invest in the media, resulting in most newspapers and the so-called mainstream avoiding informing the public on these matters. In contrast, in all major nations, there exists a strong culture of public ownership over assets vital to the very existence of the state. Few people are aware of the fact that in France, as early as 1997, an authentic "school of economic warfare" (École de Guerre Économique) was created. Its goals include training leaders and developing strategies to defend the national productive fabric from foreign threats, effectively serving as an economic intelligence force. Those who closely follow the economic dynamics within the EU will have noticed that for years France's presence in the Italian productive fabric has been growing, taking over key roles in companies and strategic infrastructure. Recently, they have even taken over control of the Italian Stock Exchange. On these issues, our Senator Adolfo Urso, with determination and courage, leads a patriotic battle, including within COPASIR (Parliamentary Committee for the Security of the Republic).

There are assets that national States hold tightly because they are deemed vital to the very existence of the nation. In Italy, in recent decades, there has been a lack of attention to this important issue. And when attention has indeed been paid, it has not been Italian interests that were safeguarded. One day, when I have the strength to do so, I will propose the establishment of an inquiry commission to uncover who was too distracted and who was too compliant. I do not exclude the possibility that we might ultimately face the greatest scandal in Italy's history.

In the 1990s in Russia, the oil wells and the gas deposits ended up in the hands of the oligarchs; in Italy, the same thing happened with our infrastructures. Instead of "liberating" the economy and the productive sectors from the excessive state control, privatization or selling off cheaply was the preferred option. A certain kind of policy literally gave friends of friends chunks of the country, obtaining funding and jobs in return. Thus were born the private monopolies in the strategic infrastructures, thanks to which our own fortunate "oligarchs" who were able to comfortably sit on "oil wells" prospered for decades. Without giving anything back to the community. The result of this is that we who invented the telephone with Antonio Meucci are currently the only European country to not have the ownership of the telecommunications network. And that a civilization famous around the world for the bridges and roads it was able to build now sees its roads and bridges collapse, as happened to Ponte Morandi in Genoa. How did we allow all this to happen? Why, despite the initial indignation and anger for the forty-three victims in Genoa and the promises made by those in government, has nothing really changed since then? Today, if we want to make Italy great again, we have no choice: we have to reverse this negative process. In Brothers of Italy's vision the Italian state should be the owner and control strategic infrastructures like ports, airports, railways, highways, telecommunications and digital networks, water and electricity supplies. These can all be managed either publicly or privately, as long as the national interest always comes first and foremost. They definitely must not be under the control of foreign powers. Are these ideas revolutionary? Autarkic? The truth of the matter is that this is how things go in the free nations in the world.

* * *

Yes, there are a lot of public works to be carried out. Meanwhile, if it is true that you practically can't do anything anymore without the internet, how can it still be that entire areas in Italy do not have an adequate connection? Installing broadband throughout the territory, even in the more internal areas, to counter the phenomenon of depopulation and to create favorable technological conditions so that companies can be competitive is the least that we can expect from our government.

We need to submit Italy to a massive "rehabilitation," and I'm not talking about the bitter medicines they gave us when we were children. I'm talking about an efficient railway system for commuters, freight, and transportation. Transportation on rail is quick, economical, and ecological. It is the future even more than the past. The challenge is bringing the high-speed and high-capability trainline as far as Lecce on the Adriatic coastline, and as far as Reggio Calabria, and after that Sicily by way of the bridge over the Strait of Messina.

Why does a peninsula at the center of the Mediterranean behave as though it were Switzerland and didn't have the sea? A "blue economy" linked to the sea should be one of our main features. We should, at a minimum, have a Ministry of the Sea. We should invest in the docks and dockland connections to intercept the freight traffic generated by the doubling of the Suez Canal, and create a real logistic platform at the heart of the Mediterranean. Instead, at the present time, the great ships arriving from the East prefer to reach Holland instead of offloading their cargo in Italy, where they would be forced to deal with myriad logistic difficulties.

Sometimes I think that Italy would do well to have a good "mental coach," of the kind that explains the simple things that you should be able to understand on your own: "You weigh over three hundred pounds, you're as strong as a bull, but not particularly agile, maybe you should consider playing football instead of doing gymnastics." Why do we fail to exploit our strengths? Italy is a nation with the most recognizable brand in the world. The Made in Italy brand guarantees quality, but beauty and prestige as well. We could prosper on that alone. Italy's economic and industrial policy vision should be something we can take for granted: gradually reconverting all that cannot be identified with the Italian brand into something with a strong identity. Our entire food and agriculture sector, of course, but also high tech, construction work, fashion, furniture, design. No one will ever again be willing to pay more for a screw manufactured in Italy rather than one made in China, but everyone is willing to pay the high prices of a pair of shoes or a car because they are made in Italy. Our once-glorious automotive sector ended up with the FIAT-FCA group—first craftily moving its headquarters to the Netherlands and the United Kingdom—and now, with the Stellantis operation, under French control. This scandal, which puts thousands of jobs in Italy and all the companies within the industry at risk, unfolded in total and culpable silence from the government, media, and political forces. Everyone except Brothers of Italy, of course. Clearly, we are an "inconvenient" party, because with us in government carrying out such destruction wouldn't have been so easy. And who knows, maybe that's why the major newspapers controlled by the "FIAT galaxy" pay so much attention to us.

I often describe Brothers of Italy as "a proudly pro-productivity party." But for us, being on the side of businesses means something very specific and quite different from the kind of industrial policies we've seen in recent years. It means supporting those who produce and hire in Italy. This is achievable if we listen to the real productive fabric of the country instead of the major economic and financial powers. Our proposals in this area are numerous. Let's start with implementing a tax principle of "the more you hire, the less you pay," to benefit those who create jobs in Italy, and penalize multinationals and tech giants that contribute very little to the nation's economic growth. For us, those who do business in Italy are heroes—especially after the tragedy of COVID-19. Heroes who must be supported in every possible way, not treated like criminals or tax evaders. Fewer taxes, less fiscal oppression, less bureaucracy, certainly. But above all, more freedom and more respect from the state.

It is not befitting of a civilized nation to uphold the barbarity of reversing the burden of proof in tax matters. In Italy, if the state accuses you of being a tax evader, it's not the state that must prove it; it's you who must prove it's not true. This is not a fight against tax evasion; it is bullying by a state that is weak with the strong and strong with the weak. The fight against tax evasion should focus on tackling bank evasion, where profits and resources are transferred to tax havens; fake relocations of headquarters abroad; the fraudulent cooperatives beloved by the Left; and "carousel fraud" schemes involving VAT in large companies, which siphon off billions from the Treasury. It should also address the "open-and-close" practices of Chinese, Bangladeshi, and other non-EU businesses that sprout up like mushrooms, pay no taxes, and then change their business identity before the state can catch up with them. This is how Italian businesses are forced to close while foreign ones proliferate. There is a solution, and we have proposed it: a deposit requirement for non-EU businesses as an advance payment on their taxes. This proposal, however, has been systematically rejected by Parliament.

Just like our proposal to adopt in Italy the same cash limit that exists in Germany and much of Europe, where, guess what, there is no limit. What credibility does the argument have that eliminating cash is necessary to combat tax evasion when I can go to Austria or Germany and spend as much cash as I want? The truth is that the crusade in favor of electronic money serves only to make yet another gift to the banking and financial sector, which profits from every electronic transaction but not from cash, as well as to monitor the citizens. Exactly. We've heard

Five-Star-Movement parliamentarians talk about "immoral spending," and left-wing representatives openly say: "We need to know who spends and on what." Well, I think that a free citizen has the right to spend their money as they see fit, without having to explain themselves to a voyeuristic state peering through the keyhole.

We need less state intrusion into people's private lives and more state presence when we step outside our homes, because only institutions can guarantee the security that is a prerequisite for freedom. Why is it that the same state that demands to monitor every expense and every action of ours does not monitor public squares and cities to protect them from crime? Large swaths of Italy have become no-go zones dominated by drug dealing and delinquency, with the mafias controlling entire neighborhoods. That is where the strength of the state needs to be felt. With a greater presence of law enforcement—who must be respected, strengthened, better paid, and equipped—with cameras in high-risk areas, and even with the army when necessary. Uniforms don't scare me at all; what scares me is those who claim to be frightened by uniforms. Just as I am frightened by the criminal gangs that think they can act with impunity. And too often they can. Because justice is another major issue in our country.

In this maddening Italy, it is often the honest people, more than the criminals, who fear justice. I believe justice should not be a topic that's disputed at the stadium, and I have always deliberately avoided both the extremists of guaranteed protections and the extremists of heavy-handedness. Let's just say I feel like a guarantor during the trial phase and a supporter of strict enforcement during the penalty phase. In other words, until you're proven guilty, you must have all the safeguards and protections of a modern state. But if it's established that you are guilty, then you must serve your sentence without question. Certainty in the rights of the accused, certainty in the punishment of the convicted. Today, the exact opposite is true.

I dream of a justice system that citizens—especially the innocent—can approach without fear, without being subjected to a media crusade during the investigation and determination phase. To achieve this, we must have the courage to reform our justice system. The judiciary is a power that must be above suspicion, free from battles between political factions, self-interest, and divisions that often prevent the best from rising to the top.

The climate of decadence reminiscent of a late empire, so starkly revealed by the Palamara Affair (Luca Palamara, a former judge, was investigated for corruption and forced to resign) calls for an urgent and radical reform of the judiciary, starting with its self-governing body, the Superior Council of the Judiciary (CSM). We must do this not only to restore a sense of trust, but above all for the many Italian magistrates who have always done their duty honestly, and have been the first victims, in their careers, of what has become known as the Palamara system.

Moreover, the relationship between business and labor needs to be repaired. In a fabric largely made up of micro-, small-, and medium-sized enterprises, it cannot be as conflictual as a certain Marxist union rhetoric would have it. Instead, it must be based on collaboration. Promoting statutes and experiences of worker participation in the destiny of their companies, encouraging widespread shareholding, increasing corporate welfare policies in an era when public bodies are increasingly struggling to provide quality social services, and strengthening the role of bargaining linked to territories and company dimensions to overcome the rigidity of national contracts without losing labor safeguards. These are just some of the elements of a participatory renaissance that a modern nation, built on social cohesion, must pursue.

This perspective speaks to us about the relationship between employers and their employees, about safeguards and guarantees.

And yet, there is an Italy that is completely excluded from this perspective: thousands of self-employed workers, freelancers, and professionals who dramatically symbolize a major divide that needs to be healed—the divide between those who are protected and those who are not. The COVID-19 crisis tragically highlighted this fact. While a broad group of employees were rightly provided months of job safeguards like layoff freezes and wage guarantee funds (albeit insufficient and paid late), the self-employed were shamefully neglected. The future must be one of a system of social safety nets that is equal for everyone: a form of "unemployment benefit" for anyone who loses their job, whether they are employees or self-employed, and a minimum "solidarity allowance" for those who cannot work for objective reasons. This would replace the vote-catching and counterproductive measure of the "reddito di cittadinanza" (a basic income provided by the state social welfare program).

These are issues that may sometimes seem distant, but in reality, they directly affect the lives of each and every one of us. The same is true for foreign policy, which by its very name seems unrelated to us, yet profoundly influences our security, our well-being, our energy supplies, our trade, and even our standard of living.

For me, dealing with foreign policy means first and foremost promoting and safeguarding our national interests. For many others, it seems to mean cheerleading for this or that economic power. We in Brothers of Italy are not "pro" anything or anyone; puppets have strings, not us. We approach every issue in foreign policy from an Italian perspective. I've found that this characteristic of ours is greatly appreciated abroad, much more so than those who act like cheerleaders with colorful pom-poms, badges, and T-shirts—like our leftist counterparts do with Obama, Macron, Merkel, or Biden. I'm reminded of an aphorism by a Spartan king cited by Plutarch: "While speaking with a foreigner who boasted about being considered a Spartan sympathizer by his fellow citizens, the king replied: it would be better for you to be known as a patriot than a Spartan sympathizer." In short, act like a patriot, and you'll be treated with respect; act like a servant, and you'll be treated as one.

For too long, Italian politics has focused only on domestic matters, underestimating how important it is to influence what happens beyond our borders to change our country's destiny.

I have always been drawn to proud peoples, to those who take pride in their history and culture. This is one reason I am enthralled by Americans' patriotism and their deep attachment to their national flag. It is no longer a matter of being pro- or anti-USA but about recognizing that Europe and the United States share an indissoluble bond and must face the challenges of the future together.

Of course, America is complex, and it won't be easy for us to engage with Joe Biden's administration, which has already shown how destabilizing an ideological approach to so-called "human rights" can be, wielded selectively to target new adversaries. But there is also a deeper America, represented by the seventy-five million voters who supported Donald Trump in November 2020, who cannot simply be dismissed as a group of fanatics wearing horns and bison pelts. Many of their concerns are ours as well. With this deeper America, we European conservatives will continue to engage in an increasingly stable and fruitful way.

This alliance will primarily aim to curb the rise of China and its expansionism. Beijing no longer seems to have any limits. Its interests stretch from African and Latin American raw materials to strategic European infrastructure like ports and railways. In the background looms the Belt and Road Initiative, the so-called "New Silk Road" announced with great fanfare by President Xi Jinping—a colossal project involving over sixty-eight nations globally. I am convinced that allowing the mass outsourcing of entire European industrial sectors to China was a serious mistake, but it would be an even greater one to persist in treating as an equal a power that does not play by the same rules as we do.

For this reason, we must keep up good relations with Russia to prevent it from aligning fully with China. Such an alliance would be highly detrimental for European and Western interests. Of course, this requires effort on both sides, and Moscow must also take significant steps forward toward the international community. I often smile when recalling Berlusconi's visits to Atreju, where he would recount moments as Prime Minister when he worked to prevent a war from breaking out between Russia and Georgia. I'm not sure if it happened exactly as he described, but I vividly remember what became known as the "Spirit of Pratica di Mare," the name of the NATO summit that took place near Rome and included Russia in a spirit of cordial and positive cooperation. Those days feel very distant now, but Russia remains part of our shared European values, defending Christian identity and combating Islamic fundamentalism. However, it must do so peacefully with its neighbors, and European states bordering on the Russian bear must be able to face the future calmly, without fearing the return of Moscow's aggressive imperial policies. We need a balance that ensures a lasting and definitive peace between Europe and Russia. This will not be achieved through the shortsighted muscle-flexing policies that were so favored by Obama and now Biden. If we approach this wisely, both the West and Russia will emerge stronger and more secure, leaving the Chinese dragon a little more isolated.

Our history and geographic position compel us to prioritize the Mediterranean. On its shores, for far too long, Erdoğan's neo-Ottoman ambitions for Turkey have been materializing. Turkey has been transformed in just a few decades from a secular and moderately Muslim state into an Islamist country under the influence of Qatar and the Muslim Brotherhood. Illegal drilling near Cyprus, at the expense of Italian and French interests, and its intervention in Libya are just the latest in a long series of provocations and attempts to blackmail Europe. But today Turkey has extended its sphere of influence, sending jihadist mercenaries to fight in Nagorno-Karabakh and increasing its foothold in the Horn of Africa. Most importantly, it has become a sponsor of political Islam, funding the opening of mosques and Islamic cultural centers across Europe. Yet, the EU has still not definitively revoked Turkey's status as a candidate for membership. I believe it is time to say no, once and for all, to Turkey joining the European Union. This does not mean waging war against Turkey. It means acknowledging that it is a third party, distant from our values and interests, with which we can perhaps engage in trade agreements but cannot share the same political space. Frankly, that seems like the bare minimum. Given that Mario Draghi has already taken a bold step by unexpectedly calling Erdoğan "a dictator," I expect him to follow through and demand in Brussels that Turkey's path to EU membership be stopped.

South of our shores lies the vast, often forgotten continent of Africa, which I have already mentioned with both fondness and respect. Fondness first, then respect. It is a well-known fact that addressing the root causes of migration is directly and tightly linked to Africa's stability and economic development. Until we restore political stability and economic sovereignty to these peoples, they will remain prone to all kinds of turbulence and the scourge of the Islamist militias.

Islamic fundamentalism is indeed another plague of our time. The military defeat of ISIS in Syria and Iraq has not eradicated it permanently. It lives on in dormant terrorist cells in Europe, in militias like Boko Haram and Al-Shabaab in Africa, in the preaching of dangerous imams around the world, and inside many Western countries. I think of the persecuted Christians around the world, all too often forgotten by a Europe that seems to have lost its spiritual bearings, where cultural relativism puts everything and everyone on the same level. From Asia to the Middle East, from countries like Egypt and Nigeria to the Congo and Somalia, and even to the horrifying news of children being beheaded in Mozambique, thousands of people risk their lives every day simply for practicing their faith. We can no longer look the other way. We must use every form of pressure to ensure this does not continue. The many women fighting against the darkness of Salafist Islam, which seeks to subjugate them also come to mind. Here, too, we can no longer remain silent, and it is no coincidence that Brothers of Italy continues to lead such battles, with Daniela Santanchè at the helm. This is especially true when it happens not only in countries like Saudi Arabia but also in cities like London, Paris, Brussels, and Berlin, where entire neighborhoods are governed according to sharia law.

And Italy cannot help but look toward Latin America, with which it shares very close cultural and identity ties. South Americans naturally feel connected to Spain, due to their colonial past, and to Italy, thanks to the many of our compatriots who, over the centuries, have shaped those lands. Yet, while Madrid cultivates these privileged relationships, we completely neglect them—sometimes even betraying those in Latin America who look to Italy with hope. I think, among others, of Venezuelans who are fighting against Nicolás Maduro's corrupt and communist regime. The economic and social situation in Venezuela is increasingly dire. Due to the failed policies pursued by the Chavists, exacerbated by the COVID-19 pandemic, a genuine humanitarian emergency is under way. Over six million people have already fled abroad in their desperate search for safety, food, medicine, and other basic necessities—many of them Italians. But these are forgotten refugees, inconvenient for the mainstream because they are Christians, of European descent, and fleeing communism. It's easier to look the other way.

Foreign policy also means addressing the needs of Italians around the world. As taught by the late and great Mirko Tremaglia, wherever there is one of our compatriots, there is an important bastion of Italian identity to be protected and valued. This network comprises over four million people living abroad with Italian passports and nearly sixty million people of Italian extraction, to whom we must pay greater attention—every day, not just during elections. Unfortunately, due to the incompetence of the political class, many young Italians are once again choosing to emigrate in search of better opportunities. We need to reverse this trend and ensure it becomes a matter of free choice, not necessity.

We have many tools at our disposal to promote our national interest. But without a doubt, the most formidable is our culture and, in particular, our language—beloved and widely studied worldwide. The year 2021 marks the Dante celebrations, commemorating seven hundred years since the death of the great poet. Dante's figure is central to the history of our nation and the formation of its shared culture. The "father of the Italian language" is rightly considered one of the highest examples of Italian genius and talent worldwide. We should follow Dante's example, spreading the Italian language abroad and defending it at home from the excessive use of English words and unpalatable technical neologisms. Everything Italian is admired around the world; we must always be proud of this and never forget it.

* * *

While the world talks about Italy, we talk about the First, Second, and Third Republic. I'm tired of these labels, and in the end, very little has changed between these supposed phases of our Republic. The only real change would be to shift from a "Republic of the Palace" to a "Republic of the Italians." And this can only happen through a presidential reform of the constitution. There is a close link between the direct election of the head of state (and/or government, depending on the presidential model) and popular sovereignty. This is the crux of the matter. A free and "mature" people chooses and elects its leaders without leaving the "Palace" room to alter their will. A people under guardianship, considered incapable of self-determination, must instead settle for a mediated form of democracy where it can have its say—but in the end, others decide who will be the head of government, and even the head of state.

During the Cold War years, presidentialism was simply unthinkable: Italy did not have the freedom to choose its international positioning. Thus, a parliamentary and proportional system, where the power remained firmly in the hands of the political establishment, was the only way to ensure a sovereignty that was controlled rather than autonomous. However, with the fall of the Berlin Wall, a period of newfound independence for Italy began, and the idea of direct representation resurfaced. We moved closer to the concept of an "Italian mayor," with a majority system that included the direct selection of the prime minister. During this phase, for the first time in republican history, we experienced a semblance of governmental alternation and, more importantly, executives that reflected the prevailing popular sentiment.

Unfortunately, this phase was short-lived. In 2011, the Franco-German axis sent an unequivocal signal to Italy: "Forget about sovereignty." This message is regularly echoed by left-wing figures who brazenly claim that a Center-Right government would not be "tolerated" by the European Union or the international community. Therefore, they claim that there is no alternative but for the Democratic Party to stay in office, even if it loses elections. In this context, any idea of electing the head of state directly, instituting a strong premiership, or abandoning proportional representation had to be shelved. The objective is all too clear: to continue ensuring an Italy with limited sovereignty.

This is why the political challenge surrounding presidentialism is essentially the primary confrontation between patriots and the Left. Ours is not merely a battle of principle. A nation with diminished sovereignty, like Italy, is vulnerable to foreign interference; it is at the mercy of economic and financial power; it is weak on the international stage. Lacking full sovereignty means accepting a European framework that is detrimental to Italy. Presidentialism, therefore, is not just a trivial embellishment—it is the mother of all reform. A nation without control over itself pays in terms of economic growth, wealth, jobs, dignity, and its future.

So yes, I will continue to fight to ensure that Italy one day has a President of the Republic chosen directly by its citizens and a government that answers directly to the people. I know this is the prospect that most of all sends shock waves through the current system of power in Italy and Europe, which is why I also know it is the right thing to do.

Moreover, many of the battles I am waging are earning me powerful and dangerous enemies. But I, despite my small stature, have certain advantages. First, I am afraid of nothing and no one, and the only thing that scares me, as you have learned from these pages, is disappointing myself and those who believe in me. Second, I cannot be blackmailed because I do nothing I would be ashamed of and do not accept help from those who might demand something in return. Third, I am not alone, and the people who have chosen to join me in this fight are, on average, very similar to me. Fourth, and last of all, I have always been underestimated, and in the end, this is a stroke of luck.

Certainly, it is possible that one day things will change. Most likely, if I reach a point where I can change things that too many prefer to keep the same, then I will realize just how determined certain powers can be. I have taken this into account and decided to stand on the battlefield anyway. Just like in the Middle Ages, those who fought in the front lines knew they might be the first to fall, hit by an arrow, or like those who, during the

Great War, advanced while praying that the cannon fire would miss them. Today, arrows and cannons are no longer used; the methods to strike are much more insidious and sophisticated. I have taken this into account too, but I will not give up. This is the war of our times, and I am a soldier.

For Ginevra

"Look! I can see Mamma's flag!" Those were your words one morning as I took you to school, pointing to the Italian flag. You were just about to turn three, and since that day, you've repeated those words over and over.

I've always been so proud that you associate me with the symbol I fight for each and every day. And yet, I often wonder whether one day, when you're old enough to understand, you'll be proud of me too. I wonder whether you'll forgive me for all the moments I couldn't spend with you, for the things I couldn't teach you, for your small everyday victories I missed. And each day I wonder whether it's the right thing to sacrifice the chance to experience you as I would like to, the way you probably want me to so that I can fulfill my many commitments. Some nights, I lie down beside you while you're asleep, and I whisper in your ear, "Your Mamma's right here," as though I'm pleading for your forgiveness for all the hours I wasn't. My guilt about you never leaves me, Gì, nor does my fear of not being the mother I should be. I try to comfort myself that I can teach you no greater lesson than leading by example. I fool myself into thinking that my unshakable determination, my devotion, and my belief that nothing in life is free has driven me to give it my all—the totality of my anger and love with which I fight for what I believe. This, I believe, is my greatest lesson to you. Yet, there are a million things I wish to tell you—about what I've learned from life and how I hope you'll face it. All this floods my mind when I take you to school, letting go of your little hand and watching you, with your small backpack, facing the world on your own. I know it's the right way, but each time my heart quivers.

Be good, my love. Remember that your heart sees more clearly than your eyes ever can. Stay deeply rooted in the ground, always keep your eyes trained on the sky. Be content with what you have, but never with what you know or what you have achieved. Keep searching. It is in our nature as human beings to desire endlessly. If you try to satisfy that longing with material things, your journey will be fleeting and unfulfilled. Even if you owned everything in the world, you'd realize you have almost nothing. Improve yourself, elevate yourself, surpass your limits: this is the only true wealth that will never slip away like sand between your fingers.

Don't be aloof—every person you meet has something to teach you. And don't let the chaos of life distract you because the wonders of the world pass us by so quickly, we risk missing them in a blur. Whatever you want won't just come knocking at your door; you must chase it. Take the long road—shortcuts are just an illusion. Never be ashamed to speak your truth. Don't agree with others just to make life easier. Yes, telling the truth can be painful at times, but only by believing something deeply will you have the strength to defend it. So, whenever necessary, don't be afraid to swim against the tide. It will be hard, of course, but it will also make you stronger, more resilient, more determined.

Never stop being good or being generous, even when others fail to show you the same in return. Selfishness, cruelty, and blind ambition lead nowhere. Love is what powers the world. And remember, love only exists if you share it.

Keep laughing like you did this morning, my sweet, and we'll figure out all the rest.